The Oxford Poetry Library

GENERAL EDITOR: FRANK KERMODE

JOHN DRYDEN (1631–1700) developed late as a poet. His poems written after the Restoration of Charles II in 1660 won him the office of Poet Laureate (1668) and for the period 1660 to 1685 he may be said to have dominated the literary scene, especially with his satires *MacFlecknoe* (probably written 1676), *Absalom and Achitophel* (1681), and *The Medal* (1682). He turned briefly to religious engagement with *Religio Laici* (1682) and *The Hind and the Panther* (1687). On the accession of William III in 1688, Dryden, as a convert to Roman Catholicism, could no longer comment publicly upon public affairs, and turned increasingly towards translation as a means of expression and sometimes covert commentary on politics and society. In his later years he formed an association with Jacob Tonson which was to initiate the future model for relationships between writers and publishers. The products of this relationship culminated in the complete translation of Virgil (1697) and *Fables Ancient and Modern*, published in 1700, the year of Dryden's death.

Throughout his life Dryden also wrote plays of disputable value, and, in a large body of prose commentary, he began the practice of literary criticism in England.

KEITH WALKER is Senior Lecturer in English Language and Literature at University College London. He has written on eighteenth-century literature, and has edited the poems of John Wilmot Earl of Rochester.

FRANK KERMODE, retired King Edward VII Professor of English Literature at Cambridge, is the author of many books, including *Romantic Image*, *The Sense of an Ending*, *The Classic*, *The Genius of Secrecy*, *Forms of Attention*, and *History and Value*; he is also co-editor with John Hollander of *The Oxford Anthology of English Literature*.

THE OXFORD POETRY LIBRARY

GENERAL EDITOR: FRANK KERMODE

Matthew Arnold	*Miriam Allott*
William Blake	*Michael Mason*
Byron	*Jerome McGann*
Samuel Taylor Coleridge	*Heather Jackson*
John Dryden	*Keith Walker*
Thomas Hardy	*Samuel Hynes*
George Herbert	*Louis Martz*
Gerald Manley Hopkins	*Catherine Phillips*
Ben Jonson	*Ian Donaldson*
John Keats	*Elizabeth Cook*
Andrew Marvell	*Frank Kermode and Keith Walker*
John Milton	*Jonathan Goldberg and Stephen Orgel*
Alexander Pope	*Pat Rogers*
Sir Philip Sidney	*Katherine Duncan-Jones*
Henry Vaughan	*Louis Martz*
William Wordsworth	*Stephen Gill and Duncan Wu*

The Oxford Poetry Library

John Dryden

Edited by
KEITH WALKER

Oxford   New York

OXFORD UNIVERSITY PRESS

1994

Oxford University Press, Walton Street, Oxford OX2 6DP

Oxford New York Toronto
Delhi Bombay Calcutta Madras Karachi
Kuala Lumpur Singapore Hong Kong Tokyo
Nairobi Dar es Salaam Cape Town
Melbourne Auckland Madrid
and associated companies in
Berlin Ibadan

Oxford is a trade mark of Oxford University Press

British Library Cataloguing in Publication Data
Data available

Library of Congress Cataloging in Publication Data
Dryden, John, 1631–1700.
[Poems. Selections]
John Dryden / edited by Keith Walker.
p.   cm. — (The Oxford poetry library)
Reprinted from the Oxford authors edition of
selections from the works of John Dryden, 1987.
Includes bibliographical references (p.   ) and index.
I. Walker, Keith, 1936–   . II. Title. III. Series.
PR3412.W35   1994   821'.4—dc20   93-34645
ISBN 0-19-282264-0

1 3 5 7 9 10 8 6 4 2

Typeset by J&L Composition Ltd, Filey, North Yorkshire
Printed in Great Britain by
Biddles Ltd
Guildford and King's Lynn

Contents

Introduction

Dryden's poetry is straightforward, bold, and energetic. He was in the public eye for some forty years, holding positions at court for a long period of that time. He was indisputably perceived as the leading writer of his day. He excelled in all the types of writing practised at the time. He wrote more, and in more genres than anyone. He accumulated to himself (it is an odd distinction) a huge mass of attacks, ranging from the reasoned to the scabrous. Dryden explained his attitudes and intentions in a large number of prologues, epilogues, prefaces, defences, and vindications—thereby quite casually producing the first body of what we now call 'criticism' in English. And yet his life and character remain something of a mystery. The manuscript of John Aubrey's 'Brief Life' of Dryden is headed 'John Dryden, esq., Poet Laureate. He will write it for me himself'. The rest of the page remains blank.

1631–1659

Dryden was born in Northamptonshire at Aldwincle where his maternal grandfather was rector. His family was puritan. His cousin, Sir Gilbert Pickering, was to be one of the judges at Charles I's trial, and high in Cromwell's favour. Gilbert was a 'committee-man' of the Commonwealth, responsible for ejecting ministers and sequestrating estates on behalf of the government.

Dryden went up to Westminster School as a King's Scholar, perhaps in 1645. Here he received a thorough education in the classics from Dr Richard Busby. Before he left Westminster he published his first poem, an elegy for Lord Hastings, among thirty-three similar poems, some by fellow schoolboys.

In 1650 Dryden went up to Cambridge. Trinity College was at the time at the forefront of the study of the 'new science', which was not formally part of the University curriculum (that was dominated by Aristotle), and his manifest interest in the natural sciences may have been stimulated while he was there.

He took his BA in 1654. His father's death in 1654 left him a modest, but never adequate, income. He was to live in London until his death, returning to Northampton for vacations from time to time. Almost uniquely among the English poets, he never travelled outside England.

In London Dryden worked as a secretary for the protectorate. He appeared alongside Marvell and Milton at Cromwell's funeral in 1658 and the next year published *Heroic Stanzas* on the death of Cromwell, which came out alongside elegies by Edmund Waller and Thomas Sprat, later historian of the Royal Society. *Heroic Stanzas* was the first work of Dryden's maturity as a poet. It was sometimes represented as containing praise for regicide and Dryden was attacked for the poem at the restoration, but he never disowned it, and his publisher issued a reprint about 1692.

1660–1678

At the restoration of the monarchy Dryden, like any civil servant today when a new government comes to power, transferred his allegiance to the new regime. He welcomed the new government in two panegyrics to the king, and one each to the Lord Chancellor and to Sir Robert Howard, a staunch royalist whose sister, Lady Elizabeth, he was to marry in 1663. She bore him three sons, and outlived him.

The poems to the king and others suggest that Dryden was looking for a patron. Although he could hardly have realized the fact at the time, he had already found a patron of sorts in his publisher Henry Herringman for whom he worked from before 1660 until 1679. Dryden's career spans a period when poets were ceasing to write for aristocratic patrons, and finding their living in writing for publishers and thus ultimately for the reading public.

With the opening of the theatres after the puritan ban there came the possibility of a new kind of employment. Dryden's first play, the comedy *The Wild Gallant*, failed in 1663, and he did not write another comedy for nearly six years, but his tragicomedy *The Rival Ladies* had better success the following year.

Dryden established himself as the leading dramatist of the period with *The Indian Queen* written in collaboration with Sir Robert Howard (1664) and its sequel *The Indian Emperor* (1665) which was written partly to recover some of the money spent on scenery and costumes, as the prologue engagingly admits. *The Indian Queen* and *The Indian Emperor* were heroic tragedies of the kind Dryden was later to be particularly associated with. The line was continued with *Tyrannic Love* (1669) and *The Conquest of Granada* in two parts

(1671, 1672), which pushed the heroic play as far into heroic absurdity as it was capable of going. *Aureng-Zebe* followed in 1675, Dryden's last play in rhymed couplets for some time.

There were two London theatrical companies. At first, Dryden worked for the King's Company of which he was a shareholder and for which he engaged himself to write three plays a year, a promise he proved unable to keep. He fell out with the King's Company in 1678 and moved to the better managed Duke's Company.

During the 1660s and the 1670s we may suppose Dryden to have made the bulk of his earned income from the theatre (a playwright received the profits from the third night of a play's run), but he found the stage uncongenial. We should, however, note the range and experimental variety of Dryden's output for the stage. Between 1663 and his death he wrote, collaborated in, or adapted nearly thirty plays, including comedies, tragedies, political plays, operas, and a masque.

In 1671 *The Rehearsal* by the Duke of Buckingham and others was acted. It satirized the heroic plays, and seems to have had a vogue alongside the plays which it mocked. Dryden appears as 'Mr Bays', a nickname which stuck. Dryden was to have a terrible revenge ten years later, portraying Buckingham as 'Zimri' in *Absalom and Achitophel*.

In 1665 the Great Plague closed the theatres. Dryden retreated to Charlton in Wiltshire, the seat of his father-in-law, the Earl of Berkshire, where he had leisure to read and reflect. He wrote *An Essay of Dramatic Poesy* here, and in 1666 he made a bold bid for poetic fame in a 'modern' epic (that is, without mythology and legend), *Annus Mirabilis*. The publication of Milton's *Paradise Lost* two months after *Annus Mirabilis* we may suppose effectively pre-empted the possibility of Dryden's ever fulfilling his often proclaimed intention of writing an epic on classical lines. Still, he was almost the only poet of his time to have taken proper note of *Paradise Lost*. It is true that he turned it into a rhymed 'opera' (really a dramatic poem), but the presence of *Paradise Lost* broods over and enriches *MacFlecknoe* and *Absalom and Achitophel*.

In 1668 Dryden was rewarded with the office of Poet Laureate, and two years later with the additional office of Historiographer Royal. These posts brought a welcome, if irregularly paid, addition to his income.

1678–1688

Probably in 1676, spurred on by some wounding reference to him in the dedication to Thomas Shadwell's play *The Virtuoso*, Dryden began a period of heroic satires with *MacFlecknoe* (which was not immediately published). This line of satire (as we can conveniently call it, though the poems are very different from one another) continued with *Absalom and Achitophel* (1681) and *The Medal* (1682). *MacFlecknoe*'s concerns may loosely be described as the politics of the theatre. The other two satires are very much concerned with the politics of the nation in the troubled years 1679–83, years of 'the popish plot', attempts to prevent the succession to the throne of the king's brother James on the grounds that he was a Roman Catholic, and the births of the Tory and Whig parties. Dryden's position was one of support for legitimacy, the king, and the duke. He was to remain recklessly loyal to James until his death.

Possibly out of this loyalty to James, Dryden converted to Roman Catholicism some time in the middle 1680s. Certainly his poems record a mind seriously occupied with questions of religion, faith, and authority. He wrote *Religio Laici* (1682) from the position of a member of the Church of England; *The Hind and the Panther* (1687) celebrates his conversion to the Church of Rome.

1688–1700

James was deposed in 1688; catholics had been a legally disadvantaged minority even under the catholic James. Under the protestant William of Orange Dryden could not keep his public offices, but was forced to turn away from public concerns and involvement in public affairs. The despised Thomas Shadwell succeeded him in the office of Poet Laureate. Despite a law which forbade catholics to live in London, Dryden lived on, apparently tolerated. He wrote the occasional play and poem, but the bulk of his writing consisted in translating, an occupation he found more congenial than the writing of plays. It has recently been suggested that Dryden, aided by Jacob Tonson, his publisher from 1679, acted as the Poundian figure of his age, 'invigorating the talents of others', a group of young translators, among them Addison and Congreve, whose work was to bear fruit in Samuel Garth's great composite translation of Ovid's *Metamorphoses* in 1717, in which Dryden's translations figure largely.

Dryden's pension was £1,075 in arrears when Charles II died in 1685. It was not possible for him to write poems which commented on public affairs. A few poems were commissioned, among them *A Song for St Cecilia's Day, 1687*, and *Eleonora* (1692), but Dryden had to turn to translating to support his family. His translations form the vast bulk of his poems, totalling nearly 40,000 lines. In the last two decades of the seventeenth century, Dryden translated Virgil complete; from Ovid, two whole books of the *Metamorphoses*, and parts of six others, along with Book I of *The Art of Love*, three *Epistles* and three books of the *Amores*; substantial passages of Lucretius; Persius complete; five Satires of Juvenal; four poems of Horace and four of Theocritus; and the first book of the *Iliad*. Besides, there are translations of three tales from Boccaccio and rehandlings of four tales from Chaucer.

The summit of Dryden's career as a translator was *The Works of Virgil* (1697), which was published by subscription. This was not a new method, for John Ogilby's *Virgil* (1654) had employed it; but it had never before achieved so much success. The publication of the translation of Virgil was a national event, and may have consoled Dryden for the epic he had always wished to write. It brought him £1,400 and showed the means by which Pope, a boy of just nine at the time, would achieve financial independence as a poet.

Dryden's last volume, *Fables*, is more relaxed. It seems a miscellany of translations with a few original poems. But the plan of the volume we might think based on that of Ovid's *Metamorphoses*, that collection of interlocked stories in which narratives melt into one another. For all its seeming casual diversity, *Fables* forms a unity, beautifully bringing together the concerns of Dryden's last years. Dryden died in 1700 two months after *Fables* was published.

Chronology

1682	*The Medal* and *Religio Laici.*
1684	Dryden edits *Miscellany Poems* for Tonson, the first of a series (1684, 1685, 1693, 1694, and 1704).
1685	James II king. Dryden converts to Roman Catholicism about this time.
1687	*The Hind and the Panther. A Song for St Cecilia's Day.*
1688	James II deposed. Tonson publishes first collected edition of Dryden's poems.
1689	Dryden loses his public posts.
1691	*King Arthur* by Dryden and Purcell.
1692	*The Satires of Juvenal and Persius.*
1693	Dryden writes his last play, *Love Triumphant.*
1697	*The Works of Virgil. Alexander's Feast.*
1698	Dryden attacked in Jeremy Collier's *Short View of the Immorality and Profaneness of the English Stage.*
1700	*Fables.* Dryden dies 1 May.

Note on the Text

DRYDEN had close, even intimate, relations with both his publishers, Henry Herringman and Jacob Tonson, and we may suppose him to have had some control over the publication of his works. Virtually none of his manuscripts has survived. The poems in this edition are normally given whole, and are based on the earliest published versions. The ordering of selections is based on the date of publication except when we know this to have been separated considerably from the date of composition.

Dryden almost invariably elides the final letter of 'the' and 'to' when an initial vowel follows in the next word. In modernizing, I have spelt such words out in full.

MacFlecknoe

All human things are subject to decay,
And when fate summons, monarchs must obey.
This Flecknoe found, who, like Augustus, young
Was called to empire, and had governed long;
In prose and verse, was owned, without dispute,
Through all the realms of Nonsense, absolute.
This aged prince, now flourishing in peace,
And blest with issue of a large increase,
Worn out with business, did at length debate
To settle the succession of the state;   10
And, pondering which of all his sons was fit
To reign, and wage immortal war with wit,
Cried: ''Tis resolved; for nature pleads, that he
Should only rule, who most resembles me.
Shadwell alone my perfect image bears,
Mature in dullness from his tender years:
Shadwell alone, of all my sons, is he
Who stands confirmed in full stupidity.
The rest to some faint meaning make pretence,
But Shadwell never deviates into sense.   20
Some beams of wit on other souls may fall,
Strike through, and make a lucid interval;
But Shadwell's genuine night admits no ray;
His rising fogs prevail upon the day.
Besides, his goodly fabric fills the eye,
And seems designed for thoughtless majesty;
Thoughtless as monarch oaks that shade the plain,
And, spread in solemn state, supinely reign.
Heywood and Shirley were but types of thee,
Thou last great prophet of tautology.   30
Even I, a dunce of more renown than they,
Was sent before but to prepare thy way:
And, coarsely clad in Norwich drugget, came
To teach the nations in thy greater name.
My warbling lute, the lute I whilom strung,
When to King John of Portugal I sung,
Was but the prelude to that glorious day,
When thou on silver Thames didst cut thy way,

With well-timed oars before the royal barge,
Swelled with the pride of thy celestial charge;   40
And big with hymn, commander of a host,
The like was ne'er in Epsom blankets tossed.
Methinks I see the new Arion sail,
The lute still trembling underneath thy nail.
At thy well-sharpened thumb from shore to shore
The treble squeaks for fear, the basses roar;
Echoes from Pissing Alley "Shadwell" call,
And "Shadwell" they resound from Ashton Hall.
About thy boat the little fishes throng,
As at the morning toast that floats along.   50
Sometimes, as prince of thy harmonious band,
Thou wield'st thy papers in thy threshing hand.
St. André's feet ne'er kept more equal time,
Not e'en the feet of thy own *Psyche's* rhyme;
Though they in number as in sense excel:
So just, so like tautology, they fell,
That, pale with envy, Singleton forswore
The lute and sword, which he in triumph bore,
And vowed he ne'er would act Villerius more.'
Here stopped the good old sire, and wept for joy   60
In silent raptures of the hopeful boy.
All arguments, but most his plays, persuade,
That for anointed dullness he was made.
    Close to the walls which fair Augusta bind,
(The fair Augusta much to fears inclined,)
An ancient fabric raised to inform the sight,
There stood of yore, and Barbican it hight:
A watchtower once; but now, so fate ordains,
Of all the pile an empty name remains.
From its old ruins brothel-houses rise,   70
Scenes of lewd loves, and of polluted joys,
Where their vast courts the mother-strumpets keep,
And, undisturbed by watch, in silence sleep.
Near these a nursery erects its head,
Where queens are formed, and future heroes bred;
Where unfledged actors learn to laugh and cry,
Where infant punks their tender voices try,
And little Maximins the gods defy.
Great Fletcher never treads in buskins here,

Nor greater Jonson dares in socks appear;   80
But gentle Simkin just reception finds
Amidst this monument of vanished minds:
Pure clenches the suburban muse affords,
And Panton waging harmless war with words.
Here Flecknoe, as a place to fame well known,
Ambitiously designed his Shadwell's throne;
For ancient Dekker prophesied long since,
That in this pile should reign a mighty prince,
Born for a scourge of wit, and flail of sense;
To whom true dullness should some *Psyches* owe,   90
But worlds of *Misers* from his pen should flow;
Humourists and *Hypocrites* it should produce,
Whole Raymond families, and tribes of Bruce.
   Now Empress Fame had published the renown
Of Shadwell's coronation through the town.
Roused by report of Fame, the nations meet,
From near Bunhill, and distant Watling Street.
No Persian carpets spread the imperial way,
But scattered limbs of mangled poets lay;
From dusty shops neglected authors come,   100
Martyrs of pies, and relics of the bum.
Much Heywood, Shirley, Ogilby there lay,
But loads of Shadwell almost choked the way.
Bilked stationers for yeomen stood prepared,
And Herringman was captain of the guard.
The hoary prince in majesty appeared,
High on a throne of his own labours reared.
At his right hand our young Ascanius sate,
Rome's other hope, and pillar of the State.
His brows thick fogs, instead of glories, grace,   110
And lambent dullness played around his face.
As Hannibal did to the altars come,
Sworn by his sire a mortal foe to Rome;
So Shadwell swore, nor should his vow be vain,
That he till death true dullness would maintain;
And, in his father's right, and realm's defence,
Ne'er to have peace with wit, nor truce with sense.
The king himself the sacred unction made,
As king by office, and as priest by trade.
In his sinister hand, instead of ball,   120

He placed a mighty mug of potent ale;
Love's Kingdom to his right he did convey,
At once his sceptre, and his rule of sway;
Whose righteous lore the prince had practised young,
And from whose loins recorded *Psyche* sprung.
His temples, last, with poppies were o'erspread,
That nodding seemed to consecrate his head.
Just at that point of time, if fame not lie,
On his left hand twelve reverend owls did fly.
So Romulus, 'tis sung, by Tiber's brook,   130
Presage of sway from twice six vultures took.
The admiring throng loud acclamations make,
And omens of his future empire take.
The sire then shook the honours of his head,
And from his brows damps of oblivion shed
Full on the filial dullness: long he stood,
Repelling from his breast the raging god;
At length burst out in this prophetic mood:
    'Heavens bless my son, from Ireland let him reign
To far Barbadoes on the western main;   140
Of his dominion may no end be known,
And greater than his father's be his throne;
Beyond *Love's Kingdom* let him stretch his pen!'
He paused, and all the people cried, 'Amen'.
Then thus continued he: 'My son, advance
Still in new impudence, new ignorance.
Success let others teach, learn thou from me
Pangs without birth, and fruitless industry.
Let *Virtuosos* in five years be writ;
Yet not one thought accuse thy toil of wit.   150
Let gentle George in triumph tread the stage,
Make Dorimant betray, and Loveit rage;
Let Cully, Cockwood, Fopling, charm the pit,
And in their folly show the writer's wit.
Yet still thy fools shall stand in thy defence,
And justify their author's want of sense.
Let 'em be all by thy own model made
Of dullness, and desire no foreign aid;
That they to future ages may be known,
Not copies drawn, but issue of thy own.   160
Nay, let thy men of wit too be the same,

All full of thee, and differing but in name.
But let no alien Sedley interpose,
To lard with wit thy hungry *Epsom* prose.
And when false flowers of rhetoric thou wouldst cull,
Trust nature, do not labour to be dull;
But write thy best, and top; and, in each line,
Sir Formal's oratory will be thine:
Sir Formal, though unsought, attends thy quill,
And does thy northern dedications fill.   170
Nor let false friends seduce thy mind to fame,
By arrogating Jonson's hostile name.
Let father Flecknoe fire thy mind with praise,
And uncle Ogilby thy envy raise.
Thou art my blood, where Jonson has no part:
What share have we in nature, or in art?
Where did his wit on learning fix a brand,
And rail at arts he did not understand?
Where made he love in Prince Nicander's vein,
Or swept the dust in *Psyche's* humble strain?   180
Where sold he bargains, "whip-stitch, kiss my arse",
Promised a play and dwindled to a farce?
When did his muse from Fletcher scenes purloin,
As thou whole Etherege dost transfuse to thine?
But so transfused, as oil on water's flow,
His always floats above, thine sinks below.
This is thy province, this thy wondrous way,
New humours to invent for each new play:
This is that boasted bias of thy mind,
By which one way, to dullness, 'tis inclined;   190
Which makes thy writings lean on one side still,
And, in all changes, that way bends thy will.
Nor let thy mountain-belly make pretence
Of likeness; thine's a tympany of sense.
A tun of man in thy large bulk is writ,
But sure thou'rt but a kilderkin of wit.
Like mine, thy gentle numbers feebly creep;
Thy tragic muse gives smiles, thy comic sleep.
With whate'er gall thou settst thyself to write,
Thy inoffensive satires never bite.   200
In thy felonious heart though venom lies,
It does but touch thy Irish pen, and dies.

Thy genius calls thee not to purchase fame
In keen iambics, but mild anagram.
Leave writing plays, and choose for thy command
Some peaceful province in acrostic land.
There thou mayst wings display and altars raise,
And torture one poor word ten thousand ways.
Or, if thou wouldst thy different talents suit,
Set thy own songs, and sing them to thy lute.'   210
   He said: but his last words were scarcely heard;
For Bruce and Longvil had a trap prepared,
And down they sent the yet declaiming bard.
Sinking he left his drugget robe behind,
Borne upwards by a subterranean wind.
The mantle fell to the young prophet's part,
With double portion of his father's art.

from Absalom and Achitophel

A POEM

In pious times, ere priestcraft did begin,
Before polygamy was made a sin;
When man on many multiplied his kind,
Ere one to one was cursedly confined;
When nature prompted, and no law denied
Promiscuous use of concubine and bride;
Then Israel's monarch after heaven's own heart,
His vigorous warmth did variously impart
To wives and slaves; and, wide as his command,
Scattered his maker's image through the land.   10
Michal, of royal blood, the crown did wear;
A soil ungrateful to the tiller's care:
Not so the rest; for several mothers bore
To godlike David several sons before.
But since like slaves his bed they did ascend,
No true succession could their seed attend.
Of all this numerous progeny was none
So beautiful, so brave, as Absalom:
Whether, inspired by some diviner lust,

His father got him with a greater gust; 20
Or that his conscious destiny made way,
By manly beauty, to imperial sway.
Early in foreign fields he won renown,
With kings and states allied to Israel's crown:
In peace the thoughts of war he could remove,
And seemed as he were only born for love.
Whate'er he did was done with so much ease,
In him alone 'twas natural to please:
His motions all accompanied with grace;
And paradise was opened in his face. 30
With secret joy indulgent David viewed
His youthful image in his son renewed:
To all his wishes nothing he denied,
And made the charming Annabel his bride.
What faults he had (for who from faults is free?)
His father could not, or he would not see.
Some warm excesses which the law forbore,
Were construed youth that purged by boiling o'er,
And Amnon's murder, by a specious name,
Was called a just revenge for injured fame. 40
Thus praised and loved the noble youth remained,
While David, undisturbed, in Sion reigned.
But life can never be sincerely blest;
Heaven punishes the bad, and proves the best.
The Jews, a headstrong, moody, murmuring race,
As ever tried the extent and stretch of grace;
God's pampered people, whom, debauched with ease,
No king could govern, nor no God could please
(Gods they had tried of every shape and size,
That god-smiths could produce, or priests devise); 50
These Adam-wits, too fortunately free,
Began to dream they wanted liberty;
And when no rule, no precedent was found,
Of men by laws less circumscribed and bound,
They led their wild desires to woods and caves,
And thought that all but savages were slaves.
They who, when Saul was dead, without a blow,
Made foolish Ishbosheth the crown forgo;
Who banished David did from Hebron bring,
And with a general shout proclaimed him king: 60

Those very Jews, who, at their very best,
Their humour more than loyalty expressed,
Now wondered why so long they had obeyed
An idol monarch, which their hands had made;
Thought they might ruin him they could create,
Or melt him to that golden calf, a state.
But these were random bolts; no formed design,
Nor interest made the factious crowd to join:
The sober part of Israel, free from stain,
Well knew the value of a peaceful reign,   70
And, looking backward with a wise affright,
Saw seams of wounds, dishonest to the sight:
In contemplation of whose ugly scars
They cursed the memory of civil wars.
The moderate sort of men, thus qualified,
Inclined the balance to the better side;
And David's mildness managed it so well,
The bad found no occasion to rebel.
But when to sin our biased nature leans,
The careful devil is still at hand with means;   80
And providently pimps for ill desires.
The Good Old Cause revived, a plot requires:
Plots, true or false, are necessary things,
To raise up commonwealths, and ruin kings.
  The inhabitants of Old Jerusalem
Were Jebusites, the town so called from them;
And theirs the native right—
But when the chosen people grew more strong,
The rightful cause at length became the wrong;
And every loss the men of Jebus bore,   90
They still were thought God's enemies the more.
Thus worn and weakened, well or ill content,
Submit they must to David's government:
Impoverished and deprived of all command,
Their taxes doubled as they lost their land;
And what was harder yet to flesh and blood,
Their gods disgraced, and burnt like common wood.
This set the heathen priesthood in a flame;
For priests of all religions are the same:
Of whatsoe'er descent their godhead be,   100

Stock, stone, or other homely pedigree,
In his defence his servants are as bold,
As if he had been born of beaten gold.
The Jewish rabbins, though their enemies,
In this conclude them honest men and wise:
For 'twas their duty, all the learned think,
To espouse his cause, by whom they eat and drink.
From hence began that Plot, the nation's curse,
Bad in itself, but represented worse;
Raised in extremes, and in extremes decried;   110
With oaths affirmed, with dying vows denied.
Not weighed or winnowed by the multitude;
But swallowed in the mass, unchewed and crude.
Some truth there was, but dashed and brewed with lies,
To please the fools, and puzzle all the wise.
Succeeding times did equal folly call,
Believing nothing, or believing all.
The Egyptian rites the Jebusites embraced;
Where gods were recommended by their taste.
Such savoury deities must needs be good,   120
As served at once for worship and for food.
By force they could not introduce these gods,
For ten to one in former days was odds;
So fraud was used (the sacrificer's trade):
Fools are more hard to conquer than persuade.
Their busy teachers mingled with the Jews,
And raked for converts even the court and stews:
Which Hebrew priests the more unkindly took,
Because the fleece accompanies the flock.
Some thought they God's anointed meant to slay   130
By guns, invented since full many a day:
Our author swears it not; but who can know
How far the Devil and Jebusites may go?
This Plot, which failed for want of common sense,
Had yet a deep and dangerous consequence:
For, as when raging fevers boil the blood,
The standing lake soon floats into a flood,
And every hostile humour, which before
Slept quiet in its channels, bubbles o'er;
So several factions from this first ferment   140
Work up to foam, and threat the government.

Some by their friends, more by themselves thought wise,
Opposed the power to which they could not rise.
Some had in courts been great, and thrown from thence,
Like fiends were hardened in impenitence.

Some, by their monarch's fatal mercy, grown
From pardoned rebels kinsmen to the throne,
Were raised in power and public office high;
Strong bands, if bands ungrateful men could tie.
   Of these the false Achitophel was first,   150
A name to all succeeding ages cursed:
For close designs and crooked counsels fit;
Sagacious, bold, and turbulent of wit;
Restless, unfixed in principles and place;
In power unpleased, impatient of disgrace:
A fiery soul, which, working out its way,
Fretted the pigmy body to decay,
And o'er-informed the tenement of clay.
A daring pilot in extremity;
Pleased with the danger, when the waves went high,   160
He sought the storms; but, for a calm unfit,
Would steer too nigh the sands, to boast his wit.
Great wits are sure to madness near allied,
And thin partitions do their bounds divide;
Else why should he, with wealth and honour blest,
Refuse his age the needful hours of rest?
Punish a body which he could not please;
Bankrupt of life, yet prodigal of ease?
And all to leave what with his toil he won,
To that unfeathered two-legged thing, a son,   170
Got, while his soul did huddled notions try;
And born a shapeless lump, like anarchy.
In friendship false, implacable in hate;
Resolved to ruin or to rule the state.
To compass this the triple bond he broke,
The pillars of the public safety shook;
And fitted Israel for a foreign yoke:
Then seized with fear, yet still affecting fame,
Usurped a patriot's all-atoning name. . . .

. . . .

Achitophel, grown weary to possess   200

A lawful fame, and lazy happiness,
Disdained the golden fruit to gather free,
And lent the crowd his arm to shake the tree.
Now, manifest of crimes contrived long since,
He stood at bold defiance with his prince;
Held up the buckler of the people's cause
Against the crown, and skulked behind the laws.
The wished occasion of the Plot he takes;
Some circumstances finds, but more he makes.
By buzzing emissaries fills the ears   210
Of listening crowds with jealousies and fears
Of arbitrary counsels brought to light,
And proves the king himself a Jebusite. . . .
                .   .   .   .

Him he attempts with studied arts to please,
And sheds his venom in such words as these:
    'Auspicious prince, at whose nativity   230
Some royal planet ruled the southern sky;
Thy longing country's darling and desire;
Their cloudy pillar and their guardian fire:
Their second Moses, whose extended wand
Divides the seas, and shows the promised land;
Whose dawning day in every distant age
Has exercised the sacred prophets' rage:
The people's prayer, the glad diviners' theme,
The young men's vision, and the old men's dream!
Thee, saviour, thee, the nation's vows confess,   240
And, never satisfied with seeing, bless:
Swift unbespoken pomps thy steps proclaim,
And stammering babes are taught to lisp thy name.
How long wilt thou the general joy detain,
Starve and defraud the people of thy reign?
Content ingloriously to pass thy days
Like one of virtue's fools that feeds on praise,
Till thy fresh glories, which now shine so bright,
Grow stale and tarnish with our daily sight.
Believe me, royal youth, thy fruit must be   250
Or gathered ripe, or rot upon the tree.
Heaven has to all allotted, soon or late,
Some lucky revolution of their fate;
Whose motions if we watch and guide with skill

(For human good depends on human will),
Our fortune rolls as from a smooth descent,
And from the first impression takes the bent:
But, if unseized, she glides away like wind,
And leaves repenting folly far behind.
Now, now she meets you with a glorious prize,   260
And spreads her locks before her as she flies.
Had thus old David, from whose loins you spring,
Not dared, when fortune called him, to be king,
At Gath an exile he might still remain,
And heaven's anointing oil had been in vain.
Let his successful youth your hopes engage,
But shun the example of declining age:
Behold him setting in his western skies,
The shadows lengthening as the vapours rise.
He is not now, as when on Jordan's sand   270
The joyful people thronged to see him land,
Covering the beach, and blackening all the strand;
But, like the prince of angels, from his height
Comes tumbling downward with diminished light,
Betrayed by one poor plot to public scorn
(Our only blessing since his cursed return);
Those heaps of people which one sheaf did bind,
Blown off and scattered by a puff of wind.
What strength can he to your designs oppose,
Naked of friends, and round beset with foes? . . .   280
      .   .   .   .

   Some of their chiefs were princes of the land:
In the first rank of these did Zimri stand;
A man so various, that he seemed to be
Not one, but all mankind's epitome:
Stiff in opinions, always in the wrong;
Was everything by starts, and nothing long;
But, in the course of one revolving moon,
Was chemist, fiddler, statesman, and buffoon: 550
Then all for women, painting, rhyming, drinking,
Besides ten thousand freaks that died in thinking.
Blest madman, who could every hour employ,
With something new to wish, or to enjoy!
Railing and praising were his usual themes;
And both (to show his judgment) in extremes:

So over-violent, or over-civil,
That every man, with him, was God or devil.
In squandering wealth was his peculiar art:
Nothing went unrewarded but desert.   560
Beggared by fools, whom still he found too late,
He had his jest, and they had his estate.
He laughed himself from court; then sought relief
By forming parties, but could ne'er be chief;
For, spite of him, the weight of business fell
On Absalom and wise Achitophel:
Thus, wicked but in will, of means bereft,
He left not faction, but of that was left. . . .
          .   .   .   .

   To speak the rest, who better are forgot,   630
Would tire a well-breathed witness of the Plot.
Yet, Corah, thou shalt from oblivion pass:
Erect thyself, thou monumental brass,
High as the serpent of thy metal made,
While nations stand secure beneath thy shade.
What though his birth were base, yet comets rise
From earthy vapours, ere they shine in skies.
Prodigious actions may as well be done
By weaver's issue as by prince's son.
This arch-attestor for the public good   640
By that one deed ennobles all his blood
Who ever asked the witnesses' high race,
Whose oath with martyrdom did Stephen grace?
Ours was a Levite, and as times went then,
His tribe were God almighty's gentlemen.
Sunk were his eyes, his voice was harsh and loud,
Sure signs he neither choleric was nor proud:
His long chin proved his wit; his saintlike grace
A church vermilion, and a Moses' face.
His memory, miraculously great,   650
Could plots exceeding man's belief, repeat;
Which therefore cannot be accounted lies,
For human wit could never such devise.
Some future truths are mingled in his book;
But where the witness failed, the prophet spoke:
Some things like visionary flights appear;
The spirit caught him up, the Lord knows where;

And gave him his rabbinical degree,
Unknown to foreign university.
His judgment yet his memory did excel;   660
Which pieced his wondrous evidence so well,
And suited to the temper of the times,
Then groaning under Jebusitic crimes.
Let Israel's foes suspect his heavenly call,
And rashly judge his writ apocryphal;
Our laws for such affronts have forfeits made;
He takes his life, who takes away his trade.
Were I myself in witness Corah's place,
The wretch who did me such a dire disgrace,
Should whet my memory, though once forgot,   670
To make him an appendix of my plot.
His zeal to heaven made him his prince despise,
And load his person with indignities;
But zeal peculiar privilege affords,
Indulging latitude to deeds and words;
And Corah might for Agag's murder call,
In terms as coarse as Samuel used to Saul.
What others in his evidence did join
(The best that could be had for love or coin),
In Corah's own predicament will fall;   680
For witness is a common name to all. . . .

. . . .

From the Second Part of
Absalom and Achitophel

Now stop your noses, readers, all and some,
For here's a tun of midnight work to come,
Og, from a treason-tavern rolling home
Round as a globe, and liquored every chink,
Goodly and great he sails behind his link.
With all this bulk there's nothing lost in Og,
For every inch that is not fool is rogue:
A monstrous mass of foul corrupted matter,
As all the devils had spewed to make the batter.
When wine has given him courage to blaspheme,   10

He curses God, but God before cursed him;
And if man could have reason, none has more,
That made his paunch so rich, and him so poor.
With wealth he was not trusted, for heaven knew
What 'twas of old to pamper up a Jew;
To what would he on quail and pheasant swell,
That e'en on tripe and carrion could rebel?
But though heaven made him poor (with reverence
   speaking),
He never was a poet of God's making.
The midwife laid her hand on his thick skull,   20
With this prophetic blessing: *be thou dull*;
Drink, swear, and roar, forbear no lewd delight
Fit for thy bulk, do anything but write:
Thou art of lasting make, like thoughtless men,
A strong nativity—but for the pen;
Eat opium, mingle arsenic in thy drink,
Still thou mayst live, avoiding pen and ink.
I see, I see, 'tis counsel given in vain,
For treason botched in rhyme will be thy bane;
Rhyme is the rock on which thou art to wreck,   30
'Tis fatal to thy fame and to thy neck:
Why should thy metre good King David blast?
A psalm of his will surely be thy last.
Darest thou presume in verse to meet thy foes,
Thou whom the penny pamphlet foiled in prose?
Doeg, whom God for mankind's mirth has made,
O'ertops thy talent in thy very trade;
Doeg to thee, thy paintings are so coarse,
A poet is, though he's the poets' horse.
A double noose thou on thy neck dost pull,   40
For writing treason, and for writing dull;
To die for faction is a common evil,
But to be hanged for nonsense is the devil:
Hadst thou the glories of thy king expressed,
Thy praises had been satire at the best;
But thou in clumsy verse, unlicked, unpointed,
Hast shamefully defied the Lord's anointed:
I will not rake the dunghill of thy crimes,
For who would read thy life that reads thy rhymes?
But of King David's foes, be this the doom,   50

> May all be like the young man Absalom;
> And for my foes may this their blessing be,
> To talk like Doeg, and to write like thee.

To the Memory of Mr Oldham

Farewell, too little and too lately known,
Whom I began to think and call my own;
For sure our souls were near allied; and thine
Cast in the same poetic mould with mine.
One common note on either lyre did strike,
And knaves and fools we both abhorred alike:
To the same goal did both our studies drive,
The last set out the soonest did arrive.
Thus Nisus fell upon the slippery place,
While his young friend performed and won the race.   10
O early ripe—to thy abundant store
What could advancing age have added more?
It might (what nature never gives the young)
Have taught the numbers of thy native tongue.
But satire needs not those, and wit will shine
Through the harsh cadence of a rugged line:
A noble error, and but seldom made,
When poets are by too much force betrayed.
Thy generous fruits, though gathered ere their prime
Still showed a quickness; and maturing time   20
But mellows what we write to the dull sweets of rhyme.
Once more, hail and farewell; farewell thou young
But ah too short, Marcellus of our tongue;
Thy brows with ivy, and with laurels bound;
But fate and gloomy night encompass thee around.

The entire Episode of Nisus and Euryalus, translated from the Fifth and Ninth Books of Virgil's Aeneid

I

From thence his way the Trojan hero bent,
Into a grassy plain with mountains pent,
Whose brows were shaded with surrounding wood.

Full in the midst of this fair valley stood
A native theatre, which rising slow,
By just degrees, o'erlooked the ground below:
A numerous train attend in solemn state:
High on the new-raised turf their leader sate.
Here those who in the rapid race delight,
Desire of honour and the prize invite:　　　　　　10
The Trojans and Sicilians mingled stand,
With Nisus and Euryalus the foremost of the band;
Euryalus with youth and beauty crowned,
Nisus for friendship to the boy renowned.
Diores next, of Priam's regal race,
Then Salius, joined with Patron, took his place:
But from Epirus one derived his birth,
The other owed it to Arcadian earth.
Then two Sicilian youths; the name of this
Was Helymus, of that was Panopes:　　　　　　20
Two jolly huntsmen in the forest bred,
And owning old Acestes for their head.
With many others of obscurer name,
Whom time has not delivered o'er to fame.
　To these Aeneas in the midst arose,
And pleasingly did thus his mind expose.
'Not one of you shall unrewarded go;
On each I will two Cretan spears bestow,
Pointed with polished steel; a battle axe too,
With silver studded; these in common share,　　　30
The foremost three shall olive garlands wear;
The victor, who shall first the race obtain,
Shall for his prize a well-breathed courser gain,
Adorned with trappings; to the next in fame,
The quiver of an Amazonian dame
With feathered Thracian arrows well supplied
Hung on a golden belt, and with a jewel tied;
The third this Grecian helmet must content.'
He said; to their appointed base they went:
With beating hearts the expected sign receive,　　40
And starting all at once, the station leave.
Spread out, as on the wings of winds they flew
And seized the distant goal with eager view;
Shot from the crowd, swift Nisus all o'erpassed,

Not storms, nor thunder equal half his haste:
The next, but though the next, yet far disjoined,
Came Salius; then a distant space behind,
Euryalus the third;
Next Helymus, whom young Diores plied,
Step after step, and almost side by side,   50
His shoulders pressing, and in longer space,
Had won, or left at least a doubtful race.
   Now spent, the goal they almost reach at last,
When eager Nisus, hapless in his haste,
Slipped first, and slipping, fell upon the plain,
Moist with the blood of oxen lately slain;
The careless victor had not marked his way
But treading where the treacherous puddle lay,
His heels flew up, and on the grassy floor,
He fell besmeared with filth and holy gore.   60
Nor mindless then Euryalus of thee,
Nor of the sacred bonds of amity,
He strove the immediate rival to oppose
And caught the foot of Salius as he rose;
So Salius lay extended on the plain:
Euryalus springs out the prize to gain,
And cuts the crowd; applauding peals attend
The conqueror to the goal, who conquered through his friend.
Next Helymus and then Diores came,
By two misfortunes, now the third in fame.   70
   But Salius enters, and exclaiming loud
For justice, deafens and disturbs the crowd:
Urges his cause may in the court be heard,
And pleads the prize is wrongfully conferred.
But favour for Euryalus appears,
His blooming beauty and his graceful tears
Had bribed the judges to protect his claim:
Besides Diores does as loud exclaim,
Who vainly reaches at the last reward,
If the first palm on Salius be conferred.   80
Then thus the prince: 'Let not disputes arise;
Where fortune placed it, I award the prize.
But give me leave her errors to amend,
At least to pity a deserving friend.'
Thus having said,
A lion's hide, amazing to behold,

Ponderous with bristles, and with paws of gold,
He gave the youth; which Nisus grieved to view;
'If such rewards to vanquished men are due,'
Said he, 'and falling is to rise by you,   90
What prize may Nisus from your bounty claim,
Who merited the first rewards and fame?
In falling did both equal fortune try,
Would fortune make me fall as happily.'
With this he pointed to his face, and showed
His hands and body all besmeared with blood;
The indulgent father of the people smiled,
And caused to be produced a massy shield
Of wonderous art by Didymaon wrought,
Long since from Neptune's bars in triumph brought;   100
With this, the graceful youth he gratified,
Then the remaining presents did divide.

2

The Trojan camp the common danger shared;
By turns they watched the walls, and kept the nightly guard.
To warlike Nisus fell the gate by lot,
(Whom Hyrtacus on huntress Ida got,
And sent to sea Aeneas to attend,)
Well could he dart the spear and shafts unerring send.
Beside him stood Euryalus, his ever-faithful friend.
No youth in all the Trojan host was seen
More beautiful in arms, or of a nobler mien;
Scarce was the down upon his chin begun;   10
One was their friendship, their desire was one;
With minds united in the field they warred
And now were both by choice upon the guard.
   Then Nisus thus:
'Or do the gods this warlike warmth inspire,
Or makes each man a god of his desire?
A noble ardour boils within my breast,
Eager of action, enemy of rest,
That urges me to fight, or undertake
Some deed that may my fame immortal make.   20
Thou seest the foe secure: how faintly shine
Their scattered fires; the most, in sleep supine,
Dissolved in ease, and drunk with victory;

The few awake the fuming flaggon ply,
All hushed around; now hear what I revolve
Within my mind, and what my labouring thoughts resolve.
Our absent lord both camp and council mourn;
By message both would hasten his return;
The gifts proposed if they confer on thee,
(For fame is recompense enough to me)   30
Methinks beneath yon hill, I have espied
A way that safely will my passage guide.'
Euryalus stood listening while he spoke,
With love of praise and noble envy struck;
Then to his ardent friend exposed his mind:
'All this alone, and leaving me behind!
Am I unworthy, Nisus, to be joined,
Thinkst thou my share of honour I will yield,
Or send thee unassisted to the field?
Not so my father taught my childhood arms,   40
Born in a siege, and bred amongst alarms;
Nor is my youth unworthy of my friend,
Or of the heaven-born hero I attend.
The thing called life with ease I can disclaim
And think it oversold to purchase fame.'
    To whom his friend:
'I could not think, alas, thy tender years
Would minister new matter to my fears;
Nor is it just thou shouldst thy wish obtain,
So Jove in triumph bring me back again   50
To those dear eyes, or if a god there be
To pious friends propitious more than he.
But if some one, as many sure there are,
Of adverse accidents in doubtful war,
If one should reach my head there let it fall,
And spare thy life, I would not perish all:
Thy youth is worthy of a longer date;
Do thou remain to mourn thy lover's fate,
To bear my mangled body from the foe,
Or buy it back, and funeral rites bestow,   60
Or if hard fortune shall my corpse deny
Those dues, with empty marble to supply.
O let not me the widow's tears renew,
Let not a mother's curse my name pursue;

Thy pious mother, who in love to thee
Left the fair coast of fruitful Sicily,
Her age committing to the seas and wind,
When every weary matron stayed behind.'
To this, Euryalus: 'Thou pleadst in vain,
And but delayst the cause thou canst not gain: 70
No more, 'tis loss of time.' With that he wakes
The nodding watch; each to his office takes.

   The guard relieved, in company they went
To find the council at the royal tent.
Now every living thing lay void of care,
And sleep, the common gift of nature, share;
Meantime the Trojan peers in council sate
And called their chief commanders to debate
The weighty business of the endangered state,
What next was to be done, who to be sent   80
To inform Aeneas of the foe's intent.
In midst of all the quiet camp they held
Nocturnal council; each sustains a shield
Which his o'erlaboured arm can hardly rear;
And leans upon a long projected spear.

   Now Nisus and his friend approach the guard
And beg admittance, eager to be heard,
The affair important, not to be deferred.
Ascanius bids them be conducted in;
Then thus, commanded, Nisus does begin.   90
'Ye Trojan fathers lend attentive ears,
Nor judge our undertaking by our years.
The foes securely drenched in sleep and wine
Their watch neglect; their fires but thinly shine.
And where the smoke in thickening vapours flies
Covering the plain, and clouding all the skies,
Betwixt the spaces we have marked a way,
Close by the gate and coasting by the sea.
This passage undisturbed, and unespied
Our steps will safely to Aeneas guide,   100
Expect each hour to see him back again
Loaded with spoils of foes in battle slain.
Snatch we the lucky minute while we may,
Nor can we be mistaken in the way:
For, hunting in the vale, we oft have seen

The rising turrets with the stream between,
And know its winding course, with every ford.'
He paused, and old Alethes took the word.
'Our country gods, in whom our trust we place,
Will yet from ruin save the Trojan race;   110
While we behold such springing worth appear,
In youth so brave, and breasts so void of fear.'
(With this he took the hand of either boy,
Embraced them closely both, and wept for joy:)
'Ye brave young men, what equal gifts can we,
What recompense for such desert, decree?
The greatest sure and best you can receive,
The gods your virtue and your fame will give:
The rest, our grateful general will bestow;
and young Ascanius, till his manhood, owe.'   120
'And I whose welfare in my father lies,'
(Ascanius adds) 'by all the deities,
By our great country, and our household gods,
By hoary Vesta's rites and dark abodes,
Adjure you both, on you my fortune stands,
That and my faith I plight into your hands,
Make me but happy in his safe return,
(For I no other loss but only his can mourn,)
Nisus your gift shall two large goblets be,
Of silver, wrought with curious imagery,   130
And high embossed, which, when old Priam reigned,
My conquering sire, at sacked Arisba gained.
And, more, two tripods cast in antique mould,
With two great talents of the finest gold:
Besides a bowl which Tyrian art did grave,
The present that Sidonian Dido gave.
But if in conquered Italy we reign,
When spoils by lot the victors shall obtain—
Thou sawest the courser by proud Turnus pressed,
That, and his golden arms, and sanguine crest,   140
And shield, from lot exempted, thou shalt share;
With these, twelve captive damsels young and fair:
Male slaves as many; well appointed all
With vests and arms, shall to thy portion fall:
And, last, a fruitful field to thee shall rest,
The large demesnes the Latian king possessed.

But thou, whose years are more to mine allied,
No fate my vowed affection shall divide
From thee, O wondrous youth! be ever mine,
Take full possession; all my soul is thine: 150
My life's companion, and my bosom friend—
One faith, one fame, one fate shall both attend.
My peace shall be committed to thy care,
And to thy conduct my concerns in war.'
    Then thus the bold Euryalus replied:
'Whatever fortune, good or bad, betide,
The same shall be my age, as now my youth;
No time shall find me wanting to my truth.
This only from your bounty let me gain
(And this not granted, all rewards are vain)   160
Of Priam's royal race my mother came—
And sure the best that ever bore the name—
Whom neither Troy, nor Sicily could hold
From me departing; but o'erspent and old,
My fate she followed. Ignorant of this
Whatever danger, neither parting kiss,
Nor pious blessing taken, her I leave,
And in this only act of all my life deceive.
By this your hand and conscious night, I swear,
My youth so sad a farewell could not bear.   170
Be you her patron, fill my vacant place,
(Permit me to presume so great a grace)
Support her age forsaken and distressed,
That hope alone will fortify my breast,
Against the worst of fortunes and of fears.'
He said; the assistants shed presaging tears,
But above all, Ascanius moved to see
That image of paternal piety.
Then thus replied:
'So great beginnings in so green an age   180
Exact that faith which firmly I engage.
Thy mother all the privilege shall claim
Creusa had, and only want the name.
Whate'er event thy enterprise shall have,
'Tis merit to have borne a son so brave.
By this my head a sacred oath I swear,
(My father used it) what returning here

Crowned with success, I for thyself prepare,
Thy parent and thy family shall share.'
He said: and weeping while he spoke the word,   190
From his broad belt he drew a shining sword,
Magnificent with gold. Lycaon made,
And in an ivory scabbard sheathed the blade.
This was his gift. While Mnestheus did provide
For Nisus' arms a grizly lion's hide,
And true Alethes changed with him his helm of temper tried.
    Thus armed they went; the noble Trojans wait
Their going forth, and follow to the gate
With prayers and vows. Above the rest appears
Ascanius, manly far above his years,   200
And messages committed to their care;
Which all in winds were lost, and empty air.
The trenches first they passed, then took their way
Where their proud foes in pitched pavilions lay:
To many fatal, ere themselves were slain.
The careless host dispersed upon the plain
They found, who drunk with wine supinely snore.
Unharnessed chariots stand upon the shore
Midst wheels, and reins, and arms, the goblet by,
A medley of debauch and war, they lie.   210
Observing Nisus showed his friend the sight
Then thus: 'Behold a conquest without fight.
Occasion calls the sword to be prepared;
The way lies there; stand thou upon the guard,
And look behind, while I securely go
To cut an ample passage through the foe.'
Softly he spoke; then stalking took his way
With his drawn sword, where haughty Rhamnes lay,
His head raised high, on tapestry beneath,
And heaving from his breast, he puffed his breath—   220
A king and prophet by king Turnus loved;
But fate by prescience cannot be removed.
Three sleeping slaves he soon subdues, then spies
Where Remus with his proud retinue lies.
His armour-bearer first, and next he kills
His charioteer entrenched betwixt the wheels
And his loved horses; last invades their lord,
Full on his neck he aims the fatal sword;

The gasping head flies off. A purple flood
Flows from the trunk, that wallows in the blood 230
Which, by the spurning heels dispersed around
The bed besprinkles, and bedews the ground.
Then Lamyrus with Lamus and the young
Serranus, who with gaming did prolong
The night; oppressed with wine and slumber lay
The beauteous youth, and dreamt of lucky play—
More lucky, had it been protracted till the day.
 The famished lion thus with hunger bold,
O'erleaps the fences of the nightly fold,
The peaceful flock devours, and tears, and draws; 240
Wrapped up in silent fear, they lie and pant beneath his paws.
Nor with less rage Euryalus employs
The vengeful sword, nor fewer foes destroys;
But on the ignoble crowd his fury flew,
Which Fadus, Herbesus, and Rhoetus slew,
With Abaris; in sleep the rest did fall;
But Rhoetus waking, and observing all,
Behind a mighty jar he slunk for fear;
The sharp edged iron found and reached him there,
Full as he rose, he plunged it in his side— 250
The cruel sword returned in crimson dyed.
The wound a blended stream of wine and blood
Pours out; the purple soul comes floating in the flood.
 Now where Messapus quartered they arrive;
The fires were fainting there, and just alive;
The warlike horses, tied in order, fed;
Nisus the discipline observed, and said:
'Our eagerness of blood may both betray:
Behold the doubtful glimmering of the day,
Foe to these nightly thefts. No more, my friend, 260
Here let our glutted execution end;
A lane through slaughtered bodies we have made.'
The bold Euryalus, though loath, obeyed.
Rich arms and arras which they scattered find,
and plate, a precious load they leave behind.
Yet fond of gaudy spoils, the boy would stay
To make the proud caparisons his prey,
Which decked a neighbouring steed—
Nor did his eyes less longingly behold

The girdle studded o'er with nails of gold   270
Which Rhamnes wore. (This present long ago
On Remulus did Caedicus bestow,
And absent joined in hospitable ties;
He dying to this heir bequeathed the prize,
Till by the conquering Rutuli oppressed
He fell, and they the glorious gift possessed.)
These gaudy spoils Euryalus now bears,
And vainly on his brawny shoulders wears:
Messapus' helm, he found amongst the dead
Garnished with plumes, and fitted to his head.   280
They leave the camp and take the safest road.
  Meantime a squadron of their foes abroad,
Three hundred horse with bucklers armed, they spied,
Whom Volcens by the king's command did guide;
To Turnus these were from the city sent,
And to perform their message sought his tent.
Approaching near their utmost lines they draw;
When bending towards the left, their captain saw
The faithful pair (for through the doubtful shade
His glittering helm Euryalus betrayed,   290
On which the moon with full reflection played.)
''Tis not for naught' cried Volcens from the crowd,
'These men go there,' then raised his voice aloud:
'Stand, stand! why thus in arms? and whither bent?
From whence, to whom, and on what errand sent?'
Silent they make away, and haste their flight
To neighbouring woods, and trust themselves to night.
The speedy horsemen spur their steeds to get
'Twixt them and home; and every path beset,
And all the windings of the well known wood;   300
(Black was the brake, and thick with oak it stood,
With fern all horrid, and perplexing thorn,
Where tracks of bears had scarce a passage worn.)
The darkness of the shades, his heavy prey,
And fear, misled the younger from his way.
But Nisus hit the turns with happier haste,
Who now, unknowing, had the danger passed,
And Alban lakes, (from Alba's name so called)
Where king Latinus then his oxen stalled,
Till turning at the length, he stood his ground,   310

And vainly cast his longing eyes around
For his lost friend.
'Ah! wretch,' he cried, 'where have I left behind,
Where shall I hope, the unhappy youth to find?
Or what way take?' Again he ventures back
And treads the mazes of his former track
Through the wild wood; at last he hears the noise
Of trampling horses, and the riders' voice.
The sound approached; and suddenly he viewed
His foes enclosing, and his friend pursued,   320
Forelaid, and taken, while he strove in vain
The covert of the neighbouring wood to gain.
What should he next attempt? what arms employ
With fruitless force to free the captive boy?
Or tempt unequal numbers with the sword,
And die by him whom living he adored?
Resolved on death, his dreadful spear he shook,
And casting to the moon a mournful look,
'Fair queen,' said he, 'who dost in woods delight,
Grace of the stars, and goddess of the night,   330
Be present, and direct my dart aright.
If e'er my pious father for my sake
Did on the altars grateful offerings make,
Or I increased them with successful toils
And hung thy sacred roof with savage spoils—
Through the brown shadows guide my flying spear
To reach this troop.' Then, poising from his ear
The quivering weapon, with full force he threw;
Through the divided shades the deadly javelin flew;
On Sulmo's back it splits; the double dart   340
Drove deeper onward, and transfixed his heart.
He staggers round, his eyeballs roll in death,
And with short sobs, he gasps away his breath.
All stand amazed; a second javelin flies
From his stretched arm, and hisses through the skies.
The lance through Tagus' temples forced its way
And in his brain-pan warmly buried lay.
Fierce Volcens foams with rage; and gazing round
Descried no author of the fatal wound,
Nor where to fix revenge. 'But thou,' he cries   350
'Shalt pay for both,' and at the prisoner flies

With his drawn sword. Then struck with deep despair
That fatal sight the lover could not bear
But from the covert rushed in open view
And sent his voice before him as he flew,
'Me, me, employ your sword on me alone;
The crime confessed; the fact was all my own.
He neither could nor durst, the guiltless youth,
Ye moon and stars bear witness to the truth,
His only fault, if that be to offend,   360
Was too much loving his unhappy friend.'
Too late alas he speaks;
The sword which unrelenting fury guides
Driven with full force had pierced his tender sides;
Down fell the beauteous youth; the gaping wound
Gushed out a crimson stream and stained the ground;
His nodding neck reclines on his white breast
Like a fair flower, in furrowed fields oppressed
By the keen share, or poppy on the plain
Whose heavy head is overcharged with rain.   370
   Disdain, despair, and deadly vengeance vowed,
Drove Nisus headlong on the hostile crowd.
Volcens he seeks; at him alone he bends;
Borne back, and pushed by his surrounding friends
He still pressed on, and kept him still in sight,
Then whirled aloft his sword with all his might.
The unerring weapon flew, and winged with death
Entered his gaping mouth, and stopped his breath.
Dying he slew, and staggering on the plain
Sought for the body of his lover slain.   380
Then quietly on his dear breast he fell,
Content in death to be revenged so well.
   O happy pair! for if my verse can give
Eternity your fame shall ever live,
Fixed as the Capitol's foundation lies,
And spread wher'er the Roman eagle flies.

The Latter Part of the Third Book of Lucretius

AGAINST THE FEAR OF DEATH

What has this bugbear, death, to frighten man,
If souls can die, as well as bodies can?
For, as before our birth we felt no pain,
When Punic arms infested land and main,
When heaven and earth were in confusion hurled,
For the debated empire of the world,
Which awed with dreadful expectation lay,
Sure to be slaves, uncertain who should sway:
So, when our mortal frame shall be disjoined,
The lifeless lump uncoupled from the mind,   10
From sense of grief and pain we shall be free;
We shall not feel, because we shall not be.
Though earth in seas, and seas in heaven were lost,
We should not move, we only should be tossed.
Nay, e'en suppose when we have suffered fate,
The soul could feel in her divided state,
What's that to us? for we are only we,
While souls and bodies in one frame agree.
Nay, though our atoms should revolve by chance,
And matter leap into the former dance;   20
Though time our life and motion could restore,
And make our bodies what they were before;
What gain to us would all this bustle bring?
The new-made man would be another thing.
When once an interrupting pause is made,
That individual being is decayed.
We, who are dead and gone, shall bear no part
In all the pleasures, nor shall feel the smart,
Which to that other mortal shall accrue,
Whom of our matter time shall mould anew.   30
For backward if you look on that long space
Of ages past, and view the changing face
Of matter, tossed, and variously combined
In sundry shapes, 'tis easy for the mind
From thence to infer, that seeds of things have been

In the same order as they now are seen;
Which yet our dark remembrance cannot trace,
Because a pause of life, a gaping space,
Has come betwixt, where memory lies dead,
And all the wandering motions from the sense are fled.   40
For, whosoe'er shall in misfortunes live,
Must *be*, when those misfortunes shall arrive;
And since the man who *is* not, feels not woe,
(For death exempts him, and wards off the blow,
Which we, the living, only feel and bear,)
What is there left for us in death to fear?
When once that pause of life has come between,
'Tis just the same as we had never been.

And therefore if a man bemoan his lot,
That after death his mouldering limbs shall rot,   50
Or flames, or jaws of beasts devour his mass,
Know, he's an unsincere, unthinking ass.
A secret sting remains within his mind;
The fool is to his own cast offals kind.
He boasts no sense can after death remain,
Yet makes himself a part of life again,
As if some other he could feel the pain.
If, while he live, this thought molest his head,
What wolf or vulture shall devour me dead?
He wastes his days in idle grief, nor can   60
Distinguish 'twixt the body and the man;
But thinks himself can still himself survive,
And what when dead he feels not, feels alive.
Then he repines that he was born to die,
Nor knows in death there is no other he,
No living he remains his grief to vent,
And o'er his senseless carcase to lament.
If, after death, 'tis painful to be torn
By birds and beasts, then why not so to burn,
Or drenched in floods of honey to be soaked,   70
Embalmed to be at once preserved and choked;
Or on an airy mountain's top to lie,
Exposed to cold and heaven's inclemency;
Or crowded in a tomb, to be oppressed
With monumental marble on thy breast?
But to be snatched from all thy household joys,

From thy chaste wife, and thy dear prattling boys,
Whose little arms about thy legs are cast,
And climbing for a kiss prevent their mother's haste,
Inspiring secret pleasure through thy breast;   80
All these shall be no more; thy friends oppressed,
Thy care and courage now no more shall free;
'Ah! wretch,' thou criest, 'ah! miserable me!
One woeful day sweeps children, friends, and wife,
And all the brittle blessings of my life!'
Add one thing more, and all thou say'st is true;
Thy want and wish of them is vanished too;
Which well considered were a quick relief
To all thy vain imaginary grief.
For thou shalt sleep, and never wake again,   90
And, quitting life, shalt quit thy living pain.
But we, thy friends, shall all those sorrows find,
Which in forgetful death thou leav'st behind;
No time shall dry our tears, nor drive thee from our mind.
The worst that can befall thee, measured right,
Is a sound slumber, and a long goodnight.
Yet thus the fools, that would be thought the wits,
Disturb their mirth with melancholy fits;
When healths go round, and kindly brimmers flow,
Till the fresh garlands on their foreheads glow,   100
They whine, and cry: 'Let us make haste to live,
Short are the joys that human life can give.'
Eternal preachers, that corrupt the draught,
And pall the god that never thinks with thought;
Idiots with all that thought, to whom the worst
Of death, is want of drink, and endless thirst,
Or any fond desire as vain as these.
For, e'en in sleep, the body, wrapped in ease,
Supinely lies, as in the peaceful grave;
And wanting nothing, nothing can it crave.   110
Were that sound sleep eternal, it were death;
Yet the first atoms then, the seeds of breath,
Are moving near to sense; we do but shake
And rouse that sense, and straight we are awake.
Then death to us, and death's anxiety,
Is less than nothing, if a less could be;
For then our atoms, which in order lay,

Are scattered from their heap, and puffed away,
And never can return into their place,
When once the pause of life has left an empty space.   120
  And, last, suppose great nature's voice should call
To thee, or me, or any of us all,
'What dost thou mean, ungrateful wretch, thou vain,
Thou mortal thing, thus idly to complain,
And sigh and sob, that thou shalt be no more?
For if thy life were pleasant heretofore,
If all the bounteous blessings I could give
Thou hast enjoyed, if thou hast known to live,
And pleasure not leaked through thee like a sieve,
Why dost thou not give thanks as at a plenteous feast,   130
Crammed to the throat with life, and rise and take thy rest?
But if my blessings thou hast thrown away,
If undigested joys passed through, and would not stay,
Why dost thou wish for more to squander still?
If life be grown a load, a real ill,
And I would all thy cares and labours end,
Lay down thy burden, fool, and know thy friend.
To please thee, I have emptied all my store;
I can invent, and can supply no more,
But run the round again, the round I ran before.   140
Suppose thou art not broken yet with years,
Yet still the selfsame scene of things appears,
And would be ever, couldst thou ever live;
For life is still but life, there's nothing new to give.'
What can we plead against so just a bill?
We stand convicted, and our cause goes ill.
But if a wretch, a man oppressed by fate,
Should beg of nature to prolong his date,
She speaks aloud to him with more disdain,
'Be still, thou martyr fool, thou covetous of pain.'   150
But if an old decrepit sot lament,
'What, thou,' she cries, 'who hast outlived content!
Dost thou complain, who hast enjoyed my store?
But this is still the effect of wishing more.
Unsatisfied with all that nature brings;
Loathing the present, liking absent things;
From hence it comes, thy vain desires, at strife
Within themselves, have tantalised thy life,

And ghastly death appeared before thy sight,
Ere thou hadst gorged thy soul and senses with delight.   160
Now leave those joys unsuiting to thy age
To a fresh comer, and resign the stage.'
    Is nature to be blamed if thus she chide?
No, sure; for 'tis her business to provide
Against this ever-changing frame's decay,
New things to come, and old to pass away.
One being, worn, another being makes;
Changed, but not lost; for nature gives and takes:
New matter must be found for things to come,
And these must waste like those, and follow nature's doom.   170
All things, like thee, have time to rise and rot,
And from each other's ruin are begot:
For life is not confined to him or thee;
'Tis given to all for use, to none for property.
Consider former ages past and gone,
Whose circles ended long ere thine begun,
Then tell me, fool, what part in them thou hast?
Thus mayst thou judge the future by the past.
What horror seest thou in that quiet state,
What bugbear dreams to fright thee after fate?   180
No ghost, no goblins, that still passage keep;
But all is there serene, in that eternal sleep.
For all the dismal tales that poets tell
Are verified on earth, and not in hell.
No Tantalus looks up with fearful eye,
Or dreads the impending rock to crush him from on high;
But fear of chance on earth disturbs our easy hours,
Or vain imagined wrath of vain imagined powers.
No Tityus torn by vultures lies in hell;
Nor could the lobes of his rank liver swell   190
To that prodigious mass for their eternal meal;
Not though his monstrous bulk had covered o'er
Nine spreading acres, or nine thousand more;
Not though the globe of earth had been the giant's floor;
Nor in eternal torments could he lie,
Nor could his corpse sufficient food supply.
But he's the Tityus, who, by love oppressed,
Or tyrant passion preying on his breast,
And ever anxious thoughts, is robbed of rest.

The Sisyphus is he, whom noise and strife   200
Seduce from all the soft retreats of life,
To vex the government, disturb the laws;
Drunk with the fumes of popular applause,
He courts the giddy crowd to make him great,
And sweats and toils in vain, to mount the sovereign seat.
For still to aim at power, and still to fail,
Ever to strive, and never to prevail,
What is it but in reason's true account,
To heave the stone against the rising mount?
Which urged, and laboured, and forced up with pain,   210
Recoils, and rolls impetuous down, and smokes along the plain.
Then still to treat thy ever-craving mind
With every blessing, and of every kind,
Yet never fill thy ravening appetite,
Though years and seasons vary thy delight,
Yet nothing to be seen of all the store,
But still the wolf within thee barks for more;
This the fable's moral, which they tell
Of fifty foolish virgins damned in hell
To leaky vessels, which the liquor spill;   220
To vessels of their sex, which none could ever fill.
As for the dog, the furies, and their snakes,
The gloomy caverns, and the burning lakes,
And all the vain infernal trumpery,
They neither are, nor were, nor e'er can be.
But here on earth the guilty have in view
The mighty pains to mighty mischiefs due:
Racks, prisons, poisons, the Tarpeian rock,
Stripes, hangmen, pitch, and suffocating smoke;
And last, and most, if these were cast behind,   230
The avenging horror of a conscious mind,
Whose deadly fear anticipates the blow,
And sees no end of punishment and woe,
But looks for more, at the last gasp of breath:
This makes a hell on earth, and life a death.
    Meantime, when thoughts of death disturb thy head,
Consider, Ancus, great and good, is dead;
Ancus, thy better far, was born to die,
And thou, dost thou bewail mortality?
So many monarchs with their mighty state,   240

Who ruled the world, were overruled by fate.
That haughty king, who lorded o'er the main,
And whose stupendous bridge did the wild waves restrain,
(In vain they foamed, in vain they threatened wreck,
While his proud legions marched upon their back):
Him death, a greater monarch, overcame;
Nor spared his guards the more, for their immortal name.
The Roman chief, the Carthaginian dread,
Scipio, the thunderbolt of war, is dead,
And like a common slave, by fate in triumph led.   250
The founders of invented arts are lost,
And wits who made eternity their boast.
Where now is Homer, who possessed the throne?
The immortal work remains, the mortal author's gone.
Democritus, perceiving age invade,
His body weakened, and his mind decayed,
Obeyed the summons with a cheerful face;
Made haste to welcome death, and met him half the race.
That stroke e'en Epicurus could not bar,
Though he in wit surpassed mankind, as far   260
As does the midday sun the midnight star.
And thou, dost thou disdain to yield thy breath,
Whose very life is little more than death?
More than one half by lazy sleep possessed;
And when awake, thy soul but nods at best,
Day-dreams and sickly thoughts revolving in thy breast,
Eternal troubles haunt thy anxious mind,
Whose cause and cure thou never hop'st to find;
But still uncertain, with thyself at strife,
Thou wanderest in the labyrinth of life.   270
     Oh, if the foolish race of man, who find
A weight of cares still pressing on their mind,
Could find as well the cause of this unrest,
And all this burden lodged within the breast;
Sure they would change their course, nor live as now,
Uncertain what to wish or what to vow.
Uneasy both in country and in town,
They search a place to lay their burden down.
One, restless in his palace, walks abroad,
And vainly thinks to leave behind the load,   280
But straight returns; for he's as restless there,

And finds there's no relief in open air.
Another to his villa would retire,
And spurs as hard as if it were on fire;
No sooner entered at his country door,
But he begins to stretch, and yawn, and snore,
Or seeks the city, which he left before.
Thus every man o'erworks his weary will,
To shun himself, and to shake off his ill;
The shaking fit returns, and hangs upon him still.   290
No prospect of repose, nor hope of ease,
The wretch is ignorant of his disease;
Which known, would all his fruitless trouble spare,
For he would know the world not worth his care:
Then would he search more deeply for the cause,
And study nature well, and nature's laws:
For in this moment lies not the debate,
But on our future, fixed, eternal state;
That never-changing state, which all must keep,
Whom death has doomed to everlasting sleep.   300
     Why are we then so fond of mortal life,
Beset with dangers, and maintained with strife?
A life, which all our care can never save;
One fate attends us, and one common grave.
Besides we tread but a perpetual round;
We ne'er strike out, but beat the former ground,
And the same mawkish joys in the same track are found.
For still we think an absent blessing best,
Which cloys, and is no blessing when possessed;
A new arising wish expels it from the breast.   310
The feverish thirst of life increases still;
We call for more and more, and never have our fill;
Yet know not what tomorrow we shall try,
What dregs of life in the last draught may lie.
Nor, by the longest life we can attain,
One moment from the length of death we gain;
For all behind belongs to his eternal reign.
When once the fates have cut the mortal thread,
The man as much to all intents is dead,
Who dies today, and will as long be so,   320
As he who died a thousand years ago.

The Ninth Ode of the First Book of Horace

I

Behold yon mountain's hoary height,
  Made higher with new mounts of snow;
Again behold the winter's weight
  Oppress the labouring woods below;
And streams, with icy fetters bound,
Benumbed and cramped to solid ground.

II

With well-heaped logs dissolve the cold,
  And feed the genial hearth with fires;
Produce the wine, that makes us bold,
  And sprightly wit and love inspires: 10
For what hereafter shall betide,
God, if 'tis worth his care, provide.

III

Let him alone, with what he made,
  To toss and turn the world below;
At his command the storms invade;
  The winds by his commission blow;
Till with a nod he bids them cease,
And then the calm returns, and all is peace.

IV

Tomorrow and her works defy,
  Lay hold upon the present hour,   20
And snatch the pleasures passing by,
  To put them out of fortune's power:
Nor love, nor love's delights disdain;
Whate'er thou gettest today is gain.

V

Secure those golden early joys
  That youth unsoured with sorrow bears,
Ere withering time the taste destroys,
  With sickness and unwieldy years.

For active sports, for pleasing rest,
This is the time to be possessed;   30
The best is but in season best.

VI

The pointed hour of promised bliss,
    The pleasing whisper in the dark,
The half-unwilling willing kiss,
    The laugh that guides thee to the mark,
When the kind nymph would coyness feign,
And hides but to be found again;
These, these are joys the gods for youth ordain.

A Song for St Cecilia's Day, 1687

I

From harmony, from heavenly harmony,
    This universal frame began:
  When nature underneath a heap
    Of jarring atoms lay,
  And could not heave her head,
The tuneful voice was heard from high,
    'Arise, ye more than dead.'
Then cold, and hot, and moist, and dry,
In order to their stations leap,
    And Music's power obey.   10
From harmony, from heavenly harmony,
    This universal frame began;
    From harmony to harmony
Through all the compass of the notes it ran,
The diapason closing full in man.

II

What passion cannot music raise and quell?
    When Jubal struck the corded shell,
  His listening brethren stood around,
  And, wondering, on their faces fell
  To worship that celestial sound: 20

Less than a God they thought there could not dwell
   Within the hollow of that shell
   That spoke so sweetly and so well.
What passion cannot music raise and quell?

III

   The trumpet's loud clangour
     Excites us to arms,
   With shrill notes of anger
     And mortal alarms.
The double double double beat
     Of the thundering drum,
   Cries 'hark! the foes come:
Charge, charge! 'tis too late to retreat.'

IV

   The soft complaining flute,
   In dying notes discovers
   The woes of hopeless lovers;
Whose dirge is whispered by the warbling lute.

V

   Sharp violins proclaim
Their jealous pangs, and desperation,
Fury, frantic indignation,
Depth of pains, and height of passion,
   For the fair, disdainful dame.

VI

   But, oh! what art can teach,
   What human voice can reach,
The sacred organ's praise?
Notes inspiring holy love,
Notes that wing their heavenly ways
     To mend the choirs above.

VII

Orpheus could lead the savage race;
And trees unrooted left their place,
   Sequacious of the lyre:

But bright Cecilia raised the wonder higher;
When to her organ vocal breath was given,
An angel heard, and straight appeared,
    Mistaking earth for heaven.

GRAND CHORUS

As from the power of sacred lays
    The spheres began to move,
And sung the great creator's praise
    To all the blessed above;
So when the last and dreadful hour
This crumbling pageant shall devour,   60
The trumpet shall be heard on high,
The dead shall live, the living die,
And Music shall untune the sky.

The Lady's Song

I

A choir of bright beauties in spring did appear,
To choose a May-lady to govern the year:
All the nymphs were in white, and the shepherds in green,
The garland was given, and Phyllis was queen;
But Phyllis refused it, and sighing did say,
I'll not wear a garland while Pan is away.

II

While Pan and fair Syrinx are fled from our shore,
The Graces are banished, and Love is no more;
The soft god of pleasure, that warmed our desires,
Has broken his bow, and extinguished his fires,   10
And vows that himself and his mother will mourn,
Till Pan and fair Syrinx in triumph return.

III

Forbear your addresses, and court us no more,
For we will perform what the deity swore:
But, if you dare think of deserving our charms,

Away with your sheep-hooks, and take to your arms;
Then laurels and myrtles your brows shall adorn,
When Pan, and his son, and fair Syrinx, return.

The Sixth Satire of Juvenal

In Saturn's reign, at nature's early birth,
There was that thing called chastity on earth;
When in a narrow cave, their common shade,
The sheep, the shepherds, and their gods were laid;
When reeds, and leaves, and hides of beasts, were spread,
By mountain-housewives, for their homely bed,
And mossy pillows raised, for the rude husband's head.
Unlike the niceness of our modern dames,
(Affected nymphs, with new-affected names,)
The Cynthias, and the Lesbias of our years,   10
Who for a sparrow's death dissolve in tears.
Those first unpolished matrons, big and bold,
Gave suck to infants of gigantic mould;
Rough as their savage lords, who ranged the wood,
And, fat with acorns, belched their windy food.
For when the world was buxom, fresh, and young,
Her sons were undebauched, and therefore strong;
And whether born in kindly beds of earth,
Or struggling from the teeming oaks to birth,
Or from what other atoms they begun,   20
No sires they had, or, if a sire, the sun.
Some thin remains of chastity appeared
E'en under Jove, but Jove without a beard;
Before the servile Greeks had learned to swear
By heads of kings; while yet the bounteous year
Her common fruits in open plains exposed;
Ere thieves were feared, or gardens were enclosed.
At length uneasy justice upwards flew,
And both the sisters to the stars withdrew;
From that old era whoring did begin,   30
So venerably ancient is the sin.
Adulterers next invade the nuptial state,
And marriage-beds creaked with a foreign weight;

All other ills did iron times adorn,
But whores and silver in one age were born.
　　Yet thou, they say, for marriage dost provide;
Is this an age to buckle with a bride?
They say thy hair the curling art is taught,
The wedding-ring perhaps already bought;
A sober man like thee to change his life!　　　　　　40
What fury would possess thee with a wife?
Art thou of every other death bereft,
No knife, no ratsbane, no kind halter left?
(For every noose compared to hers is cheap.)
Is there no city bridge from whence to leap?
Wouldst thou become her drudge, who dost enjoy
A better sort of bedfellow, thy boy?
He keeps thee not awake with nightly brawls,
Nor, with a begged reward, thy pleasure palls;
Nor, with insatiate heavings, calls for more,　　　　50
When all thy spirits were drained out before.
But still Ursidius courts the marriage-bait,
Longs for a son to settle his estate,
And takes no gifts, though every gaping heir
Would gladly grease the rich old bachelor.
What revolution can appear so strange,
As such a lecher such a life to change?
A rank, notorious whoremaster, to choose
To thrust his neck into the marriage-noose?
He who so often in a dreadful fright　　　　　　　60
Had in a coffer scaped the jealous cuckold's sight,
That he to wedlock dotingly betrayed,
Should hope, in this lewd town, to find a maid!
The man's grown mad! to ease his frantic pain,
Run for the surgeon, breathe the middle vein;
But let a heifer with gilt horns be led
To Juno, regent of the marriage-bed;
And let him every deity adore,
If his new bride prove not an arrant whore,
In head and tail and every other pore.　　　　　　70
On Ceres' feast, restrained from their delight,
Few matrons there, but curse the tedious night;
Few whom their fathers dare salute, such lust
Their kisses have, and come with such a gust.

With ivy now adorn thy doors, and wed;
Such is thy bride, and such thy genial bed.
Thinkst thou one man is for one woman meant?
She sooner with one eye would be content.

And yet, 'tis noised, a maid did once appear
In some small village, though fame says not where.   80
'Tis possible; but sure no man she found;
'Twas desert all about her father's ground.
And yet some lustful god might there make bold;
Are Jove and Mars grown impotent and old?
Many a fair nymph has in a cave been spread,
And much good love without a feather-bed.
Whither wouldst thou to choose a wife resort,
The park, the mall, the playhouse, or the court?
Which way soever thy adventures fall,
Secure alike of chastity in all.   90

One sees a dancing-master capering high,
And raves, and pisses, with pure ecstasy;
Another does with all his motions move,
And gapes, and grins, as in the feat of love;
A third is charmed with the new opera notes,
Admires the song, but on the singer dotes.
The country lady in the box appears,
Softly she warbles over all she hears,
And sucks in passion both at eyes and ears.

The rest (when now the long vacation's come,   100
The noisy hall and theatres grown dumb)
Their memories to refresh, and cheer their hearts,
In borrowed breeches act the players' parts.
The poor, that scarce have wherewithal to eat,
Will pinch, to make the singing-boy a treat;
The rich, to buy him, will refuse no price,
And stretch his quail-pipe, till they crack his voice.
Tragedians, acting love, for lust are sought,
(Though but the parrots of a poet's thought.)
The pleading lawyer, though for counsel used,   110
In chamber-practice often is refused.
Still thou wilt have a wife, and father heirs,
(The product of concurring theatres.)
Perhaps a fencer did thy brows adorn,
And a young swordsman to thy lands is born.

Thus Hippia loathed her old patrician lord,
And left him for a brother of the sword.
To wondering Pharos with her love she fled,
To show one monster more than Afric bred;
Forgetting house and husband left behind,   120
E'en children too, she sails before the wind;
False to them all, but constant to her kind.
But, stranger yet, and harder to conceive,
She could the playhouse and the players leave.
Born of rich parentage, and nicely bred,
She lodged on down, and in a damask bed;
Yet daring now the dangers of the deep,
On a hard mattress is content to sleep.
Ere this, 'tis true, she did her fame expose;
But that great ladies with great ease can lose.   130
The tender nymph could the rude ocean bear,
So much her lust was stronger than her fear.
But had some honest cause her passage pressed,
The smallest hardship had disturbed her breast.
Each inconvenience makes their virtue cold;
But womankind in ills is ever bold.
Were she to follow her own lord to sea,
What doubts and scruples would she raise to stay?
Her stomach sick, and her head giddy grows,
The tar and pitch are nauseous to her nose;   140
But in love's voyage nothing can offend,
Women are never sea-sick with a friend.
Amidst the crew she walks upon the board,
She eats, she drinks, she handles every cord;
And if she spew, 'tis thinking of her lord.
Now ask, for whom her friends and fame she lost?
What youth, what beauty, could the adulterer boast?
What was the face, for which she could sustain
To be called mistress to so base a man?
The gallant of his days had known the best;   150
Deep scars were seen indented on his breast,
And all his battered limbs required their needful rest;
A promontory wen, with grisly grace,
Stood high upon the handle of his face:
His blear eyes ran in gutters to his chin;
His beard was stubble, and his cheeks were thin.

But 'twas his fencing did her fancy move;
'Tis arms and blood and cruelty they love.
But should he quit his trade, and sheathe his sword,
Her lover would begin to be her lord. 160
   This was a private crime; but you shall hear
What fruits the sacred brows of monarchs bear:
The good old sluggard but began to snore,
When, from his side, up rose the imperial whore;
She, who preferred the pleasures of the night
To pomps, that are but impotent delight,
Strode from the palace, with an eager pace,
To cope with a more masculine embrace.
Muffled she marched, like Juno in a cloud,
Of all her train but one poor wench allowed; 170
One whom in secret service she could trust,
The rival and companion of her lust.
To the known brothel-house she takes her way,
And for a nasty room gives double pay;
That room in which the rankest harlot lay.
Prepared for fight, expectingly she lies,
With heaving breasts, and with desiring eyes.
The fair unbroken belly lay displayed
Where once the brave Britannicus was laid.
Bare was her bosom, bare the field of lust, 180
Eager to swallow every sturdy thrust.
Still as one drops, another takes his place,
And baffled, still succeeds to like disgrace.
At length, when friendly darkness is expired,
And every strumpet from her cell retired,
She lags behind and lingering at the gate,
With a repining sigh submits to fate;
All filth without, and all afire within,
Tired with the toil, unsated with the sin.
Old Caesar's bed the modest matron seeks, 190
The steam of lamps still hanging on her cheeks
In ropy smut; thus foul, and thus bedight,
She brings him back the product of the night.
   Now should I sing what poisons they provide,
With all their trumpery of charms beside,
And all their arts of death,—it would be known,
Lust is the smallest sin the sex can own.

Caesinia still, they say, is guiltless found
Of every vice, by her own lord renowned;
And well she may, she brought ten thousand pound.   200
She brought him wherewithal to be called chaste:
His tongue is tied in golden fetters fast:
He sighs, adores, and courts her every hour;
Who would not do as much for such a dower?
She writes love-letters to the youth in grace,
Nay, tips the wink before the cuckold's face;
And might do more, her portion makes it good;
Wealth has the privilege of widowhood.

These truths with his example you disprove,
Who with his wife is monstrously in love: 210
But know him better; for I heard him swear,
'Tis not that she's his wife, but that she's fair.
Let her but have three wrinkles in her face,
Let her eyes lessen, and her skin unbrace,
Soon you will hear the saucy steward say
'Pack up with all your trinkets, and away;
You grow offensive both at bed and board;
Your betters must be had to please my lord.'

Meantime she's absolute upon the throne,
And knowing time is precious, loses none.   220
She must have flocks of sheep, with wool more fine
Than silk, and vineyards of the noblest wine;
Whole droves of pages for her train she craves,
And sweeps the prisons for attending slaves.
In short, whatever in her eyes can come,
Or others have abroad, she wants at home.
When winter shuts the seas, and fleecy snows
Make houses white, she to the merchant goes;
Rich crystals of the rock she takes up there,
Huge agate vases, and old china ware;   230
Then Berenice's ring her finger proves,
More precious made by her incestuous loves,
And infamously dear; a brother's bribe,
E'en God's anointed, and of Judah's tribe;
Where barefoot they approach the sacred shrine,
And think it only sin to feed on swine.

But is none worthy to be made a wife
In all this town? Suppose her free from strife,

Rich, fair, and fruitful, of unblemished life;
Chaste as the Sabines, whose prevailing charms,   240
Dismissed their husbands' and their brothers' arms;
Grant her, besides, of noble blood, that ran
In ancient veins, ere heraldry began;
Suppose all these, and take a poet's word,
A black swan is not half so rare a bird.
A wife, so hung with virtues, such a freight,
What mortal shoulders could support the weight!
Some country girl, scarce to a curtsey bred,
Would I much rather than Cornelia wed;
If supercilious, haughty, proud, and vain,   250
She brought her father's triumphs in her train.
Away with all your Carthaginian state;
Let vanquished Hannibal without doors wait,
Too burly, and too big, to pass my narrow gate.
   'O Paean!' cries Amphion, 'bend thy bow
Against my wife, and let my children go!'
But sullen Paean shoots at sons and mothers too.
His Niobe and all his boys he lost;
E'en her, who did her numerous offspring boast,
As fair and fruitful as the sow that carried   260
The thirty pigs, at one large litter farrowed.
   What beauty or what chastity, can bear
So great a price, if stately and severe,
She still insults, and you must still adore?
Grant that the honey's much, the gall is more.
Upbraided with the virtues she displays,
Seven hours in twelve you loathe the wife you praise.
Some faults, though small, intolerable grow;
For what so nauseous and affected too,
As those that think they due perfection want,   270
Who have not learnt to lisp the Grecian cant?
In Greece, their whole accomplishments they seek:
Their fashion, breeding, language, must be Greek;
But, raw in all that does to Rome belong,
They scorn to cultivate their mother tongue.
In Greek they flatter, all their fears they speak;
Tell all their secrets, nay, they scold in Greek:
E'en in the feat of love, they use that tongue.
Such affectations may become the young;

But thou, old hag, of threescore years and three,   280
Is showing of thy parts in Greek for thee?
Ζωὴ καὶ ψυχή! All those tender words
The momentary trembling bliss affords;
The kind soft murmurs of the private sheets
Are bawdy, while thou speakst in public streets.
Those words have fingers; and their force is such,
They raise the dead, and mount him with a touch.
But all provocatives from thee are vain;
No blandishment the slackened nerve can strain:
It looks but on thy face and falls again.   290
   If then thy lawful spouse thou canst not love,
What reason should thy mind to marriage move?
Why all the charges of the nuptial feast,
Wine and desserts, and sweetmeats to digest?
The endowing gold that buys the dear delight,
Given for thy first and only happy night?
If thou art thus uxoriously inclined,
To bear thy bondage with a willing mind,
Prepare thy neck, and put it in the yoke;
But for no mercy from thy woman look.   300
For though, perhaps, she loves with equal fires,
To absolute dominion she aspires,
Joys in the spoils, and triumphs o'er thy purse;
The better husband makes the wife the worse.
Nothing is thine to give, or sell, or buy,
All offices of ancient friendship die,
Nor hast thou leave to make a legacy.
By thy imperious wife thou art bereft
A privilege, to pimps and panders left;
Thy testament's her will; where she prefers   310
Her ruffians, drudges, and adulterers,
Adopting all thy rivals for thy heirs.
   'Go drag that slave to death!'—'Your reason? why
Should the poor innocent be doomed to die?
What proofs? For, when man's life is in debate,
The judge can ne'er too long deliberate.'
'Call'st thou that slave a man?' the wife replies;
'Proved, or unproved the crime, the villain dies.
I have the sovereign power to save or kill
And give no other reason but my will.'   320

Thus the she-tyrant reigns, till pleased with change,
Her wild affections to new empires range;
Another subject-husband she desires;
Divorced from him, she to the first retires
While the last wedding-feast is scarcely o'er,
And garlands hang yet green upon the door.
So still the reckoning rises; and appears
In total sum, eight husbands in five years.
The title for a tombstone might be fit,
But that it would too commonly be writ.   330

Her mother living, hope no quiet day;
She sharpens her, instructs her how to flay
Her husband bare, and then divides the prey.
She takes love-letters, with a crafty smile,
And, in her daughter's answer, mends the style.
In vain the husband sets his watchful spies;
She cheats their cunning, or she bribes their eyes.
The doctor's called; the daughter, taught the trick,
Pretends to faint, and in full health is sick.
The panting stallion in the closet stands,   340
Hears all, and thinks, and loves, and helps it with his hands.
Canst thou, in reason, hope, a bawd so known,
Should teach her other manners than her own?
Her interest is in all the advice she gives
'Tis on the daughter's rents the mother lives.

No cause is tried at the litigious bar
But women plaintiffs or defendants are;
They form the process, all the briefs they write,
The topics furnish, and the pleas indict,
And teach the toothless lawyer how to bite.   350

They turn viragoes too; the wrestler's toil
They try, and smear the naked limbs with oil;
Against the post their wicker shields they crush,
Flourish the sword, and at the plastron push.
Of every exercise the mannish crew
Fulfils the parts, and oft excels us too;
Prepared not only in feigned fights to engage,
But rout the gladiators on the stage.
What sense of shame in such a breast can lie,
Inured to arms, and her own sex to fly?   360
Yet to be wholly man she would disclaim;

To quit her tenfold pleasure at the game,
For frothy praises and an empty name.
Oh what a decent sight 'tis to behold
All thy wife's magazine by auction sold!
The belt, the crested plume, the several suits
Of armour, and the Spanish leather boots!
Yet these are they, that cannot bear the heat
Of figured silks, and under sarcenet sweat.
Behold the strutting Amazonian whore,   370
She stands in guard with her right foot before;
Her coats tucked up, and all her motions just,
She stamps, and then cries, 'Hah!' at every thrust;
But laugh to see her, tired with many a bout,
Call for the pot, and like a man piss out.
The ghosts of ancient Romans, should they rise,
Would grin to see their daughters play a prize.
   Besides, what endless brawls by wives are bred!
The curtain-lecture makes a mournful bed.
Then, when she has thee sure within the sheets,   380
Her cry begins, and the whole day repeats.
Conscious of crimes herself, she teases first;
Thy servants are accused; thy whore is cursed;
She acts the jealous, and at will she cries;
For women's tears are but the sweat of eyes.
Poor cuckold fool! thou think'st that love sincere,
And suckst between her lips the falling tear;
But search her cabinet, and thou shalt find
Each tiller there with love-epistles lined.
Suppose her taken in a close embrace,   390
This you would think so manifest a case,
No rhetoric could defend, no impudence outface;
And yet e'en then she cries, 'The marriage-vow
A mental reservation must allow;
And there's a silent bargain still implied,
The parties should be pleased on either side,
And both may for their private needs provide.
Though men yourselves, and women us you call,
Yet *homo* is a common name for all.'
There's nothing bolder than a woman caught;   400
Guilt gives them courage to maintain their fault.
   You ask, from whence proceed these monstrous crimes?

Once poor, and therefore chaste, in former times
Our matrons were; no luxury found room,
In low-roofed houses, and bare walls of loam;
Their hands with labour hardened while 'twas light,
And frugal sleep supplied the quiet night;
While pinched with want, their hunger held them straight,
When Hannibal was hovering at the gate:
But wanton now, and lolling at our ease,   410
We suffer all the inveterate ills of peace,
And wasteful riot; whose destructive charms,
Revenge the vanquished world of our victorious arms.
No crime, no lustful postures are unknown,
Since poverty, our guardian god, is gone;
Pride, laziness, and all luxurious arts,
Pour like a deluge in from foreign parts:
Since gold obscene, and silver found the way,
Strange fashions, with strange bullion, to convey,
And our plain simple manners to betray.   420
     What care our drunken dames to whom they spread?
Wine no distinction makes of tail or head,
Who lewdly dancing at a midnight ball,
For hot eringoes and fat oysters call:
Full brimmers to their fuddled noses thrust,
Brimmers, the last provocatives of lust;
When vapours to their swimming brains advance,
And double tapers on the table dance.
     Now think what bawdy dialogues they have,
What Tullia talks to her confiding slave,   430
At Modesty's old statue; when by night
They make a stand, and from their litters light;
They straighten with their hands the nameless place
And spouting thence bepiss her venerable face;
Before the conscious moon they get astride,
By turns are ridden, and by turns they ride.
The good man early to the levee goes,
And treads the nasty puddle of his spouse.
     The secrets of the goddess named the good
Are e'en by boys and barbers understood: 440
Where the rank matrons, dancing to the pipe,
Jig with their bums, and are for action ripe;
With music raised, they spread abroad their hair

And toss their heads like an enamoured mare,
Confess their itching in their ardent eyes
While tears of wine run trickling down their thighs.
Laufella lays her garland by, and proves
The mimic lechery of manly loves,
Provokes to flats some battered household whore,
And heaving up the rubster does adore,   450
Ranked with the lady the cheap sinner lies;
For here not blood, but virtue, gives the prize.
Nothing is feigned in this venereal strife,
'Tis downright lust, and acted to the life.
So full, so fierce, so vigorous, and so strong,
That looking on would make old Nestor young.
Impatient of delay, a general sound,
A universal groan of lust goes round;
For then, and only then, the sex sincere is found.
'Now is the time of action; now begin,'   460
They cry, 'and let the lusty lovers in.
The whoresons are asleep; then bring the slaves
And watermen, a race of strong-backed knaves;
Bring anything that's man: if none be nigh,
Asses have better parts their places to supply.'

  I wish, at least, our sacred rites were free
From those pollutions of obscenity:
But 'tis well known what singer, how disguised,
A lewd audacious action enterprised;
Into the fair, with women mixed, he went,   470
Armed with a huge two-handed instrument,
A grateful present to those holy choirs,
Where the mouse, guilty of his sex, retires,
And e'en male pictures modestly are veiled:
Yet no profaneness on that age prevailed;
No scoffers at religious rites were found,
Though now at every altar they abound.

  I hear your cautious council; you would say,
'Keep close your women under lock and key:'
But, who shall keep those keepers? Women, nursed   480
In craft; begin with those, and bribe them first.
The sex is turned all whore; they love the game,
And mistresses and maids are both the same.

  The poor Ogulnia, on the poet's day,

Will borrow clothes and chair to see the play;
She, who before had mortgaged her estate,
And pawned the last remaining piece of plate.
Some are reduced their utmost shifts to try;
But women have no shame of poverty.
They live beyond their stint, as if their store, 490
The more exhausted, would increase the more:
Some men, instructed by the labouring ant,
Provide against the extremities of want;
But womankind, that never knows a mean,
Down to the dregs their sinking fortune drain:
Hourly they give, and spend, and waste, and wear,
And think no pleasure can be bought too dear.

There are, who in soft eunuchs place their bliss,
To shun the scrubbing of a bearded kiss,
And scape abortion; but their solid joy 500
Is when the page, already past a boy,
Is caponed late, and to the gelder shown,
With his two-pounders to perfection grown;
When all the navel-string could give, appears;
All but the beard, and that's the barber's loss, not theirs.
Seen from afar, and famous for his ware,
He struts into the bath among the fair;
The admiring crew to their devotions fall,
And, kneeling, on their new Priapus call.
Carved for my lady's use, with her he lies; 510
And let him drudge for her, if thou art wise,
Rather than trust him with thy favourite boy;
He proffers death, in proffering to enjoy.

If songs they love, the singer's voice they force
Beyond his compass, till his quail-pipe's hoarse.
His lute and lyre with their embrace is worn;
With knots they trim it, and with gems adorn;
Run over all the strings, and kiss the case,
And make love to it in the master's place.

A certain lady once, of high degree, 520
To Janus vowed, and Vesta's deity,
That Pollio might in singing win the prize;
Pollio, the dear, the darling of her eyes:
She prayed, and bribed; what could she more have done
For a sick husband, or an only son?

With her face veiled, and heaving up her hands,
The shameless suppliant at the altar stands;
The forms of prayer she solemnly pursues,
And, pale with fear, the offered entrails views.
Answer, ye powers; for if you heard her vow,   530
Your godships sure had little else to do.

   This is not all; for actors they implore;
An impudence unknown to heaven before.
The haruspex, tired with this religious rout,
Is forced to stand so long, he gets the gout.
But suffer not thy wife abroad to roam:
If she love singing, let her sing at home;
Not strut in streets with Amazonian pace,
For that's to cuckold thee before thy face.

   Their endless itch of news comes next in play;   540
They vent their own, and hear what others say;
Know what in Thrace, or what in France is done;
The intrigues betwixt the stepdame and the son;
Tell who loves who, what favours some partake,
And who is jilted for another's sake;
What pregnant widow in what month was made;
How oft she did, and, doing, what she said.

   She first beholds the raging comet rise,
Knows whom it threatens, and what lands destroys.
Still for the newest news she lies in wait,   550
And takes reports just entering at the gate.
Wrecks, floods, and fires, whatever she can meet,
She spreads, and is the fame of every street.

   This is a grievance; but the next is worse;
A very judgment, and her neighbours' curse;
For if their barking dog disturb her ease,
No prayer can bend her, no excuse appease.
The unmannered malefactor is arraigned;
But first the master, who the cur maintained,
Must feel the scourge. By night she leaves her bed,   560
By night her bathing equipage is led,
That marching armies a less noise create;
She moves in tumult, and she sweats in state.
Meanwhile, her guests their appetites must keep;
Some gape for hunger, and some gasp for sleep.
At length she comes, all flushed; but ere she sup,

Swallows a swingeing preparation-cup,
And then, to clear her stomach, spews it up.
The deluge-vomit all the floor o'erflows,
And the sour savour nauseates every nose.   570
She drinks again, again she spews a lake;
Her wretched husband sees, and dares not speak;
But mutters many a curse against his wife,
And damns himself for choosing such a life.

But of all plagues, the greatest is untold;
The book-learned wife, in Greek and Latin bold;
The critic-dame, who at her table sits,
Homer and Virgil quotes, and weighs their wits,
And pities Dido's agonizing fits.
She has so far the ascendant of the board,   580
The prating pedant puts not in one word;
The man of law is nonplussed in his suit,
Nay, every other female tongue is mute.
Hammers and beating anvils you would swear,
And Vulcan, with his whole militia, there.
Tabors and trumpets, cease; for she alone
Is able to redeem the labouring moon.
E'en wit's a burden, when it talks too long;
But she, who has no continence of tongue,
Should walk in breeches, and should wear a beard,   590
And mix among the philosophic herd.
O what a midnight curse has he, whose side
Is pestered with a mood and figure bride!
Let mine, ye Gods! (if such must be my fate,)
No logic learn, nor history translate,
But rather be a quiet, humble fool;
I hate a wife to whom I go to school,
Who climbs the grammar-tree, distinctly knows
Where noun, and verb, and participle grows;
Corrects her country-neighbour; and, abed,   600
For breaking Priscian's breaks her husband's head.

The gaudy gossip, when she's set agog,
In jewels dressed, and at each ear a bob,
Goes flaunting out, and in her trim of pride,
Thinks all she says or does is justified.
When poor, she's scarce a tolerable evil;
But rich, and fine, a wife's a very devil.

She duly, once a month, renews her face;
Meantime it lies in daub and hid in grease.
Those are the husband's nights; she craves her due,   610
He takes fat kisses, and is stuck in glue.
But to the loved adulterer when she steers,
Fresh from the bath, in brightness she appears:
For him the rich Arabia sweats her gum,
And precious oils from distant Indies come,
How haggardly soe'er she looks at home.
The eclipse then vanishes, and all her face
Is opened, and restored to every grace;
The crust removed, her cheeks as smooth as silk
Are polished with a wash of asses' milk;   620
And should she to the furthest north be sent,
A train of these attend her banishment.
But hadst thou seen her plastered up before,
'Twas so unlike a face, it seemed a sore.

    'Tis worth our while, to know what all the day
They do, and how they pass their time away;
For, if o'ernight the husband has been slack,
Or counterfeited sleep, and turned his back,
Next day, be sure, the servants go to wrack.
The chambermaid and dresser are called whores,   630
The page is stripped, and beaten out of doors;
The whole house suffers for the master's crime,
And he himself is warned to wake another time.

    She hires tormentors by the year; she treats
Her visitors, and talks, but still she beats.
Beats while she paints her face, surveys her gown,
Casts up the day's account, and still beats on:
Tired out, at length, with an outrageous tone,
She bids them in the devil's name be gone.
Compared with such a proud, insulting dame,   640
Sicilian tyrants may renounce their name.

    For if she hastes abroad to take the air,
Or goes to Isis' church, (the bawdy house of prayer,)
She hurries all her handmaids to the task;
Her head, alone, will twenty dressers ask.
Psecas, the chief, with breast and shoulders bare,
Trembling, considers every sacred hair;
If any straggler from his rank be found,

A pinch must for the mortal sin compound.
Psecas is not in fault; but in the glass,   650
The dame's offended at her own ill face.
That maid is banished; and another girl
More dexterous manages the comb and curl.
The rest are summoned on a point so nice,
And first the grave old woman gives advice;
The next is called, and so the turn goes round,
As each for age, or wisdom, is renowned:
Such counsel, such deliberate care they take,
As if her life and honour lay at stake:
With curls on curls, they build her head before,   660
And mount it with a formidable tower.
A giantess she seems; but look behind,
And then she dwindles to the pigmy kind.
Duck-legged, short-waisted, such a dwarf she is,
That she must rise on tiptoes for a kiss.
Meanwhile her husband's whole estate is spent;
He may go bare, while she receives his rent.
She minds him not; she lives not as a wife,
But like a bawling neighbour, full of strife:
Near him in this alone, that she extends   670
Her hate to all his servants and his friends.
    Bellona's priests, a eunuch at their head,
About the streets a mad procession lead:
The venerable gelding, large, and high,
O'erlooks the herd of his inferior fry.
His awkward clergymen about him prance,
And beat the timbrels to their mystic dance;
Guiltless of testicles, they tear their throats,
And squeak in treble their unmanly notes.
Meanwhile his cheeks the mitred prophet swells,   680
And dire presages of the year foretells;
Unless with eggs (his priestly hire) they haste
To expiate, and avert the autumnal blast;
And add beside a murrey-coloured vest,
Which, in their places, may receive the pest,
And thrown into the flood, their crimes may bear,
To purge the unlucky omens of the year.
The astonished matrons pay, before the rest;
That sex is still obnoxious to the priest.

Through ice they beat, and plunge into the stream,   690
If so the god has warned them in a dream.
Weak in their limbs, but in devotion strong,
On their bare hands and feet they crawl along
A whole field's length, the laughter of the throng.
Should Io (Io's priest, I mean) command
A pilgrimage to Meroe's burning sand,
Through deserts they would seek the secret spring,
And holy water for lustration bring.
How can they pay their priests too much respect,
Who trade with heaven, and earthly gains neglect?   700
With him domestic gods discourse by night;
By day, attended by his choir in white,
The bald-pate tribe runs madding through the street,
And smile to see with how much ease they cheat.
The ghostly sire forgives the wife's delights,
Who sins, through frailty, on forbidden nights,
And tempts her husband in the holy time,
When carnal pleasure is a mortal crime.
The sweating image shakes its head, but he,
With mumbled prayers, atones the deity.   710
The pious priesthood the fat goose receive,
And they once bribed, the godhead must forgive.
    No sooner these remove, but full of fear,
A gipsy Jewess whispers in your ear,
And begs an alms; a high-priest's daughter she,
Versed in their Talmud, and divinity,
And prophesies beneath a shady tree.
Her goods a basket, and old hay her bed,
She strolls, and telling fortunes, gains her bread:
Farthings and some small moneys are her fees;   720
Yet she interprets all your dreams for these.
Foretells the estate when the rich uncle dies
And sees a sweetheart in the sacrifice.
Such toys, a pigeon's entrails can disclose,
Which yet the Armenian augur far outgoes;
In dogs, a victim more obscene, he rakes;
And murdered infants for inspection takes:
For gain his impious practice he pursues,
For gain will his accomplices accuse.
    More credit yet is to Chaldeans given;   730

What they foretell is deemed the voice of heaven.
Their answers, as from Hammon's altar, come;
Since now the Delphian oracles are dumb,
And mankind, ignorant of future fate,
Believes what fond astrologers relate.

Of these the most in vogue is he, who, sent
Beyond seas, is returned from banishment;
His art who to aspiring Otho sold,
And sure succession to the crown foretold;
For his esteem is in his exile placed;   740
The more believed, the more he was disgraced.
No astrologic wizard honour gains,
Who has not oft been banished, or in chains.
He gets renown, who, to the halter near,
But narrowly escapes, and buys it dear.

From him your wife inquires the planets' will,
When the black jaundice shall her mother kill;
Her sister's and her uncle's end would know,
But first consults his art, when you shall go;
And what's the greatest gift that heaven can give,   750
If after her the adulterer shall live.
She neither knows, nor cares to know, the rest,
If Mars and Saturn shall the world infest;
Or Jove and Venus, with their friendly rays,
Will interpose, and bring us better days.

Beware the woman too, and shun her sight,
Who in these studies does herself delight,
By whom a greasy almanac is borne,
With often handling, like chafed amber worn:
Not now consulting, but consulted, she   760
Of the twelve houses, and their lords, is free.
She, if the scheme a fatal journey show,
Stays safe at home, but lets her husband go.
If but a mile she travel out of town,
The planetary hour must first be known,
And lucky moment, if her eye but aches,
Or itches, its decumbiture she takes.
No nourishment receives in her disease,
But what the stars and Ptolemy shall please.

The middle sort, who have not much to spare,   770
To chiromancers' cheaper art repair,

Who clap the pretty palm, to make the lines more fair.
But the rich matron who has more to give,
Her answers from the Brahmin will receive;
Skilled in the globe and sphere, he gravely stands,
And with his compass measures seas and lands.

   The poorest of the sex have still an itch
To know their fortunes, equal to the rich.
The dairymaid inquires, if she shall take
The trusty tailor, and the cook forsake,   780

   Yet these, though poor, the pain of childbed bear,
And without nurses their own infants rear:
You seldom hear of the rich mantle spread
For the babe, born in the great lady's bed:
Such is the power of herbs, such arts they use
To make them barren, or their fruit to lose.
But thou, whatever slops she will have bought,
Be thankful and supply the deadly draught;
Help her to make manslaughter; let her bleed,
And never want for savin at her need.   790
For if she holds till her nine months be run,
Thou may'st be father to an Ethiop's son;
A boy who, ready gotten to thy hands,
By law is to inherit all thy lands;
One of that hue, that should he cross the way,
His omen would discolour all the day.

   I pass the foundling by, a race unknown,
At doors exposed, whom matrons make their own;
And into noble families advance
A nameless issue, the blind work of chance.   800
Indulgent fortune does her care employ,
And smiling, broods upon the naked boy:
Her garment spreads, and laps him in the fold,
And covers with her wings from nightly cold:
Gives him her blessing, puts him in a way,
Sets up the farce, and laughs at her own play.
Him she promotes; she favours him alone,
And makes provision for him as her own.

   The craving wife the force of magic tries,
And philtres for the unable husband buys;   810
The potion works not on the part designed,
But turns his brain, and stupefies his mind.

The sotted moon-calf gapes, and staring on,
Sees his own business by another done:
A long oblivion, a benumbing frost,
Constrains his head, and yesterday is lost.
Some nimbler juice would make him foam and rave,
Like that Caesinia to her Caius gave,
Who plucking from the forehead of the foal
His mother's love, infused it in the bowl;   820
The boiling blood ran hissing in his veins,
Till the mad vapour mounted to his brains.
The thunderer was not half so much on fire,
When Juno's girdle kindled his desire.
What woman will not use the poisoning trade,
When Caesar's wife the precedent has made?
Let Agrippina's mushroom be forgot,
Given to a slavering, old, unuseful sot;
That only closed the drivelling dotard's eyes,
And sent his godhead downward to the skies;   830
But this fierce potion calls for fire and sword,
Nor spares the commons, when it strikes the lord.
So many mischiefs were in one combined;
So much one single poisoner cost mankind.

   If step-dames seek their sons-in-law to kill,
'Tis venial trespass—let them have their will;
But let the child, entrusted to the care
Of his own mother, of her bread beware;
Beware the food she reaches with her hand;
The morsel is intended for thy land.   840
Thy tutor be thy taster, ere thou eat;
There's poison in thy drink and in thy meat.

   You think this feigned; the satire in a rage
Struts in the buskins of the tragic stage;
Forgets his business is to laugh and bite,
And will of deaths and dire revenges write.
Would it were all a fable that you read!
But Drymon's wife pleads guilty to the deed.
'I', she confesses, 'in the fact was caught,
Two sons dispatching at one deadly draught.'   850
'What, two! two sons, thou viper, in one day!'
'Yes, seven,' she cries, 'if seven were in my way.'
Medea's legend is no more a lie,

Our age adds credit to antiquity.
Great ills, we grant, in former times did reign,
And murders then were done, but not for gain.
Less admiration to great crimes is due,
Which they through wrath, or through revenge pursue;
For, weak of reason, impotent of will,
The sex is hurried headlong into ill;   860
And like a cliff, from its foundations torn
By raging earthquakes, into seas is borne.
But those are fiends, who crimes from thought begin,
And cool in mischief meditate the sin.
They read the example of a pious wife,
Redeeming, with her own, her husband's life;
Yet if the laws did that exchange afford,
Would save their lap-dog sooner than their lord.
     Where'er you walk the Belides you meet,
And Clytemnestras grow in every street;   870
But here's the difference,—Agamemnon's wife
Was a gross butcher with a bloody knife;
But murder now is to perfection grown,
And subtle poisons are employed alone;
Unless some antidote prevents their arts,
And lines with balsam all the noble parts.
In such a case, reserved for such a need,
Rather than fail, the dagger does the deed.

The First Book of
Ovid's Metamorphoses

Of bodies changed to various forms I sing:
Ye gods, from whom these miracles did spring,
Inspire my numbers with celestial heat,
Till I my long laborious work complete;
And add perpetual tenor to my rhymes,
Deduced from nature's birth to Caesar's times.
     Before the seas, and this terrestrial ball,
And heaven's high canopy, that covers all,
One was the face of nature, if a face;
Rather a rude and indigested mass;   10

A lifeless lump, unfashioned, and unframed,
Of jarring seeds, and justly chaos named.
No sun was lighted up the world to view;
No moon did yet her blunted horns renew;
Nor yet was earth suspended in the sky,
Nor, poised, did on her own foundations lie;
Nor seas about the shores their arms had thrown;
But earth, and air, and water, were in one.
Thus air was void of light, and earth unstable,
And water's dark abyss unnavigable.   20
No certain form on any was imprest;
All were confused, and each disturbed the rest:
For hot and cold were in one body fixed;
And soft with hard, and light with heavy, mixed.
  But god, or nature, while they thus contend,
To these intestine discords put an end.
Then earth from air, and seas from earth, were driven,
And grosser air sunk from ethereal heaven.
Thus disembroiled, they take their proper place;
The next of kin contiguously embrace;   30
And foes are sundered by a larger space.
The force of fire ascended first on high,
And took its dwelling in the vaulted sky.
Then air succeeds, in lightness next to fire,
Whose atoms from unactive earth retire.
Earth sinks beneath, and draws a numerous throng,
Of ponderous, thick, unwieldy seeds along.
About her coasts unruly waters roar,
And, rising on a ridge, insult the shore.
Thus when the god, whatever god was he,   40
Had formed the whole, and made the parts agree,
That no unequal portions might be found,
He moulded earth into a spacious round;
Then, with a breath, he gave the winds to blow,
And bade the congregated waters flow:
He adds the running springs, and standing lakes,
And bounding banks for winding rivers makes.
Some part in earth are swallowed up, the most
In ample oceans, disembogued, are lost:
He shades the woods, the valleys he restrains   50
With rocky mountains, and extends the plains.

And as five zones the ethereal regions bind,
Five, correspondent, are to earth assigned;
The sun, with rays directly darting down,
Fires all beneath, and fries the middle zone:
The two beneath the distant poles complain
Of endless winter, and perpetual rain.
Betwixt the extremes, two happier climates hold
The temper that partakes of hot and cold.
The fields of liquid air, enclosing all,   60
Surround the compass of this earthly ball:
The lighter parts lie next the fires above;
The grosser near the watery surface move:
Thick clouds are spread, and storms engender there,
And thunder's voice, which wretched mortals fear,
And winds that on their wings cold winter bear.
Nor were those blustering brethren left at large,
On seas and shores their fury to discharge:
Bound as they are, and circumscribed in place,
They rend the world, resistless, where they pass,   70
And mighty marks of mischief leave behind;
Such is the rage of their tempestuous kind.
First, Eurus to the rising morn is sent,
(The regions of the balmy continent,)
And eastern realms, where early Persians run,
To greet the blest appearance of the sun.
Westward the wanton Zephyr wings his flight,
Pleased with the remnants of departing light;
Fierce Boreas with his offspring issues forth,
To invade the frozen waggon of the north;   80
While frowning Auster seeks the southern sphere,
And rots, with endless rain, the unwholesome year.

High o'er the clouds, and empty realms of wind,
The god a clearer space for heaven designed;
Where fields of light and liquid ether flow,
Purged from the ponderous dregs of earth below.
Scarce had the power distinguished these, when straight
The stars, no longer overlaid with weight,
Exert their heads from underneath the mass,
And upward shoot, and kindle as they pass,   90
And with diffusive light adorn their heavenly place.
Then, every void of nature to supply,

With forms of gods he fills the vacant sky:
New herds of beasts he sends, the plains to share;
New colonies of birds, to people air;
And to their oozy beds the finny fish repair.
A creature of a more exalted kind
Was wanting yet, and then was man designed;
Conscious of thought, of more capacious breast,
For empire formed, and fit to rule the rest: 100
Whether with particles of heavenly fire
The god of nature did his soul inspire;
Or earth, but new divided from the sky,
And pliant still, retained the ethereal energy;
Which wise Prometheus tempered into paste,
And, mixed with living streams, the god-like image cast.
Thus, while the mute creation downward bend
Their sight, and to their earthly mother tend,
Man looks aloft, and, with erected eyes,
Beholds his own hereditary skies.   110
From such rude principles our form began,
And earth was metamorphosed into man.

THE GOLDEN AGE

The Golden Age was first, when man yet new
No rule but uncorrupted reason knew;
And, with a native bent, did good pursue.
Unforced by punishment, unawed by fear,
His words were simple, and his soul sincere.
Needless was written law, where none oppressed;
The law of man was written in his breast.
No suppliant crowds before the judge appeared;   120
No court erected yet, nor cause was heard;
But all was safe, for conscience was their guard.
The mountain trees in distant prospect please,
Ere yet the pine descended to the seas;
Ere sails were spread, new oceans to explore;
And happy mortals, unconcerned for more,
Confined their wishes to their native shore.
No walls were yet, nor fence, nor moat, nor mound;
Nor drum was heard, nor trumpet's angry sound;
Nor swords were forged; but, void of care and crime,   130
The soft creation slept away their time.

The teeming earth, yet guiltless of the plough,
And unprovoked, did fruitful stores allow:
Content with food, which nature freely bred,
On wildings and on strawberries they fed;
Cornels and bramble-berries gave the rest,
And falling acorns furnished out a feast.
The flowers, unsown, in fields and meadows reigned;
And western winds immortal spring maintained.
In following years the bearded corn ensued   140
From earth unasked, nor was that earth renewed.
From veins of valleys milk and nectar broke,
And honey sweating through the pores of oak.

THE SILVER AGE

But when good Saturn, banished from above,
Was driven to hell, the world was under Jove.
Succeeding times a Silver Age behold,
Excelling brass, but more excelled by gold.
Then Summer, Autumn, Winter did appear,
And Spring was but a season of the year.
The sun his annual course obliquely made,   150
Good days contracted, and enlarged the bad.
Then air with sultry heats began to glow,
The winds of winds were clogged with ice and snow;
And shivering mortals, into houses driven,
Sought shelter from the inclemency of heaven.
Those houses, then, were caves, or homely sheds,
With twining osiers fenced, and moss their beds.
Then ploughs for seed the fruitful furrows broke,
And oxen laboured first beneath the yoke.

THE BRAZEN AGE

To this came next, in course the Brazen Age: 160
A warlike offspring prompt to bloody rage,
Not impious yet—

THE IRON AGE

                          Hard steel succeeded then;
And stubborn as the metal were the men.
Truth, modesty, and shame, the world forsook;

Fraud, avarice, and force, their places took.
Then sails were spread to every wind that blew;
Raw were the sailors, and the depths were new:
Trees, rudely hollowed, did the waves sustain,
Ere ships in triumph ploughed the watery plain.

   Then landmarks limited to each his right;   170
For all before was common as the light.
Nor was the ground alone required to bear
Her annual income to the crooked share;
But greedy mortals, rummaging her store,
Dug from her entrails the precious ore;
Which next to hell the prudent gods had laid,
And that alluring ill to sight displayed.
Thus cursed steel, and more accursed gold,
Gave mischief birth, and made that mischief bold;
And double death did wretched man invade,   180
By steel assaulted, and by gold betrayed.
Now (brandished weapons glittering in their hands)
Mankind is broken loose from moral bands:
No rights of hospitality remain,
The guest, by him who harboured him, is slain;
The son-in-law pursues the father's life;
The wife her husband murders, he the wife;
The step-dame poison for the son prepares;
The son inquires into his father's years.
Faith flies, and piety in exile mourns: 190
And justice, here oppressed, to heaven returns.

THE GIANTS' WAR

   Nor were the Gods themselves more safe above;
Against beleaguered heaven the Giants move.
Hills piled on hills, on mountains mountains lie,
To make their mad approaches to the sky:
Till Jove, no longer patient, took his time
To avenge with thunder their audacious crime;
Red lightning played along the firmament,
And their demolished works to pieces rent.
Singed with the flames, and with the bolts transfixed,   200
With native earth their blood the monsters mixed;
The blood, endued with animating heat,

Did in the impregnant earth new sons beget;
They, like the seed from which they sprung, accursed,
Against the gods immortal hatred nursed;
An impious, arrogant, and cruel brood,
Expressing their original from blood;
Which when the king of gods beheld from high,
(Withal revolving in his memory
What he himself had found on earth of late,   210
Lycaon's guilt, and his inhuman treat,)
He sighed, nor longer with his pity strove,
But kindled to a wrath becoming Jove.
Then called a general council of the gods;
Who, summoned, issue from their blest abodes,
And fill the assembly with a shining train.
  A way there is in heaven's expanded plain,
Which, when the skies are clear, is seen below,
And mortals by the name of Milky know.
The ground-work is of stars; through which the road   220
Lies open to the thunderer's abode.
The gods of greater nations dwell around,
And on the right and left the palace bound;
The commons where they can; the nobler sort,
With winding doors wide open, front the court.
This place, as far as earth with heaven may vie,
I dare to call the Louvre of the sky.
When all were placed, in seats distinctly known,
And he, their father, had assumed the throne,
Upon his ivory sceptre first he leant,   230
Then shook his head, that shook the firmament;
Air, earth, and seas obeyed the almighty nod,
And with a general fear confessed the god.
At length, with indignation, thus he broke
His awful silence, and the powers bespoke.
  'I was not more concerned in that debate
Of empire, when our universal state
Was put to hazard, and the giant race
Our captive skies were ready to embrace:
For though the foe was fierce, the seeds of all   240
Rebellion sprung from one original;
Now wheresoever ambient waters glide,
All are corrupt, and all must be destroyed.

Let me this holy protestation make,
By hell, and hell's inviolable lake,
I tried whatever in the godhead lay;
But gangrened members must be lopped away,
Before the nobler parts are tainted to decay.
There dwells below a race of demi-gods,
Of nymphs in waters, and of fauns in woods;　　250
Who, though not worthy yet in heaven to live,
Let them at least enjoy that earth we give.
Can these be thought securely lodged below,
When I myself, who no superior know,
I, who have heaven and earth at my command,
Have been attempted by Lycaon's hand?'
　　At this a murmur through the synod went,
And with one voice they vote his punishment.
Thus when conspiring traitors dared to doom
The fall of Caesar, and in him of Rome,　　260
The nations trembled with a pious fear,
All anxious for their earthly thunderer:
Nor was their care, O Caesar, less esteemed
By thee, than that of heaven for Jove was deemed;
Who with his hand and voice did first restrain
Their murmurs, then resumed his speech again.
The gods to silence were composed, and sate
With reverence due to his superior state.
　　'Cancel your pious cares; already he
Has paid his debt to justice, and to me.　　270
Yet what his crimes, and what my judgments were,
Remains for me thus briefly to declare.
The clamours of this vile degenerate age,
The cries of orphans, and the oppressor's rage,
Had reached the stars; "I will descend," said I,
"In hope to prove this loud complaint a lie."
Disguised in human shape, I travelled round
The world, and more than what I heard, I found.
O'er Maenalus I took my steepy way,
By caverns infamous for beasts of prey;　　280
Then crossed Cyllene, and the piny shade,
More infamous by cursed Lycaon made.
Dark night had covered heaven and earth, before
I entered his unhospitable door.

Just at my entrance, I displayed the sign
That somewhat was approaching of divine.
The prostrate people pray; the tyrant grins;
And, adding profanation to his sins,
"I'll try," said he, "and if a God appear,
To prove his deity shall cost him dear."   290
'Twas late; the graceless wretch my death prepares,
When I should soundly sleep, oppressed with cares:
This dire experiment he chose, to prove
If I were mortal, or undoubted Jove.
But first he had resolved to taste my power:
Not long before, but in a luckless hour,
Some legates, sent from the Molossian state,
Were on a peaceful errand come to treat;
Of these he murders one, he boils the flesh,
And lays the mangled morsels in a dish;   300
Some part he roasts; then serves it up so dressed,
And bids me welcome to this human feast.
Moved with disdain, the table I o'erturned,
And with avenging flames the palace burned.
The tyrant in a fright, for shelter gains
The neighbouring fields, and scours along the plains.
Howling he fled, and fain he would have spoke,
But human voice his brutal tongue forsook.
About his lips the gathered foam he churns,
And, breathing slaughter, still with rage he burns,   310
But on the bleating flock his fury turns.
His mantle, now his hide, with rugged hairs
Cleaves to his back; a famished face he bears;
His arms descend, his shoulders sink away,
To multiply his legs for chase of prey.
He grows a wolf, his hoariness remains,
And the same rage in other members reigns.
His eyes still sparkle in a narrower space,
His jaws retain the grin, and violence of his face.
    'This was a single ruin, but not one   320
Deserves so just a punishment alone.
Mankind's a monster, and the ungodly times,
Confederate into guilt, are sworn to crimes.
All are alike involved in ill, and all
Must by the same relentless fury fall.'

Thus ended he; the greater gods assent,
By clamours urging his severe intent;
The less fill up the cry for punishment.
Yet still with pity they remember man,
And mourn as much as heavenly spirits can.   330
They ask, when those were lost of human birth,
What he would do with all this waste of earth.
If his dispeopled world he would resign
To beasts, a mute, and more ignoble line.
Neglected altars must no longer smoke,
If none were left to worship and invoke.
To whom the father of the gods replied:
'Lay that unnecessary fear aside;
Mine be the care new people to provide.
I will from wondrous principles ordain   340
A race unlike the first, and try my skill again.'
  Already had he tossed the flaming brand,
And rolled the thunder in his spacious hand,
Preparing to discharge on seas and land;
But stopped, for fear, thus violently driven,
The sparks should catch his axle-tree of heaven;
Remembering, in the fates, a time, when fire
Should to the battlements of heaven aspire,
And all his blazing worlds above should burn,
And all the inferior globe to cinders turn.   350
His dire artillery thus dismissed, he bent
His thoughts to some securer punishment;
Concludes to pour a watery deluge down,
And what he durst not burn, resolves to drown.
  The northern breath, that freezes floods, he binds,
With all the race of cloud-dispelling winds;
The south he loosed, who night and horror brings,
And fogs are shaken from his flaggy wings.
From his divided beard two streams he pours;
His head and rheumy eyes distil in showers;   360
With rain his robe and heavy mantle flow,
And lazy mists are louring on his brow.
Still as he swept along, with his clenched fist,
He squeezed the clouds; the imprisoned clouds resist;
The skies, from pole to pole, with peals resound,
And showers enlarged come pouring on the ground.

Then clad in colours of a various dye,
Junonian Iris breeds a new supply
To feed the clouds: impetuous rain descends;
The bearded corn beneath the burden bends;   370
Defrauded clowns deplore their perished grain,
And the long labours of the year are vain.
     Nor from his patrimonial heaven alone
Is Jove content to pour his vengeance down;
Aid from his brother of the seas he craves,
To help him with auxiliary waves.
The watery tyrant calls his brooks and floods,
Who roll from mossy caves, their moist abodes;
And with perpetual urns his palace fill:
To whom, in brief, he thus imparts his will.   380
     'Small exhortation needs; your powers employ,
And this bad world (so Jove requires) destroy.
Let loose the reins to all your watery store;
Bear down the dams, and open every door.'
     The floods, by nature enemies to land,
And proudly swelling with their new command,
Remove the living stones that stopped their way,
And gushing from their source, augment the sea.
Then with his mace their monarch struck the ground;
With inward trembling earth received the wound,   390
And rising streams a ready passage found.
The expanded waters gather on the plain,
They float the fields, and overtop the grain;
Then rushing onwards, with a sweepy sway,
Bear flocks and folds and labouring hinds away.
Nor safe their dwellings were; for sapped by floods,
Their houses fell upon their household gods,
The solid piles, too strongly built to fall,
High o'er their heads behold a watery wall.
Now seas and earth were in confusion lost;   400
A world of waters, and without a coast.
     One climbs a cliff; one in his boat is borne,
And ploughs above, where late he sowed his corn.
Others o'er chimney-tops and turrets row,
And drop their anchors on the meads below;
Or, downward driven, they bruise the tender vine,
Or, tossed aloft, are knocked against a pine;
And where of late the kids had cropped the grass,

The monsters of the deep now take their place.
Insulting nereids on the cities ride,   410
And wondering dolphins o'er the palace glide;
On leaves and masts of mighty oaks they browse;
And their broad fins entangle in the boughs.
The frighted wolf now swims amongst the sheep;
The yellow lion wanders in the deep;
His rapid force no longer helps the boar;
The stag swims faster than he ran before.
The fowls, long beating on their wings in vain,
Despair of land and drop into the main.
Now hills and vales no more distinction know,   420
And levelled nature lies oppressed below.
The most of mortals perish in the flood,
The small remainder dies for want of food.
   A mountain of stupendous height there stands
Betwixt the Athenian and Boeotian lands,
The bound of fruitful fields, while fields they were,
But then a field of waters did appear:
Parnassus is its name, whose forky rise
Mounts through the clouds and mates the lofty skies.
High on the summit of this dubious cliff,   430
Deucalion wafting moored his little skiff.
He with his wife were only left behind
Of perished man; they two were humankind.
The mountain-nymphs and Themis they adore,
And from her oracles relief implore.
The most upright of mortal men was he;
The most sincere and holy woman, she.
   When Jupiter, surveying earth from high,
Beheld it in a lake of water lie,
That where so many millions lately lived,   440
But two, the best of either sex, survived,
He loosed the northern wind; fierce Boreas flies
To puff away the clouds, and purge the skies;
Serenely, while he blows, the vapours driven
Discover heaven to earth, and earth to heaven.
The billows fall, while Neptune lays his mace
On the rough sea, and smooths its furrowed face.
Already Triton at his call appears
Above the waves; a Tyrian robe he wears;

And in his hand a crooked trumpet bears.   450
The sovereign bids him peaceful sounds inspire,
And give the waves the signal to retire.
His writhen shell he takes, whose narrow vent
Grows by degrees into a large extent,
Then gives it breath; the blast, with doubling sound,
Runs the wide circuit of the world around.
The sun first heard it in his early east
And met the rattling echoes in the west.
The waters, listening to the trumpet's roar,
Obey the summons, and forsake the shore.   460
   A thin circumference of land appears;
And earth, but not at once, her visage rears,
And peeps upon the seas from upper grounds:
The streams, but just contained within their bounds,
By slow degrees into their channels crawl,
And earth increases as the waters fall.
In longer time the tops of trees appear,
Which mud on their dishonoured branches bear.
   At length the world was all restored to view,
But desolate, and of a sickly hue: 470
Nature beheld herself, and stood aghast,
A dismal desert, and a silent waste.
   Which when Deucalion, with a piteous look,
Beheld, he wept, and thus to Pyrrha spoke:
'O wife, O sister, oh, of all thy kind,
The best and only creature left behind,
By kindred, love, and now by dangers joined;
Of multitudes, who breathed the common air,
We two remain, a species in a pair:
The rest the seas have swallowed; nor have we   480
E'en of this wretched life a certainty.
The clouds are still above; and while I speak,
A second deluge o'er our heads may break.
Should I be snatched from hence, and thou remain,
Without relief, or partner of thy pain,
How couldst thou such a wretched life sustain?
Should I be left, and thou be lost, the sea,
That buried her I loved, should bury me.
Oh could our father his old arts inspire,
And make me heir of his informing fire,   490

That so I might abolished man retrieve,
And perished people in new souls might live!
But heaven is pleased, nor ought we to complain,
That we, the examples of mankind, remain.'
  He said; the careful couple join their tears,
And then invoke the gods with pious prayers.
Thus in devotion having eased their grief,
From sacred oracles they seek relief,
And to Cephisus' brook their way pursue;
The stream was troubled, but the ford they knew.   500
With living waters in the fountain bred,
They sprinkle first their garments, and their head,
Then took the way which to the temple led.
The roofs were all defiled with moss and mire,
The desert altars void of solemn fire.
Before the gradual prostrate they adored,
The pavement kissed, and thus the saint implored.
  'O righteous Themis, if the powers above
By prayers are bent to pity and to love;
If human miseries can move their mind;   510
If yet they can forgive, and yet be kind;
Tell how we may restore, by second birth,
Mankind, and people desolated earth.'
Then thus the gracious goddess, nodding, said:
'Depart, and with your vestments veil your head:
And stooping lowly down, with loosened zones,
Throw each behind your backs your mighty mother's bones.'
Amazed the pair, and mute with wonder, stand,
Till Pyrrha first refused the dire command.
'Forbid it heaven,' said she, 'that I should tear   520
Those holy relics from the sepulchre.'
They pondered the mysterious words again,
For some new sense; and long they sought in vain.
At length Deucalion cleared his cloudy brow,
And said: 'The dark enigma will allow
A meaning which, if well I understand,
From sacrilege will free the god's command:
This earth our mighty mother is, the stones
In her capacious body are her bones.
These we must cast behind.' With hope, and fear,   530
The woman did the new solution hear:

The man diffides in his own augury,
And doubts the gods; yet both resolve to try.
Descending from the mount, they first unbind
Their vests, and, veiled, they cast the stones behind:
The stones (a miracle to mortal view,
But long tradition makes it pass for true,)
Did first the rigour of their kind expel,
And suppled into softness as they fell;
Then swelled, and, swelling, by degrees grew warm,   540
And took the rudiments of human form;
Imperfect shapes, in marble such are seen,
When the rude chisel does the man begin,
While yet the roughness of the stone remains,
Without the rising muscles, and the veins.
The sappy parts, and next resembling juice,
Were turned to moisture, for the body's use;
Supplying humours, blood, and nourishment:
The rest, too solid to receive a bent,
Converts to bones; and what was once a vein,   550
Its former name and nature did retain
By help of power divine, in little space,
What the man threw, assumed a manly face;
And what the wife, renewed the female race.
Hence we derive our nature, born to bear
Laborious life, and hardened into care.
    The rest of animals, from teeming earth
Produced, in various forms received their birth.
The native moisture, in its close retreat,
Digested by the sun's ethereal heat,   560
As in a kindly womb, began to breed;
Then swelled, and quickened by the vital seed:
And some in less, and some in longer space,
Were ripened into form, and took a several face.
Thus when the Nile from Pharian fields is fled,
And seeks with ebbing tides his ancient bed,
The fat manure with heavenly fire is warmed,
And crusted creatures, as in wombs, are formed:
These, when they turn the glebe, the peasants find:
Some rude, and yet unfinished in their kind;   570
Short of their limbs, a lame imperfect birth;
One half alive, and one of lifeless earth.

For heat and moisture, when in bodies joined,
The temper that results from either kind,
Conception makes; and fighting till they mix,
Their mingled atoms in each other fix.
Thus nature's hand the genial bed prepares,
With friendly discord, and with fruitful wars.

From hence the surface of the ground, with mud
And slime besmeared, (the faeces of the flood,)   580
Received the rays of heaven; and sucking in
The seeds of heat, new creatures did begin.
Some were of several sorts produced before;
But of new monsters earth created more.

Unwillingly, but yet she brought to light
Thee, Python, too, the wondering world to fright,
And the new nations with so dire a sight;
So monstrous was his bulk, so large a space
Did his vast body and long train embrace:
Whom Phoebus basking on a bank espied.   590
Ere now the god his arrows had not tried
But on the trembling deer, or mountain-goat;
At this new quarry he prepares to shoot.
Though every shaft took place, he spent the store
Of his full quiver; and 'twas long before
The expiring serpent wallowed in his gore.

Then to preserve the fame of such a deed,
For Python slain, he Pythian games decreed,
Where noble youths for mastership should strive,
To quoit, to run, and steeds and chariots drive.   600
The prize was fame. In witness of renown,
An oaken garland did the victor crown.
The laurel was not yet for triumphs borne;
But every green alike, by Phoebus worn,
Did, with promiscuous grace, his flowing locks adorn.

THE TRANSFORMATION OF DAPHNE INTO A LAUREL

The first and fairest of his loves was she,
Whom not blind fortune, but the dire decree
Of angry Cupid, forced him to desire;
Daphne her name, and Peneus was her sire.
Swelled with the pride that new success attends,   610

He sees the stripling, while his bow he bends,
And thus insults him: 'Thou lascivious boy,
Are arms like these for children to employ?
Know, such achievements are my proper claim,
Due to my vigour and unerring aim:
Resistless are my shafts, and Python late,
In such a feathered death, has found his fate.
Take up thy torch, and lay my weapons by;
With that the feeble souls of lovers fry.'
To whom the son of Venus thus replied: 620
'Phoebus, thy shafts are sure on all beside;
But mine on Phoebus; mine the fame shall be
Of all thy conquests, when I conquer thee.'

   He said, and soaring swiftly winged his flight;
Nor stopped but on Parnassus' airy height.
Two different shafts he from his quiver draws;
One to repel desire, and one to cause.
One shaft is pointed with refulgent gold,
To bribe the love, and make the lover bold;
One blunt, and tipped with lead, whose base allay   630
Provokes disdain, and drives desire away.
The blunted bolt against the nymph he dressed;
But with the sharp transfixed Apollo's breast.

   The enamoured deity pursues the chase;
The scornful damsel shuns his loathed embrace:
In hunting beasts of prey her youth employs,
And Phoebe rivals in her rural joys.
With naked neck she goes, and shoulders bare,
And with a fillet binds her flowing hair.
By many suitors sought, she mocks their pains,   640
And still her vowed virginity maintains.
Impatient of a yoke, the name of bride
She shuns, and hates the joys she never tried.
On wilds and woods she fixes her desire;
Nor knows what youth and kindly love inspire.
Her father chides her oft: 'Thou ow'st,' says he,
'A husband to thyself, a son to me.'
She, like a crime, abhors the nuptial bed;
She glows with blushes, and she hangs her head.
Then casting round his neck her tender arms,   650
Soothes him with blandishments, and filial charms:

'Give me, my lord,' she said, 'to live and die
A spotless maid, without the marriage-tie.
'Tis but a small request; I beg no more
Than what Diana's father gave before.'
The good old sire was softened to consent;
But said her wish would prove her punishment;
For so much youth, and so much beauty joined,
Opposed the state which her desires designed.

The god of light, aspiring to her bed,   660
Hopes what he seeks, with flattering fancies fed,
And is by his own oracles misled.
And as in empty fields the stubble burns,
Or nightly travellers, when day returns,
Their useless torches on dry hedges throw,
That catch the flames, and kindle all the row;
So burns the god, consuming in desire,
And feeding in his breast a fruitless fire:
Her well-turned neck he viewed, (her neck was bare,)
And on her shoulders her dishevelled hair: 670
'Oh, were it combed,' said he, 'with what a grace
Would every waving curl become her face!'
He viewed her eyes, like heavenly lamps that shone;
He viewed her lips, too sweet to view alone;
Her taper fingers, and her panting breast:
He praises all he sees; and for the rest,
Believes the beauties yet unseen are best.
Swift as the wind, the damsel fled away,
Nor did for these alluring speeches stay.
'Stay, nymph,' he cried; 'I follow, not a foe: 680
Thus from the lion trips the trembling doe;
Thus from the wolf the frightened lamb removes,
And from pursuing falcons fearful doves;
Thou shunn'st a god, and shunn'st a god that loves.
Ah! lest some thorn should pierce thy tender foot,
Or thou shouldst fall in flying my pursuit,
To sharp uneven ways thy steps decline,
Abate thy speed, and I will bate of mine.
Yet think from whom thou dost so rashly fly;
Nor basely born, nor shepherd's swain am I.   690
Perhaps thou know'st not my superior state,
And from that ignorance proceeds thy hate.

Me Claros, Delphos, Tenedos, obey;
These hands the Patareian sceptre sway.
The king of gods begot me: what shall be,
Or is, or ever was, in fate, I see.
Mine is the invention of the charming lyre;
Sweet notes, and heavenly numbers, I inspire.
Sure is my bow, unerring is my dart;
But ah! more deadly his, who pierced my heart.   700
Medicine is mine; what herbs and simples grow
In fields and forests, all their powers I know,
And am the great physician called below.
Alas, that fields and forests can afford
No remedies to heal their love-sick lord!
To cure the pains of love, no plant avails,
And his own physic the physician fails.'
    She heard not half, so furiously she flies,
And on her ear the imperfect accent dies.
Fear gave her wings; and as she fled, the wind   710
Increasing spread her flowing hair behind;
And left her legs and thighs exposed to view,
Which made the god more eager to pursue.
The god was young, and was too hotly bent
To lose his time in empty compliment;
But led by love, and fired with such a sight,
Impetuously pursued his near delight.
    As when the impatient greyhound, slipped from far,
Bounds o'er the glebe, to course the fearful hare,
She in her speed does all her safety lay,   720
And he with double speed pursues the prey;
O'erruns her at the sitting turn, and licks
His chaps in vain, and blows upon the flix;
She scapes, and for the neighbouring covert strives,
And gaining shelter doubts if yet she lives.
If little things with great we may compare,
Such was the god, and such the flying fair:
She, urged by fear, her feet did swiftly move,
But he more swiftly, who was urged by love.
He gathers ground upon her in the chase;   730
Now breathes upon her hair, with nearer pace,
And just is fastening on the wished embrace.
The nymph grew pale, and in a mortal fright,

Spent with the labour of so long a flight,
And now despairing, cast a mournful look
Upon the streams of her paternal brook:
'Oh, help,' she cried, 'in this extremest need,
If water-gods are deities indeed!
Gape, earth, and this unhappy wretch entomb,
Or change my form, whence all my sorrows come.'   740
Scarce had she finished, when her feet she found
Benumbed with cold, and fastened to the ground;
A filmy rind about her body grows,
Her hair to leaves, her arms extend to boughs;
The nymph is all into a laurel gone,
The smoothness of her skin remains alone.

  Yet Phoebus loves her still, and, casting round
Her bole his arms, some little warmth he found.
The tree still panted in the unfinished part,
Not wholly vegetive, and heaved her heart.   750
He fixed his lips upon the trembling rind;
It swerved aside, and his embrace declined.
To whom the god: 'Because thou canst not be
My mistress, I espouse thee for my tree:
Be thou the prize of honour and renown;
The deathless poet, and the poem, crown.
Thou shalt the Roman festivals adorn,
And, after poets, be by victors worn;
Thou shalt returning Caesar's triumph grace,
When pomps shall in a long procession pass;   760
Wreathed on the posts before his palace wait,
And be the sacred guardian of the gate:
Secure from thunder, and unharmed by Jove,
Unfading as the immortal powers above;
And as the locks of Phoebus are unshorn,
So shall perpetual green thy boughs adorn.'
The grateful tree was pleased with what he said,
And shook the shady honours of her head.

THE TRANSFORMATION OF IO INTO A HEIFER

An ancient forest in Thessalia grows,
Which Tempe's pleasing valley does enclose;   770
Through this the rapid Peneus takes his course,
From Pindus rolling with impetuous force;

Mists from the river's mighty fall arise,
And deadly damps enclose the cloudy skies;
Perpetual fogs are hanging o'er the wood,
And sounds of water deaf the neighbourhood.
Deep in a rocky cave he makes abode;
A mansion proper for a mourning god.
Here he gives audience; issuing out decrees
To rivers, his dependent deities.   780
On this occasion hither they resort,
To pay their homage, and to make their court;
All doubtful, whether to congratulate
His daughter's honour, or lament her fate.
Spercheus, crowned with poplar, first appears;
Then old Apidanus came, crowned with years;
Enipeus turbulent, Amphrysos tame,
And Aeas, last, with lagging waters came.
Then of his kindred brooks a numerous throng
Condole his loss, and bring their urns along: 790
Not one was wanting of the watery train,
That filled his flood, or mingled with the main,
But Inachus, who, in his cave alone,
Wept not another's losses, but his own.
For his dear Io, whether strayed, or dead,
To him uncertain, doubtful tears he shed.
He sought her through the world, but sought in vain;
And nowhere finding, rather feared her slain.
    Her, just returning from her father's brook,
Jove had beheld with a desiring look;   800
And, 'Oh, fair daughter of the flood,' he said,
'Worthy alone of Jove's imperial bed,
Happy whoever shall those charms possess!
The king of gods (nor is thy lover less,)
Invites thee to yon cooler shades, to shun
The scorching rays of the meridian sun.
Nor shalt thou tempt the dangers of the grove
Alone without a guide; thy guide is Jove.
No puny power, but he, whose high command
Is unconfined, who rules the seas and land,   810
And tempers thunder in his awful hand.
Oh, fly not!'—for she fled from his embrace.
O'er Lerna's pastures he pursued the chase,

Along the shades of the Lyrcaean plain.
At length the god, who never asks in vain,
Involved with vapours, imitating night,
Both air and earth; and then suppressed her flight,
And, mingling force with love, enjoyed the full delight.

   Meantime the jealous Juno, from on high,
Surveyed the fruitful fields of Arcady;   820
And wondered that the mist should overrun
The face of daylight and obscure the sun.
No natural cause she found, from brooks or bogs,
Or marshy lowlands, to produce the fogs:
Then round the skies she sought for Jupiter,
Her faithless husband; but no Jove was there.
Suspecting now the worst, 'Or I,' she said,
'Am much mistaken, or am much betrayed.'
With fury she precipitates her flight,
Dispels the shadows of dissembled night,   830
And to the day restores his native light.
The almighty lecher, careful to prevent
The consequence, foreseeing her descent,
Transforms his mistress in a trice; and now,
In Io's place, appears a lovely cow.
So sleek her skin, so faultless was her make,
E'en Juno did unwilling pleasure take
To see so fair a rival of her love;
And what she was, and whence, inquired of Jove,
Of what fair herd, and from what pedigree?   840
The god, half-caught, was forced upon a lie,
And said she sprang from earth. She took the word,
And begged the beauteous heifer of her lord.
What should he do? 'twas equal shame to Jove,
Or to relinquish, or betray his love;
Yet to refuse so slight a gift, would be
But more to increase his consort's jealousy.
Thus fear, and love, by turns his heart assailed;
And stronger love had sure at length prevailed,
But some faint hope remained, his jealous queen   850
Had not the mistress through the heifer seen.
The cautious goddess, of her gift possessed,
Yet harboured anxious thoughts within her breast;
As she who knew the falsehood of her Jove,

And justly feared some new relapse of love;
Which to prevent, and to secure her care,
To trusty Argus she commits the fair.
  The head of Argus (as with stars the skies,)
Was compassed round, and wore a hundred eyes.
But two by turns their lids in slumber steep;   860
The rest on duty still their station keep;
Nor could the total constellation sleep.
Thus, ever present to his eyes and mind,
His charge was still before him, though behind.
In fields he suffered her to feed by day;
But when the setting sun to night gave way,
The captive cow he summoned with a call,
And drove her back, and tied her to the stall.
On leaves of trees and bitter herbs she fed,
Heaven was her canopy, bare earth her bed,   870
So hardly lodged; and, to digest her food,
She drank from troubled streams, defiled with mud.
Her woeful story fain she would have told,
With hands upheld, but had no hands to hold.
Her head to her ungentle keeper bowed,
She strove to speak; she spoke not, but she lowed;
Affrighted with the noise, she looked around,
And seemed to inquire the author of the sound.
  Once on the banks where often she had played,
(Her father's banks,) she came, and there surveyed   880
Her altered visage, and her branching head;
And starting, from herself she would have fled.
Her fellow-nymphs, familiar to her eyes,
Beheld, but knew her not in this disguise.
E'en Inachus himself was ignorant;
And in his daughter did his daughter want.
She followed where her fellows went, as she
Were still a partner of the company:
They stroke her neck; the gentle heifer stands,
And her neck offers to their stroking hands.   890
Her father gave her grass; the grass she took,
And licked his palms, and cast a piteous look,
And in the language of her eyes she spoke.
She would have told her name, and asked relief,
But wanting words, in tears she tells her grief;

Which with her foot she makes him understand,
And prints the name of Io in the sand.
  'Ah, wretched me!' her mournful father cried;
She, with a sigh, to 'wretched me!' replied.
About her milk-white neck his arms he threw,   900
And wept, and then these tender words ensue.
'And art thou she, whom I have sought around
The world, and have at length so sadly found?
So found, is worse than lost: with mutual words
Thou answerest not, no voice thy tongue affords;
But sighs are deeply drawn from out thy breast,
And speech denied, by lowing is expressed.
Unknowing, I prepared thy bridal bed;
With empty hopes of happy issue fed.
But now the husband of a herd must be   910
Thy mate, and bellowing sons thy progeny.
Oh, were I mortal, death might bring relief!
But now my godhead but extends my grief;
Prolongs my woes, of which no end I see,
And makes me curse my immortality.'
More had he said, but fearful of her stay,
The starry guardian drove his charge away
To some fresh pasture; on a hilly height
He sat himself, and kept her still in sight.

THE EYES OF ARGUS TRANSFORMED INTO A
PEACOCK'S TRAIN

Now Jove no longer could her sufferings bear;   920
But called in haste his airy messenger,
The son of Maia, with severe decree
To kill the keeper, and to set her free.
With all his harness soon the god was sped;
His flying hat was fastened on his head;
Wings on his heels were hung, and in his hand
He holds the virtue of the snaky wand.
The liquid air his moving pinions wound,
And, in the moment, shoot him on the ground.
Before he came in sight, the crafty god   930
His wings dismissed, but still retained his rod:
That sleep-procuring wand wise Hermes took,

But made it seem to sight a shepherd's hook.
With this he did a herd of goats control;
Which by the way he met, and slyly stole.
Clad like a country swain, he piped and sung;
And, playing, drove his jolly troop along.
  With pleasure Argus the musician heeds;
But wonders much at those new vocal reeds.
And, 'Whosoe'er thou art, my friend,' said he,   940
'Up hither drive thy goats, and play by me;
This hill has browse for them, and shade for thee.'
The god, who was with ease induced to climb,
Began discourse to pass away the time;
And still, betwixt, his tuneful pipe he plies,
And watched his hour, to close the keeper's eyes.
With much ado, he partly kept awake;
Not suffering all his eyes repose to take;
And asked the stranger, who did reeds invent,
And whence began so rare an instrument.   950

THE TRANSFORMATION OF SYRINX INTO REEDS

Then Hermes thus; 'A nymph of late there was,
Whose heavenly form her fellows did surpass;
The pride and joy of fair Arcadia's plains,
Beloved by deities, adored by swains;
Syrinx her name, by sylvans oft pursued,
As oft she did the lustful gods delude:
The rural and the woodland powers disdained;
With Cynthia hunted, and her rites maintained;
Like Phoebe clad, e'en Phoebe's self she seems,
So tall, so straight, such well-proportioned limbs: 960
The nicest eye did no distinction know,
But that the goddess bore a golden bow;
Distinguished thus, the sight she cheated too.
Descending from Lycaeus, Pan admires
The matchless nymph, and burns with new desires.
A crown of pine upon his head he wore;
And thus began her pity to implore.
But ere he thus began, she took her flight
So swift, she was already out of sight;
Nor stayed to hear the courtship of the god,   970

But bent her course to Ladon's gentle flood;
There by the river stopped, and, tired before,
Relief from water-nymphs her prayers implore.
   'Now while the lustful god, with speedy pace,
Just thought to strain her in strict embrace,
He filled his arms with reeds, new rising on the place.
And while he sighs his ill success to find,
The tender canes were shaken by the wind;
And breathed a mournful air, unheard before,
That, much surprising Pan, yet pleased him more.   980
Admiring this new music, "Thou," he said,
"Who canst not be the partner of my bed,
At least shalt be the consort of my mind,
And often, often, to my lips be joined."
He formed the reeds, proportioned as they are;
Unequal in their length, and waxed with care,
They still retain the name of his ungrateful fair.'
   While Hermes piped, and sung, and told his tale,
The keeper's winking eyes began to fail,
And drowsy slumber on the lids to creep,   990
Till all the watchman was at length asleep.
Then soon the god his voice and song suppressed,
And with his powerful rod confirmed his rest;
Without delay his crooked falchion drew,
And at one fatal stroke the keeper slew.
Down from the rock fell the dissevered head,
Opening its eyes in death, and falling bled;
And marked the passage with a crimson trail:
Thus Argus lies in pieces, cold and pale;
And all his hundred eyes, with all their light,   1000
Are closed at once, in one perpetual night.
These Juno takes, that they no more may fail,
And spreads them in her peacock's gaudy tail.
   Impatient to revenge her injured bed,
She wreaks her anger on her rival's head;
With furies frights her from her native home,
And drives her gadding round the world to roam:
Nor ceased her madness and her flight, before
She touched the limits of the Pharian shore.
At length, arriving on the banks of Nile,   1010
Wearied with length of ways, and worn with toil,

She laid her down; and leaning on her knees,
Invoked the cause of all her miseries;
And cast her languishing regards above,
For help from heaven, and her ungrateful Jove.
She sighed, she wept, she lowed; 'twas all she could;
And with unkindness seemed to tax the god.
Last, with a humble prayer, she begged repose,
Or death at least to finish all her woes.
Jove heard her vows, and with a flattering look,   1020
In her behalf to jealous Juno spoke.
He cast his arms about her neck, and said,
'Dame, rest secure; no more thy nuptial bed
This nymph shall violate; by Styx I swear,
And every oath that binds the thunderer.'
The goddess was appeased; and at the word
Was Io to her former shape restored.
The rugged hair began to fall away;
The sweetness of the eyes did only stay,
Though not so large; her crooked horns decrease;   1030
The wideness of her jaws and nostrils cease;
Her hoofs to hands return, in little space:
The five long taper fingers take their place;
And nothing of the heifer now is seen,
Beside the native whiteness of the skin.
Erected on her feet, she walks again,
And two the duty of the four sustain.
She tries her tongue, her silence softly breaks,
And fears her former lowings when she speaks:
A goddess now through all the Egyptian state,   1040
And served by priests, who in white linen wait.
    Her son was Epaphus, at length believed
The son of Jove, and as a god received.
With sacrifice adored, and public prayers,
He common temples and his mother shares.
Equal in years, and rival in renown
With Epaphus, the youthful Phaeton
Like honour claims, and boasts his sire the sun.
His haughty looks, and his assuming air,
The son of Isis could no longer bear;   1050
'Thou tak'st thy mother's word too far,' said he,
'And hast usurped thy boasted pedigree.
Go, base pretender to a borrowed name!'

Thus taxed, he blushed with anger, and with shame;
But shame repressed his rage: the daunted youth
Soon seeks his mother, and inquires the truth.
'Mother,' said he, 'this infamy was thrown
By Epaphus on you, and me your son.
He spoke in public, told it to my face,
Nor durst I vindicate the dire disgrace: 1060
E'en I, the bold, the sensible of wrong,
Restrained by shame, was forced to hold my tongue.
To hear an open slander, is a curse;
But not to find an answer, is a worse.
If I am heaven-begot, assert your son
By some sure sign, and make my father known,
To right my honour, and redeem your own.'
He said, and, saying, cast his arms about
Her neck, and begged her to resolve the doubt.
   'Tis hard to judge if Clymene were moved   1070
More by his prayer, whom she so dearly loved,
Or more with fury fired, to find her name
Traduced, and made the sport of common fame.
She stretched her arms to heaven, and fixed her eyes
On that fair planet that adorns the skies;
'Now by those beams,' said she, 'whose holy fires
Consume my breast, and kindle my desires;
By him who sees both, and cheers our sight,
By him, the public minister of light,
I swear that sun begot thee; if I lie   1080
Let him his cheerful influence deny;
Let him no more this perjured creature see,
And shine on all the world but only me.
If still you doubt your mother's innocence,
His eastern mansion is not far from hence;
With little pains you to his levée go,
And from himself your parentage may know.'
With joy the ambitious youth his mother heard.
And, eager for the journey, soon prepared.
He longs the world beneath him to survey,   1090
To guide the chariot, and to give the day.
From Meroe's burning sands he bends his course,
Nor less in India feels his father's force;
His travel urging, till he came in sight,
And saw the palace by the purple light.

The Fable of Iphis and Ianthe

The fame of this, perhaps, through Crete had flown;
But Crete had newer wonders of her own,
In Iphis changed; for near the Gnossian bounds,
As loud report the miracle resounds,
At Phaestus dwelt a man of honest blood,
But meanly born, and not so rich as good,
Esteemed and loved by all the neighbourhood;
Who to his wife, before the time assigned
For childbirth came, thus bluntly spoke his mind:
'If heaven', said Ligdus, 'will vouchsafe to hear,   10
I have but two petitions to prefer;
Short pains for thee, for me a son and heir.
Girls cost as many throes in bringing forth;
Beside, when born, the tits are little worth;
Weak puling things, unable to sustain
Their share of labour, and their bread to gain.
If therefore thou a creature shalt produce,
Of so great charges, and so little use,
Bear witness, heaven, with what reluctancy,
Her hapless innocence I doom to die.'   20
He said, and tears the common grief display,
Of him who bade, and her who must obey.
    Yet Telethusa still persists to find
Fit arguments to move a father's mind;
To extend his wishes to a larger scope,
And in one vessel not confine his hope.
Ligdus continues hard; her time drew near,
And she her heavy load could scarcely bear;
When slumbering in the latter shades of night
Before the approaches of returning light,   30
She saw, or thought she saw, before her bed,
A glorious train, and Isis at their head;
Her moony horns were on her forehead placed,
And yellow sheaves her shining temples graced;
A mitre, for a crown, she wore on high;
The dog and dappled bull were waiting by;
Osiris, sought along the banks of Nile;
The silent god; the sacred crocodile;

And last a long procession moving on,
With timbrels, that assist the labouring moon.   40
Her slumbers seemed dispelled, and, broad awake,
She heard a voice, that thus distinctly spake:
'My votary, thy babe from death defend,
Nor fear to save whate'er the gods will send;
Delude with art thy husband's dire decree;
When danger calls, repose thy trust on me;
And know thou hast not served a thankless deity.'
This promise made, with night the goddess fled;
With joy the woman wakes, and leaves her bed;
Devoutly lifts her spotless hands on high,   50
And prays the powers their gift to ratify.

   Now grinding pains proceed to bearing throes,
Till its own weight the burden did disclose.
'Twas of the beauteous kind, and brought to light
With secrecy, to shun the father's sight.
The indulgent mother did her care employ,
And passed it on her husband for a boy.
The nurse was conscious of the fact alone;
The father paid his vows as for a son;
And called him Iphis, by a common name,   60
Which either sex with equal right may claim.
Iphis his grandsire was; the wife was pleased,
Of half the fraud by fortune's favour eased;
The doubtful name was used without deceit,
And truth was covered with a pious cheat.
The habit showed a boy, the beauteous face
With manly fierceness mingled female grace.

   Now thirteen years of age were swiftly run,
When the fond father thought the time drew on
Of settling in the world his only son.   70
Ianthe was his choice; so wondrous fair,
Her form alone with Iphis could compare;
A neighbour's daughter of his own degree,
And not more blessed with fortune's goods than he.

   They soon espoused; for they with ease were joined,
Who were before contracted in the mind.
Their age the same, their inclinations too,
And bred together in one school, they grew.
Thus, fatally disposed to mutual fires,

They felt, before they knew, the same desires.   80
Equal their flame, unequal was their care;
One loved with hope, one languished in despair.
The maid accused the lingering days alone;
For whom she thought a man, she thought her own.
But Iphis bends beneath a greater grief;
As fiercely burns, but hopes for no relief.
E'en her despair adds fuel to her fire;
A maid with madness does a maid desire.

   And, scarce refraining tears, 'Alas,' said she,
'What issue of my love remains for me!   90
How wild a passion works within my breast!
With what prodigious flames am I possessed!
Could I the care of providence deserve,
Heaven must destroy me, if it would preserve.
And that's my fate, or sure it would have sent
Some usual evil for my punishment;
Not this unkindly curse; to rage and burn,
Where nature shows no prospect of return.
Nor cows for cows consume with fruitless fire;
Nor mares, when hot, their fellow-mares desire;   100
The father of the fold supplies his ewes;
The stag through secret woods his hind pursues;
And birds for mates the males of their own species choose.
Her females nature guards from female flame,
And joins two sexes to preserve the game;
Would I were nothing, or not what I am!
Crete, famed for monsters, wanted of her store,
Till my new love produced one monster more.
The daughter of the sun a bull desired;
And yet e'en then a male a female fired: 110
Her passion was extravagantly new;
But mine is much the madder of the two.
To things impossible she was not bent,
But found the means to compass her intent.
To cheat his eyes she took a different shape;
Yet still she gained a lover, and a leap.
Should all the wit of all the world conspire,
Should Daedalus assist my wild desire,
What art can make me able to enjoy,
Or what can change Ianthe to a boy?   120

Extinguish then thy passion, hopeless maid,
And recollect thy reason for thy aid.
Know what thou art, and love as maidens ought,
And drive these golden wishes from thy thought.
Thou canst not hope thy fond desires to gain;
Where hope is wanting, wishes are in vain.
  And yet no guards against our joys conspire;
No jealous husband hinders our desire;
My parents are propitious to my wish,
And she herself consenting to the bliss.   130
All things concur to prosper our design;
All things to prosper any love but mine.
And yet I never can enjoy the fair;
'Tis past the power of heaven to grant my prayer.
Heaven has been kind, as far as heaven can be;
Our parents with our own desires agree;
But nature, stronger than the gods above,
Refuses her assistance to my love:
She sets the bar that causes all my pain;
One gift refused makes all their bounty vain.   140
And now the happy day is just at hand,
To bind our hearts in Hymen's holy band;
Our hearts, but not our bodies; thus accursed,
In midst of water I complain of thirst.
Why comest thou, Juno, to these barren rites,
To bless a bed defrauded of delights?
And why should Hymen lift his torch on high,
To see two brides in cold embraces lie?'
  Thus love-sick Iphis her vain passion mourns;
With equal ardour fair Ianthe burns;   150
Invoking Hymen's name, and Juno's power,
To speed the work, and haste the happy hour.
  She hopes, while Telethusa fears the day,
And strives to interpose some new delay;
Now feigns a sickness, now is in a fright
For this bad omen, or that boding sight.
But having done whate'er she could devise,
And emptied all her magazine of lies,
The time approached; the next ensuing day
The fatal secret must to light betray.   160
Then Telethusa had recourse to prayer,

She and her daughter with dishevelled hair;
Trembling with fear, great Isis they adored,
Embraced her altar, and her aid implored.
  'Fair queen, who dost on fruitful Egypt smile,
Who sway'st the sceptre of the Pharian isle,
And seven-fold falls of disemboguing Nile;
Relieve, in this our last distress,' she said,
'A suppliant mother, and a mournful maid.
Thou, goddess, thou wert present to my sight;   170
Revealed I saw thee by thy own fair light;
I saw thee in my dream, as now I see,
With all thy marks of awful majesty;
The glorious train that compassed thee around;
And heard the hollow timbrel's holy sound.
Thy words I noted, which I still retain;
Let not thy sacred oracles be vain.
That Iphis lives, that I myself am free
From shame and punishment, I owe to thee.
On thy protection all our hopes depend;   180
Thy counsel saved us, let thy power defend.'
  Her tears pursued her words, and while she spoke,
The goddess nodded, and her altar shook;
The temple doors, as with a blast of wind,
Were heard to clap; the lunar horns, that bind
The brows of Isis, cast a blaze around;
The trembling timbrel made a murmuring sound.
  Some hopes these happy omens did impart;
Forth went the mother with a beating heart,
Not much in fear, nor fully satisfied;   190
But Iphis followed with a larger stride:
The whiteness of her skin forsook her face;
Her looks emboldened with an awful grace;
Her features and her strength together grew,
And her long hair to curling locks withdrew.
Her sparkling eyes with manly vigour shone;
Big was her voice, audacious was her tone.
The latent parts, at length revealed, began
To shoot, and spread, and burnish into man.
The maid becomes a youth; no more delay   200
Your vows, but look, and confidently pay.
Their gifts the parents to the temple bear;

The votive tables this inscription wear;—
'Iphis, the man, has to the goddess paid
The vows, that Iphis offered when a maid.'
   Now when the star of day had shown his face,
Venus and Juno with their presence grace
The nuptial rites, and Hymen from above
Descending to complete their happy love;
The gods of marriage lend their mutual aid,   210
And the warm youth enjoys the lovely maid.

The Fable of Acis, Polyphemus, and Galatea

Acis, the lovely youth, whose loss I mourn,
From Faunus and the nymph Symaethis born,
Was both his parents' pleasure; but to me
Was all that love could make a lover be.
The gods our minds in mutual bonds did join;
I was his only joy, and he was mine.
Now sixteen summers the sweet youth had seen,
And doubful down began to shade his chin;
When Polyphemus first disturbed our joy,
And loved me fiercely, as I loved the boy.   10
Ask not which passion in my soul was higher,
My last aversion, or my first desire;
Nor this the greater was, nor that the less,
Both were alike, for both were in excess.
Thee, Venus, thee both heaven and earth obey;
Immense thy power, and boundless is thy sway.
The cyclops, who defied the ethereal throne,
And thought no thunder louder than his own,
The terror of the woods, and wilder far
Than wolves in plains, or bears in forests are;   20
The inhuman host, who made his bloody feasts
On mangled members of his butchered guests,
Yet felt the force of love, and fierce desire,
And burnt for me with unrelenting fire;
Forgot his caverns, and his woolly care,
Assumed the softness of a lover's air,
And combed with teeth of rakes his rugged hair.

Now with a crooked scythe his beard he sleeks,
And mows the stubborn stubble of his cheeks;
Now in the crystal stream he looks, to try   30
His simagres, and rolls his glaring eye.
His cruelty and thirst of blood are lost;
And ships securely sail along the coast.
  The prophet Telemus (arrived by chance
Where Etna's summits to the seas advance,
Who marked the tracks of every bird that flew.
And sure presages from their flying drew,)
Foretold the cyclops, that Ulysses' hand
In his broad eye should thrust a flaming brand.
The giant, with a scornful grin, replied.   40
'Vain augur, thou hast falsely prophesied:
Already love his flaming brand has tossed;
Looking on two fair eyes, my sight I lost.'
Thus warned in vain, with stalking pace he strode,
And stamped the margin of the briny flood
With heavy steps, and weary sought again
The cool retirement of his gloomy den.
  A promontory sharpening by degrees
Ends in a wedge, and overlooks the seas;
On either side below the water flows: 50
This airy walk the giant-lover chose;
Here on the midst he sat; his flocks, unled,
Their shepherd followed, and securely fed.
A pine so burly and of length so vast
That sailing ships required it for a mast,
He wielded for a staff, his steps to guide;
But laid it by, his whistle while he tried.
A hundred reeds, of a prodigious growth,
Scarce made a pipe proportioned to his mouth;
Which when he gave it wind, the rocks around,   60
And watery plains, the dreadful hiss resound.
I heard the ruffian shepherd rudely blow,
Where, in a hollow cave, I sat below.
On Acis' bosom I my head reclined;
And still preserve the poem in my mind.
  'O lovely Galatea, whiter far
Than falling snows, and rising lilies are;
More flowery than the meads, as crystal bright,

Erect as alders, and of equal height;
More wanton than a kid; more sleek thy skin,   70
Than orient shells, that on the shores are seen;
Than apples fairer, when the boughs they lade;
Pleasing, as winter suns, or summer shade;
More grateful to the sight than goodly planes,
And softer to the touch than down of swans,
Or curds new turned; and sweeter to the taste.
Than swelling grapes, that to the vintage haste;
More clear than ice, or running streams, that stray
Through garden plots, but ah! more swift than they.
   'Yet, Galatea, harder to be broke   80
Than bullocks, unreclaimed to bear the yoke,
And far more stubborn than the knotted oak;
Like sliding streams, impossible to hold,
Like them fallacious, like their fountains cold;
More warping than the willow, to decline
My warm embrace; more brittle than the vine;
Immovable, and fixed in thy disdain;
Rough as these rocks, and of a harder grain:
More violent than is the rising flood;
And the praised peacock is not half so proud;   90
Fierce as the fire, and sharp as thistles are,
And more outrageous than a mother bear;
Deaf as the billows to the vows I make,
And more revengeful than a trodden snake;
In swiftness fleeter than the flying hind,
Or driven tempests, or the driving wind.
All other faults with patience I can bear;
But swiftness is the vice I only fear.
   'Yet, if you knew me well, you would not shun
My love, but to my wished embraces run,   100
Would languish in your turn and court my stay,
And much repent of your unwise delay.
   'My palace in the living rock is made
By nature's hand; a spacious pleasing shade,
Which neither heat can pierce, nor cold invade.
My garden filled with fruits you may behold,
And grapes in clusters, imitating gold;
Some blushing bunches of a purple hue;
And these, and those, are all reserved for you.

Red strawberries in shades expecting stand,   110
Proud to be gathered by so white a hand.
Autumnal cornels later fruit provide,
And plums, to tempt you, turn their glossy side;
Not those of common kinds, but such alone,
As in Phaeacian orchards might have grown.
Nor chestnuts shall be wanting to your food,
Nor garden-fruits, nor wildings of the wood.
The laden boughs for you alone shall bear,
And yours shall be the product of the year.
    'The flocks you see are all my own, beside   120
The rest that woods and winding valleys hide,
And those that folded in the caves abide.
Ask not the numbers of my growing store;
Who knows how many, knows he has no more.
Nor will I praise my cattle; trust not me,
But judge yourself, and pass your own decree.
Behold their swelling dugs; the sweepy weight
Of ewes that sink beneath the milky freight;
In the warm folds their tender lambkins lie;
Apart from kids that call with human cry.   130
New milk in nut-brown bowls is duly served
For daily drink, the rest for cheese reserved.
Nor are these household dainties all my store;
The fields and forests will afford us more;
The deer, the hare, the goat, the savage boar,
All sorts of venison, and of birds the best;
A pair of turtles taken from the nest.
I walked the mountains, and two cubs I found,
Whose dam had left them on the naked ground;
So like, that no distinction could be seen;   140
So pretty, they were presents for a queen:
And so they shall; I took them both away,
And keep, to be companions of your play.
    'Oh raise, fair nymph, your beauteous face above
The waves; nor scorn my presents, and my love.
Come, Galatea, come, and view my face;
I late beheld it in the watery glass,
And found it lovelier than I feared it was.
Survey my towering stature, and my size:
Not Jove, the Jove you dream, that rules the skies,   150

Bears such a bulk, or is so largely spread.
My locks (the plenteous harvest of my head,)
Hang o'er my manly face, and dangling down,
As with a shady grove, my shoulders crown.
Nor think, because my limbs and body bear
A thick-set underwood of bristling hair,
My shape deformed; what fouler sight can be,
Than the bald branches of a leafless tree?
Foul is the steed without a flowing main;
And birds, without their feathers, and their train: 160
Wool decks the sheep; and man receives a grace
From bushy limbs, and from a bearded face.
My forehead with a single eye is filled,
Round as a ball, and ample as a shield.
The glorious lamp of heaven, the radiant sun,
Is nature's eye; and she's content with one.
Add, that my father sways your seas, and I,
Like you, am of the watery family.
I make you his, in making you my own;
You I adore, and kneel to you alone;   170
Jove, with his fabled thunder, I despise,
And only fear the lightning of your eyes.
Frown not, fair nymph! yet I could bear to be
Disdained, if others were disdained with me.
But to repulse the cyclops, and prefer
The love of Acis,—heavens! I cannot bear.
But let the stripling please himself; nay more,
Please you, though that's the thing I must abhor;
The boy shall find, if e'er we cope in fight,
These giant limbs endued with giant might.   180
His living bowels from his belly torn,
And scattered limbs, shall on the flood be borne,
They flood, ungrateful nymph; and fate shall find
That way for thee and Acis to be joined.
For oh! I burn with love, and thy disdain
Augments at once my passion, and my pain.
Translated Etna flames within my heart,
And thou, inhuman, wilt not ease my smart.'

     Lamenting thus in vain, he rose, and strode
With furious paces to the neighbouring wood;   190
Restless his feet, distracted was his walk,

Mad were his motions, and confused his talk;
Mad as the vanquished bull, when forced to yield
His lovely mistress, and forsake the field.
    Thus far unseen I saw; when, fatal chance
His looks directing, with a sudden glance,
Acis and I were to his sight betrayed;
Where, naught suspecting, we securely played.
From his wide mouth a bellowing cry he cast,
'I see, I see, but this shall be your last.'   200
A roar so loud made Etna to rebound,
And all the cyclops laboured in the sound.
Affrighted with his monstrous voice, I fled,
And in the neighbouring ocean plunged my head.
Poor Acis turned his back, and, 'Help,' he cried,
'Help, Galatea! help, my parent gods,
And take me, dying, to your deep abodes!'
The cylcops followed; but he sent before
A rib, which from the living rock he tore;
Though but an angle reached him of the stone,   210
The mighty fragment was enough alone,
To crush all Acis; 'twas too late to save,
But what the fates allowed to give, I gave;
That Acis to his lineage should return,
And roll among the river gods his urn.
Straight issued from the stone a stream of blood,
Which lost the purple mingling with the flood;
Then like a troubled torrent it appeared;
The torrent too in little space was cleared;
The stone was cleft, and through the yawning chink   220
New reeds arose, on the new river's brink.
The rock, from out its hollow womb, disclosed
A sound like water in its course opposed:
When (wondrous to behold!) full in the flood,
Up starts a youth, and navel-high he stood.
Horns from his temples rise; and either horn
Thick wreaths of reeds (his native growth) adorn.
Were not his stature taller than before,
His bulk augmented, and his beauty more,
His colour blue, for Acis he might pass;   230
And Acis, changed into a stream, he was.
But mine no more, he rolls along the plains
With rapid motion, and his name retains.

To my Dear Friend Mr Congreve on his Comedy called
The Double Dealer

Well then, the promised hour is come at last,
The present age of wit obscures the past.
Strong were our sires, and as they fought they writ,
Conquering with force of arms and dint of wit:
Theirs was the giant race before the flood;
And thus, when Charles returned, our empire stood.
Like Janus he the stubborn soil manured,
With rules of husbandry the rankness cured;
Tamed us to manners when the stage was rude,
And boisterous English wit with art endued.   10
Our age was cultivated thus at length;
But what we gained in skill we lost in strength.
Our builders were with want of genius cursed;
The second temple was not like the first;
Till you, the best Vitruvius, come at length,
Our beauties equal, but excel our strength.
Firm doric pillars found your solid base;
The fair corinthian crowns the higher space:
Thus all below is strength, and all above is grace.
In easy dialogue is Fletcher's praise;   20
He moved the mind, but had not power to raise.
Great Jonson did by strength of judgment please;
Yet doubling Fletcher's force, he wants his ease.
In differing talents both adorned their age;
One for the study, t' other for the stage.
But both to Congreve justly shall submit,
One matched in judgment, both o'ermatched in wit.
In him all beauties of this age we see,
Etherege's courtship, Southerne's purity,
The satire, wit, and strength, of manly Wycherley.   30
All this in blooming youth you have achieved,
Nor are your foiled contemporaries grieved.
So much the sweetness of your manners move,
We cannot envy you, because we love.
Fabius might joy in Scipio, when he saw
A beardless consul made against the law,
And join his suffrage to the votes of Rome,

Though he with Hannibal was overcome.
Thus old Romano bowed to Raphael's fame,
And scholar to the youth he taught became.   40
   O that your brows my laurel had sustained,
Well had I been deposed, if you had reigned!
The father had descended for the son;
For only you are lineal to the throne.
Thus when the state one Edward did depose,
A greater Edward in his room arose:
But now not I, but poetry, is cursed;
For Tom the second reigns like Tom the first.
But let them not mistake my patron's part,
Nor call his charity their own desert   50
Yet this I prophesy; thou shalt be seen,
(Though with some short parenthesis between,)
High on the throne of wit, and, seated there,
Not mine (that's little) but thy laurel wear.
Thy first attempt an early promise made;
That early promise this has more than paid.
So bold, yet so judiciously you dare
That your least praise is to be regular.
Time, place, and action may with pains be wrought,
But genius must be born and never can be taught.   60
This is your portion, this your native store.
Heaven, that but once was prodigal before,
To Shakespeare gave as much, he could not give him more.
   Maintain your post; that's all the fame you need;
For 'tis impossible you should proceed.
Already I am worn with cares and age,
And just abandoning the ungrateful stage;
Unprofitably kept at heaven's expense,
I live a rent-charge on his providence:
But you, whom every muse and grace adorn,   70
Whom I foresee to better fortune born,
Be kind to my remains; and oh, defend,
Against your judgment, your departed friend!
Let not the insulting foe my fame pursue,
But shade those laurels which descend to you;
And take for tribute what these lines express:
You merit more, nor could my love do less.

An Ode on the Death of Mr Henry Purcell

I

Mark how the lark and linnet sing;
  With rival notes
 They strain their warbling throats,
  To welcome in the spring.
  But in the close of night,
 When Philomel begins her heavenly lay,
  They cease their mutual spite,
 Drink in her music with delight,
And, listening and silent and silent and listening,
  and listening and silent obey.

II

So ceased the rival crew when Purcell came;   10
They sang no more, or only sang his fame.
Struck dumb, they all admired the godlike man:
   The godlike man,
   Alas! too soon retired,
   As he too late began.
We beg not hell our Orpheus to restore;
 Had he been there,
 Their sovereigns' fear
 Had sent him back before.
The power of harmony too well they know: 20
He long ere this had tuned their jarring sphere,
  And left no hell below.

III

The heavenly choir, who heard his notes from high,
Let down the scale of music from the sky;
  They handed him along,
And all the way he taught, and all the way they sung.
Ye brethren of the lyre, and tuneful voice,
Lament his lot, but at your own rejoice:
Now live secure, and linger out your days;
The gods are pleased alone with Purcell's lays,   30
  Nor know to mend their choice.

Meleager and Atalanta

From him the Calydonians sought relief;
Though valiant Meleagrus was their chief.
The cause, a boar, who ravaged far and near;
Of Cynthia's wrath, the avenging minister.
For Oeneus with autumnal plenty blessed,
By gifts to heaven his gratitude expressed;
Culled sheafs, to Ceres; to Lyaeus, wine;
To Pan and Pales, offered sheep and kine;
And fat of olives to Minerva's shrine.
Beginning from the rural gods, his hand   10
Was liberal to the powers of high command;
Each deity in every kind was blessed,
Till at Diana's fane the invidious honour ceased.
    Wrath touches e'en the gods: the Queen of Night,
Fired with disdain and jealous of her right,
'Unhonoured though I am, at least,' said she,
'Not unrevenged that impious act shall be.'
Swift as the word, she sped the boar away,
With charge on those devoted fields to prey.
No larger bulls the Egyptian pastures feed,   20
And none so large Sicilian meadows breed:
His eye-balls glare with fire suffused with blood;
His neck shoots up a thick-set thorny wood;
His bristled back a trench impaled appears,
And stands erected, like a field of spears;
Froth fills his chaps, he sends a grunting sound,
And part he churns, and part befoams the ground;
For tusks with Indian elephants he strove,
And Jove's own thunder from his mouth he drove.
He burns the leaves; the scorching blast invades   30
The tender corn, and shrivels up the blades;
Or, suffering not their yellow beards to rear,
He tramples down the spikes, and intercepts the year.
In vain the barns expect their promised load,
Nor barns at home, nor ricks are heaped abroad;
In vain the hinds the threshing-floor prepare,
And exercise their flails in empty air.
With olives ever green the ground is strowed,

And grapes ungathered shed their generous blood.
Amid the fold he rages, nor the sheep   40
Their shepherds, nor the grooms their bulls, can keep.
    From fields to walls the frighted rabble run,
Nor think themselves secure within the town;
Till Meleagrus, and his chosen crew,
Contemn the danger, and the praise pursue.
Fair Leda's twins, (in time to stars decreed,)
One fought on foot, one curbed the fiery steed;
Then issued forth famed Jason after these,
Who manned the foremost ship that sailed the seas;
Then Theseus, joined with bold Pirithous, came;   50
A single concord in a double name:
The Thestian sons, Idas who swiftly ran,
And Caeneus, once a woman, now a man.
Lynceus, with eagle's eyes, and lion's heart;
Leucippus, with his never-erring dart;
Acastus, Phileus, Phoenix, Telamon,
Echion, Lelex, and Eurytion,
Achilles' father, and great Phocus' son;
Dryas the fierce, and Hippasus the strong,
With twice-old Iolas, and Nestor then but young;   60
Laertes active, and Ancaeus bold;
Mopsus the sage, who future things foretold;
And t'other seer, yet by his wife unsold.
A thousand others of immortal fame;
Among the rest, fair Atalanta came,
Grace of the woods: a diamond buckle bound
Her vest behind, that else had flowed upon the ground,
And showed her buskined legs; her head was bare,
But for her native ornament of hair,
Which in a simple knot was tied above,   70
Sweet negligence, unheeded bait of love!
Her sounding quiver on her shoulder tied,
One hand a dart, and one a bow supplied.
Such was her face, as in a nymph displayed
A fair fierce boy, or in a boy betrayed
The blushing beauties of a modest maid.
The Calydonian chief at once the dame
Beheld, at once his heart received the flame,
With heavens averse. 'O happy youth,' he cried,

'For whom thy fates reserve so fair a bride!'   80
He sighed, and had no leisure more to say;
His honour called his eyes another way,
And forced him to pursue the now neglected prey.
  There stood a forest on a mountain's brow,
Which overlooked the shaded plains below;
No sounding axe presumed those trees to bite,
Coeval with the world, a venerable sight.
The heroes there arrived, some spread around
The toils, some search the footsteps on the ground,
Some from the chains the faithful dogs unbound.   90
Of action eager, and intent in thought,
The chiefs their honourable danger sought:
A valley stood below; the common drain
Of waters from above, and falling rain;
The bottom was a moist and marshy ground,
Whose edges were with bending osiers crowned;
The knotty bulrush next in order stood,
And all within of reeds a trembling wood.
  From hence the boar was roused, and sprung amain,
Like lightning sudden on the warrior-train;   100
Beats down the trees before him, shakes the ground,
The forest echoes to the crackling sound;
Shout the fierce youth, and clamours ring around.
All stood with their protended spears prepared,
With broad steel heads the brandished weapons glared.
The beast impetuous with his tusks aside
Deals glancing wounds; the fearful dogs divide;
All spend their mouth aloof, but none abide.
Echion threw the first, but missed his mark,
And stuck his boar-spear on a maple's bark.   110
Then Jason; and his javelin seemed to take,
But failed with over-force, and whizzed above his back.
Mopsus was next; but, ere he threw, addressed
To Phoebus thus: 'O patron, help thy priest!
If I adore and ever have adored
Thy power divine, thy present aid afford,
That I may reach the beast!' The god allowed
His prayer and smiling, gave him what he could:
He reached the savage, but no blood he drew;
Dian unarmed the javelin as it flew.   120

This chafed the boar, his nostrils' flames expire,
And his red eye-balls roll with living fire.
Whirled from a sling, or from an engine thrown,
Amid the foes so flies a mighty stone,
As flew the beast: the left wing put to flight,
The chiefs o'erborne, he rushes on the right.
Empalamos and Pelagon he laid
In dust and next to death but for their fellows' aid.
Enesimus fared worse, prepared to fly,
The fatal fang drove deep within his thigh,   130
And cut the nerves; the nerves no more sustain
The bulk; the bulk unpropped, falls headlong on the plain.
Nestor had failed the fall of Troy to see,
But leaning on his lance, he vaulted on a tree;
Then, gathering up his feet, looked down with fear,
And thought his monstrous foe was still too near.
Against a stump his tusk the monster grinds,
And in the sharpened edge new vigour finds;
Then, trusting to his arms, young Othrys found,
And ranched his hips with one continued wound.   140
Now Leda's twins, the future stars, appear;
White were their habits, white their horses were;
Conspicuous both, and both in act to throw,
Their trembling lances brandished at the foe:
Nor had they missed; but he to thickets fled,
Concealed from aiming spears, not pervious to the steed.
But Telamon rushed in, and happed to meet
A rising root, that held his fastened feet;
So down he fell, whom, sprawling on the ground,
His brother from the wooden gyves unbound.   150
   Meantime the virgin-huntress was not slow
To expel the shaft from her contracted bow.
Beneath his ear the fastened arrow stood,
And from the wound appeared the trickling blood.
She blushed for joy: but Meleagrus raised
His voice with loud applause, and the fair archer praised.
He was the first to see, and first to show
His friends the marks of the successful blow.
'Nor shall thy valour want the praises due.'
He said; a virtuous envy seized the crew.   160
They shout; the shouting animates their hearts,

And all at once employ their thronging darts;
But out of order thrown, in air they join,
And multitude makes frustrate the design.
With both his hands the proud Ancaeus takes,
And flourishes his double biting axe:
Then forward to his fate, he took a stride
Before the rest, and to his fellows cried,
'Give place, and mark the difference, if you can,
Between a woman-warrior and a man;   170
The boar is doomed; nor, though Diana lend
Her aid, Diana can her beast defend.'
Thus boasted he; then stretched, on tiptoe stood,
Secure to make his empty promise good;
But the more wary beast prevents the blow,
And upward rips the groin of his audacious foe.
Ancaeus falls; his bowels from the wound
Rush out, and clotted blood distains the ground.

    Pirithous, no small portion of the war,
Pressed on, and shook his lance; to whom from far,   180
Thus Theseus cried: 'O stay, my better part,
My more than mistress; of my heart, the heart!
The strong may fight aloof: Ancaeus tried
His force too near, and by presuming died.'
He said, and, while he spake, his javelin threw;
Hissing in air, the unerring weapon flew;
But on an arm of oak, that stood betwixt
The marksman and the mark, his lance he fixed.

    Once more bold Jason threw, but failed to wound
The boar, and slew an undeserving hound;   190
And through the dog the dart was nailed to ground.

    Two spears from Meleager's hand were sent,
With equal force, but various in the event;
The first was fixed in earth, the second stood
On the boar's bristled back, and deeply drank his blood.
Now, while the tortured savage turns around,
And flings about his foam, impatient of the wound,
The wound's great author, close at hand, provokes
His rage, and plies him with redoubled strokes;
Wheels as he wheels, and with his pointed dart   200
Explores the nearest passage to his heart.
Quick, and more quick, he spins in giddy gyres,

Then falls, and in much foam his soul expires.
This act with shouts heaven high the friendly band
Applaud, and strain in theirs the victor hand.
Then all approach the slain with vast surprise,
Admire on what a breadth of earth he lies;
And, scarce secure, reach out their spears afar,
And blood their points, to prove their partnership of war.
    But he, the conquering chief, his foot impressed   210
On the strong neck of that destructive beast;
And gazing on the nymph with ardent eyes,
'Accept,' said he, 'fair Nonacrine, my prize;
And, though inferior, suffer me to join
My labours, and my part of praise, with thine.'
At this presents her with the tusky head
And chine, with rising bristles roughly spread.
Glad, she received the gift; and seemed to take
With double pleasure, for the giver's sake.
The rest were seized with sullen discontent,   220
And a deaf murmur through the squadron went:
All envied; but the Thestian brethren showed
The least respect, and thus they vent their spleen aloud:
'Lay down those honoured spoils, nor think to share,
Weak woman as thou art, the prize of war;
Ours is the title, thine a foreign claim,
Since Meleagrus from our lineage came.
Trust not thy beauty; but restore the prize,
Which he, besotted on that face and eyes,
Would rend from us.' At this, inflamed with spite,   230
From her they snatch the gift, from him the giver's right.
    But soon the impatient prince his falchion drew,
And cried, 'Ye robbers of another's due,
Now learn the difference, at your proper cost,
Betwixt true valour and an empty boast.'
At this advanced, and, sudden as the word,
In proud Plexippus' bosom plunged the sword:
Toxeus amazed, and with amazement slow,
Or to revenge, or ward the coming blow,
Stood doubting; and while doubting thus he stood,   240
Received the steel bathed in his brother's blood.
    Pleased with the first, unknown the second news,
Althaea to the temples pays their dues

For her son's conquest; when at length appear
Her grisly brethren stretched upon the bier:
Pale at the sudden sight she changed her cheer,
And with her cheer her robes; but hearing tell
The cause, the manner, and by whom they fell,
'Twas grief no more, or grief and rage were one
Within her soul; at last 'twas rage alone;   250
Which burning upwards, in succession dries
The tears that stood considering in her eyes.
    There lay a log unlighted on the hearth:
When she was labouring in the throes of birth
For the unborn chief, the fatal sisters came,
And raised it up, and tossed it on the flame;
Then on the rock a scanty measure place
Of vital flax, and turned the wheel apace;
And turning sung, 'To this red brand and thee,
O new-born babe, we give an equal destiny;'   260
So vanished out of view. The frighted dame
Sprung hasty from her bed, and quenched the flame;
The log, in secret locked, she kept with care,
And that, while thus preserved, preserved her heir.
This brand she now produced; and first she strows
The hearth with heaps of chips, and after blows;
Thrice heaved her hand, and heaved, she thrice repressed;
The sister and the mother long contest,
Two doubtful titles in one tender breast;
And now her eyes and cheeks with fury glow,   270
Now pale her cheeks, her eyes with pity flow;
Now louring looks presage approaching storms,
And now prevailing love her face reforms:
Resolved, she doubts again; the tears, she dried
With burning rage, are by new tears supplied;
And as a ship, which winds and waves assail,
Now with the current drives, now with the gale,
Both opposite, and neither long prevail,
She feels a double force; by turns obeys
The imperious tempest, and the impetuous seas: 280
So fares Althaea's mind; she first relents
With pity, of that pity then repents:
Sister and mother long the scales divide,
But the beam nodded on the sister's side.

Sometimes she softly sighed, then roared aloud;
But sighs were stifled in the cries of blood.
   The pious impious wretch at length decreed,
To please her brothers' ghost, her son should bleed;
And when the funeral flames began to rise,
'Receive,' she said, 'a sister's sacrifice;   290
A mother's bowels burn: high in her hand,
Thus while she spoke, she held the fatal brand;
Then thrice before the kindled pile she bowed,
And the three Furies thrice invoked aloud:
'Come, come, revenging sisters, come and view
A sister paying her dead brothers' due;
A crime I punish, and a crime commit;
But blood for blood, and death for death, is fit:
Great crimes must be with greater crimes repaid,
And second funerals on the former laid.   300
Let the whole household in one ruin fall,
And may Diana's curse o'ertake us all.
Shall fate to happy Oeneus still allow
One son, while Thestius stands deprived of two?
Better three lost, than one unpunished go.
Take then, dear ghosts, (while yet, admitted new
In hell, you wait my duty,) take your due;
A costly offering on your tomb is laid,
When with my blood the price of yours is paid.
   'Ah! whither am I hurried? Ah! forgive,   310
Ye shades, and let your sister's issue live:
A mother cannot give him death; though he
Deserves it, he deserves it not from me.
   'Then shall the unpunished wretch insult the slain,
Triumphant live? not only live, but reign?
While you, thin shades, the sport of winds, are tossed
O'er dreary plains, or tread the burning coast.
I cannot, cannot bear; 'tis past, 'tis done;
Perish this impious, this detested son;
Perish his sire, and perish I withal;   320
And let the house's heir, and the hoped kingdom fall.
   'Where is the mother fled, her pious love,
And where the pains with which ten months I strove!
Ah! hadst thou died, my son, in infant years,
Thy little hearse had been bedewed with tears.

'Thou livest by me; to me thy breath resign;
Mine is the merit, the demerit thine.
Thy life by double title I require;
Once given at birth, and once preserved from fire:
One murder pay, or add one murder more,   330
And me to them who fell by thee restore.

  'I would, but cannot: my son's image stands
Before my sight;—and now their angry hands
My brothers hold, and vengeance these exact;
This pleads compassion, and repents the fact.

  'He pleads in vain, and I pronounce his doom:
My brothers, though unjustly, shall o'ercome;
But having paid their injured ghosts their due,
My son requires my death, and mine shall his pursue.'

  At this, for the last time, she lifts her hand,   340
Averts her eyes, and half-unwilling drops the brand.
The brand, amid the flaming fuel thrown,
Or drew, or seemed to draw, a dying groan;
The fires themselves but faintly licked their prey,
Then loathed their impious food, and would have shrunk away.

  Just then the hero cast a doleful cry,
And in those absent flames began to fry;
The blind contagion raged within his veins;
But he with manly patience bore his pains;
He feared not fate, but only grieved to die   350
Without an honest wound, and by a death so dry.
'Happy Ancaeus,' thrice aloud he cried,
'With what becoming fate in arms he died!'
Then called his brothers, sisters, sire, around,
And her to whom his nuptial vows were bound;
Perhaps his mother; a long sigh he drew,
And, his voice failing, took his last adieu;
For, as the flames augment, and as they stay
At their full height, then languish to decay,
They rise and sink by fits; at last they soar   360
In one bright blaze, and then descend no more:
Just so his inward heats at height impair,
Till the last burning breath shoots out the soul in air.

  Now lofty Calydon in ruins lies;
All ages, all degrees, unsluice their eyes;
And heaven and earth resound with murmurs, groans, and cries.

Matrons and maidens beat their breasts, and tear
Their habits, and root up their scattered hair.
The wretched father, father now no more,
With sorrow sunk, lies prostrate on the floor; 370
Deforms his hoary locks with dust obscene,
And curses age, and loathes a life prolonged with pain.
By steel her stubborn soul his mother freed,
And punished on herself her impious deed.

Had I a hundred tongues, a wit so large
As could their hundred offices discharge;
Had Phoebus all his Helicon bestowed,
In all the streams inspiring all the god;
Those tongues, that wit, those streams, that god in vain
Would offer to describe his sisters' pain; 380
They beat their breasts with many a bruising blow,
Till they turned livid, and corrupt the snow.
The corpse they cherish, while the corpse remains,
And exercise and rub with fruitless pains;
And when to funeral flames 'tis borne away,
They kiss the bed on which the body lay;
And when those funeral flames no longer burn,
The dust composed within a pious urn,
E'en in that urn their brother they confess,
And hug it in their arms, and to their bosoms press. 390

His tomb is raised; then, stretched along the ground,
Those living monuments his tomb surround;
E'en to his name, inscribed, their tears they pay,
Till tears and kisses wear his name away.

But Cynthia now had all her fury spent,
Not with less ruin, than a race, content;
Excepting Gorge, perished all the seed,
And her whom heaven for Hercules decreed.
Satiate at last, no longer she pursued
The weeping sisters; but with wings endued, 400
And horny beaks, and sent to flit in air,
Who yearly round the tomb in feathered flocks repair.

Sigismonda and Guiscardo

While Norman Tancred in Salerno reigned,
The title of a gracious prince he gained;
Till turned a tyrant in his latter days,
He lost the lustre of his former praise;
And from the bright meridian where he stood,
Descending, dipped his hands in lovers' blood.

   This prince of fortune's favour long possessed,
Yet was with one fair daughter only blessed;
And blessed he might have been with her alone,
But oh! how much more happy, had he none!   10
She was his care, his hope, and his delight,
Most in his thought, and ever in his sight:
Next, nay beyond his life, he held her dear;
She lived by him, and now he lived in her.
For this, when ripe for marriage, he delayed
Her nuptial bonds, and kept her long a maid,
As envy any else should share a part
Of what was his, and claiming all her heart.
At length, as public decency required,
And all his vassals eagerly desired,   20
With mind averse, he rather underwent
His people's will, than gave his own consent.
So was she torn, as from a lover's side,
And made almost in his despite a bride.

   Short were her marriage joys; for in the prime
Of youth, her lord expired before his time:
And to her father's court, in little space
Restored anew, she held a higher place;
More loved, and more exalted into grace.
This princess fresh and young, and fair, and wise,   30
The worshipped idol of her father's eyes,
Did all her sex in every grace exceed,
And had more wit beside than women need.

   Youth, health, and ease, and most an amorous mind,
To second nuptials had her thoughts inclined;
And former joys had left a secret sting behind.
But prodigal in every other grant,
Her sire left unsupplied her only want;

And she, betwixt her modesty and pride,
Her wishes, which she could not help, would hide.   40
    Resolved at last to lose no longer time,
And yet to please herself without a crime,
She cast her eyes around the court, to find
A worthy subject suiting to her mind,
To him in holy nuptials to be tied,
A seeming widow, and a secret bride.
Among the train of courtiers, one she found
With all the gifts of bounteous nature crowned,
Of gentle blood, but one whose niggard fate
Had set him far below her high estate: 50
Guiscard his name was called, of blooming age,
Now squire to Tancred, and before his page:
To him, the choice of all the shining crowd,
Her heart the noble Sigismonda vowed.
    Yet hitherto she kept her love concealed,
And with close glances every day beheld
The graceful youth; and every day increased
The raging fire that burned within her breast;
Some secret charm did all his acts attend,
And what his fortune wanted, hers could mend: 60
Till, as the fire will force its outward way,
Or, in the prison pent, consume the prey,
So long her earnest eyes on his were set,
At length their twisted rays together met;
And he, surprised with humble joy, surveyed
One sweet regard, shot by the royal maid.
Not well assured, while doubtful hopes he nursed,
A second glance came gliding like the first;
And he who saw the sharpness of the dart,
Without defence received it in his heart.   70
In public though their passion wanted speech,
Yet mutual looks interpreted for each:
Time, ways, and means of meeting were denied,
But all those wants ingenious love supplied.
The inventive god, who never fails his part,
Inspires the wit, when once he warms the heart.
    When Guiscard next was in the circle seen,
Where Sigismonda held the place of queen,
A hollow cane within her hand she brought,

But in the concave had enclosed a note;   80
With this she seemed to play, and, as in sport,
Tossed to her love, in presence of the court;
'Take it,' she said; 'and when your needs require,
This little brand will serve to light your fire.'
He took it with a bow, and soon divined
The seeming toy was not for nought designed:
But when retired, so long with curious eyes
He viewed the present, that he found the prize.
Much was in little writ; and all conveyed
With cautious care, for fear to be betrayed   90
By some false confident, or favourite maid.
The time, the place, the manner how to meet,
Were all in punctual order plainly writ:
But since a trust must be, she thought it best
To put it out of laymen's power at least,
And for their solemn vows prepared a priest.
    Guiscard (her secret purpose understood)
With joy prepared to meet the coming good;
Nor pains nor danger was resolved to spare,
But use the means appointed by the fair.   100
    Near the proud palace of Salerno stood
A mount of rough ascent, and thick with wood,
Through this a cave was dug with vast expense,
The work it seemed of some suspicious prince,
Who, when abusing power with lawless might,
From public justice would secure his flight.
The passage made by many a winding way,
Reached e'en the room in which the tyrant lay,
Fit for his purpose; on a lower floor
He lodged, whose issue was an iron door,   110
From whence, by stairs descending to the ground,
In the blind grot a safe retreat he found.
Its outlet ended in a brake o'ergrown
With brambles, choked by time, and now unknown.
A rift there was, which from the mountain's height
Conveyed a glimmering and malignant light,
A breathing-place to draw the damps away,
A twilight of an intercepted day.
The tyrant's den, whose use though lost to fame,
Was now the apartment of the royal dame;   120

The cavern only to her father known,
By him was to his darling daughter shown.
　Neglected long she let the secret rest,
Till love recalled it to her labouring breast,
And hinted as the way by heaven designed
The teacher, by the means he taught, to blind.
What will not women do, when need inspires
Their wit, or love their inclination fires!
Though jealousy of state the invention found,
Yet love refined upon the former ground.   130
That way the tyrant had reserved to fly
Pursuing hate, now served to bring two lovers nigh.
　The dame, who long in vain had kept the key,
Bold by desire, explored the secret way;
Now tried the stairs, and wading through the night,
Searched all the deep recess, and issued into light.
All this her letter had so well explained,
The instructed youth might compass what remained:
The cavern-mouth alone was hard to find,
Because the path disused was out of mind: 140
But in what quarter of the copse it lay,
His eye by certain level could survey:
Yet (for the wood perplexed with thorns he knew)
A frock of leather o'er his limbs he drew:
And thus provided, searched the brake around,
Till the choked entry of the cave he found.
　Thus, all prepared, the promised hour arrived,
So long expected, and so well contrived:
With love to friend, the impatient lover went,
Fenced from the thorns, and trod the deep descent.   150
The conscious priest, who was suborned before,
Stood ready posted at the postern door;
The maids in distant rooms were sent to rest,
And nothing wanted but the invited guest.
He came, and knocking thrice, without delay,
The longing lady heard, and turned the key;
At once invaded him with all her charms,
And the first step he made, was in her arms:
The leathern outside, boistrous as it was,
Gave way, and bent beneath her strict embrace: 160
On either side the kisses flew so thick,

That neither he nor she had breath to speak.
The holy man amazed at what he saw,
Made haste to sanctify the bliss by law;
And muttered fast the matrimony o'er,
For fear committed sin should get before.
His work performed, he left the pair alone,
Because he knew he could not go too soon;
His presence odious, when his task was done.
What thoughts he had, beseems not me to say,   170
Though some surmise he went to fast and pray,
And needed both, to drive the tempting thoughts away.

The foe once gone, they took their full delight;
'Twas restless rage, and tempest all the night:
For greedy love each moment would employ,
And grudged the shortest pauses of their joy.

Thus were their loves auspiciously begun,
And thus with secret care were carried on.
The stealth itself did appetite restore,
And looked so like a sin, it pleased the more.   180

The cave was now become a common way,
The wicket often opened, knew the key.
Love rioted secure, and long enjoyed,
Was ever eager, and was never cloyed.

But as extremes are short, of ill and good,
And tides at highest mark regorge the flood;
So fate, that could no more improve their joy,
Took a malicious pleasure to destroy.

Tancred, who fondly loved, and whose delight
Was placed in his fair daughter's daily sight,   190
Of custom, when his state affairs were done,
Would pass his pleasing hours with her alone:
And, as a father's privilege allowed,
Without attendance of the officious crowd.

It happened once, that when in heat of day
He tried to sleep, as was his usual way,
The balmy slumber fled his wakeful eyes,
And forced him, in his own despite, to rise:
Of sleep forsaken, to relieve his care,
He sought the conversation of the fair: 200
But with her train of damsels she was gone,
In shady walks the scorching heat to shun:

He would not violate that sweet recess,
And found besides a welcome heaviness
That seized his eyes; and slumber, which forgot
When called before to come, now came unsought.
From light retired, behind his daughter's bed,
He for approaching sleep composed his head;
A chair was ready, for that use designed,
So quilted, that he lay at ease reclined;   210
The curtains closely drawn, the light to screen,
As if he had contrived to lie unseen:
Thus covered with an artificial night,
Sleep did his office soon, and sealed his sight.

With heaven averse, in this ill-omened hour
Was Guiscard summoned to the secret bower,
And the fair nymph, with expectation fired,
From her attending damsels was retired:
For, true to love, she measured time so right,
As not to miss one moment of delight.   220
The garden, seated on the level floor,
She left behind, and locking every door,
Thought all secure; but little did she know,
Blind to her fate, she had enclosed her foe.
Attending Guiscard, in his leathern frock,
Stood ready, with his thrice-repeated knock:
Thrice with a doleful sound the jarring grate
Rung deaf, and hollow, and presaged their fate.
The door unlocked, to known delight they haste,
And panting in each other's arms, embraced;   230
Rush to the conscious bed, a mutual freight,
And heedless press it with their wonted weight.

The sudden bound awaked the sleeping sire,
And showed a sight no parent can desire:
His opening eyes at once with odious view
The love discovered, and the lover knew:
He would have cried; but hoping that he dreamt,
Amazement tied his tongue, and stopped the attempt.
The ensuing moment all the truth declared,
But now he stood collected, and prepared;   240
For malice and revenge had put him on his guard.

So, like a lion that unheeded lay,
Dissembling sleep, and watchful to betray,

With inward rage he meditates his prey.
The thoughtless pair, indulging their desires,
Alternate kindled and then quenched their fires;
Nor thinking in the shades of death they played,
Full of themselves, themselves alone surveyed,
And, too secure, were by themselves betrayed.
Long time dissolved in pleasure thus they lay,   250
Till nature could no more suffice their play;
Then rose the youth, and through the cave again
Returned; the princess mingled with her train.

Resolved his unripe vengeance to defer,
The royal spy, when now the coast was clear,
Sought not the garden, but retired unseen,
To brood in secret on his gathered spleen,
And methodize revenge: to death he grieved;
And, but he saw the crime, had scarce believed.
The appointment for the ensuing night he heard;   260
And therefore in the cavern had prepared
Two brawny yeomen of his trusty guard.

Scarce had unwary Guiscard set his foot
Within the farmost entrance of the grot,
When these in secret ambush ready lay,
And rushing on the sudden seized the prey:
Encumbered with his frock, without defence,
An easy prize, they led the prisoner thence,
And, as commanded, brought before the prince.
The gloomy sire, too sensible of wrong   270
To vent his rage in words, restrained his tongue;
And only said, 'Thus servants are preferred,
And trusted, thus their sovereigns they reward.
Had I not seen, had not these eyes received
So clear a proof, I could not have believed.'

He paused, and choked the rest. The youth who saw
His forfeit life abandoned to the law,
The judge the accuser, and the offence to him
Who had both power and will to avenge the crime,
No vain defence prepared; but thus replied,   280
'The faults of love by love are justified:
With unresisted might the monarch reigns,
He levels mountains, and he raises plains;
And not regarding difference of degree,

Abased your daughter, and exalted me.'
   This bold return with seeming patience heard,
The prisoner was remitted to the guard.
The sullen tyrant slept not all the night,
But lonely walking by a winking light,
Sobbed, wept, and groaned, and beat his withered breast,   290
But would not violate his daughter's rest;
Who long expecting lay, for bliss prepared,
Listening for noise, and grieved that none she heard;
Oft rose, and oft in vain employed the key,
And oft accused her lover of delay;
And passed the tedious hours in anxious thoughts away.
   The morrow came; and at his usual hour
Old Tancred visited his daughter's bower;
Her cheek (for such his custom was) he kissed,
Then blessed her kneeling, and her maids dismissed.   300
The royal dignity thus far maintained,
Now left in private, he no longer feigned;
But all at once his grief and rage appeared,
And floods of tears ran trickling down his beard.
   'O Sigismonda,' he began to say:
Thrice he began, and thrice was forced to stay,
Till words with often trying found their way:
'I thought, O Sigismonda, (but how blind
Are parents' eyes, their children's faults to find!)
Thy virtue, birth, and breeding were above   310
A mean desire, and vulgar sense of love:
Nor less than sight and hearing could convince
So fond a father, and so just a prince,
Of such an unforeseen, and unbelieved offence.
Then what indignant sorrow must I have,
To see thee lie subjected to my slave!
A man so smelling of the people's lee,
The court received him first for charity;
And since with no degree of honour graced,
But only suffered, where he first was placed: 320
A grovelling insect still; and so designed
By nature's hand, nor born of noble kind:
A thing, by neither man nor woman prized,
And scarcely known enough, to be despised.
To what has heaven reserved my age? Ah why

Should man, when nature calls, not choose to die,
Rather than stretch the span of life, to find
Such ills as fate has wisely cast behind,
For those to feel, whom fond desire to live
Makes covetous of more than life can give!   330
Each has his share of good, and when 'tis gone,
The guest, though hungry, cannot rise too soon.
But I, expecting more, in my own wrong
Protracting life, have lived a day too long.
If yesterday could be recalled again,
E'en now would I conclude my happy reign:
But 'tis too late, my glorious race is run,
And a dark cloud o'ertakes my setting sun.
Hadst thou not loved, or loving saved the shame,
If not the sin, by some illustrious name,   340
This little comfort had relieved my mind,
'Twas frailty, not unusual to thy kind:
But thy low fall beneath the royal blood,
Shows downward appetite to mix with mud:
Thus not the least excuse is left for thee,
Nor the least refuge for unhappy me.
    'For him I have resolved: whom by surprise
I took, and scarce can call it, in disguise;
For such was his attire, as with intent
Of nature, suited to his mean descent: 350
The harder question yet remains behind,
What pains a parent and a price can find
To punish an offence of this degenerate kind.
    'As I have loved, and yet I love thee more
Than ever father loved a child before;
So that indulgence draws me to forgive:
Nature, that gave thee life, would have thee live.
But, as a public parent of the state,
My justice, and thy crime, require thy fate.
Fain would I choose a middle course to steer;   360
Nature's too kind, and justice too severe:
Speak for us both, and to the balance bring
On either side, the father, and the king.
Heaven knows, my heart is bent to favour thee;
Make it but scanty weight, and leave the rest to me.'
    Here stopping with a sigh, he poured a flood

Of tears, to make his last expression good.
    She, who had heard him speak, nor saw alone
The secret conduct of her love was known,
But he was taken who her soul possessed,   370
Felt all the pangs of sorrow in her breast;
And little wanted, but a woman's heart
With cries, and tears, had testified her smart:
But inborn worth, that fortune can control,
New strung, and stiffer bent her softer soul;
The heroine assumed the woman's place,
Confirmed her mind, and fortified her face:
Why should she beg, or what could she pretend,
When her stern father had condemned her friend!
Her life she might have had; but her despair   380
Of saving his, had put it past her care:
Resolved on fate, she would not lose her breath,
But rather than not die, solicit death.
Fixed on this thought, she, not as women use
Her fault by common frailty would excuse,
But boldly justified her innocence,
And while the fact was owned, denied the offence:
Then with dry eyes, and with an open look,
She met his glance midway, and thus undaunted spoke.
    'Tancred, I neither am disposed to make   390
Request for life nor offered life to take:
Much less deny the deed; but least of all
Beneath pretended justice weakly fall.
My words to sacred truth shall be confined,
My deeds shall show the greatness of my mind.
That I have loved, I own; that still I love,
I call to witness all the powers above:
Yet more I own: to Guiscard's love I give
The small remaining time I have to live;
And if beyond this life desire can be,   400
Not fate itself shall set my passion free.
    'This first avowed; nor folly warped my mind,
Nor the frail texture of the female kind
Betrayed my virtue: for, too well I knew
What honour was, and honour had his due:
Before the holy priest my vows were tied,
So came I not a strumpet, but a bride;

This for my fame: and for the public voice:
Yet more, his merits justified my choice;
Which had they not, the first election thine,   410
That bond dissolved, the next is freely mine:
Or grant I erred, (which yet I must deny)
Had parents power e'en second vows to tie,
Thy little care to mend my widowed nights
Has forced me to recourse of marriage rites,
To fill an empty side, and follow known delights.
What have I done in this, deserving blame?
State laws may alter: nature's are the same;
Those are usurped on helpless woman-kind,
Made without our consent, and wanting power to bind.   420
    'Thou, Tancred, better shouldst have understood,
That as thy father gave thee flesh and blood,
So gavest thou me: not from the quarry hewed,
But of a softer mould, with sense endued;
E'en softer than thy own, of suppler kind,
More exquisite of taste, and more than man refined.
Nor needst thou by thy daughter to be told,
Though now thy sprightly blood with age be cold,
Thou hast been young; and canst remember still,
That when thou hadst the power, thou hadst the will;   430
And from the past experience of thy fires,
Canst tell with what a tide our strong desires
Come rushing on in youth, and what their rage requires.
    'And grant thy youth was exercised in arms,
When love no leisure found for softer charms,
My tender age in luxury was trained,
With idle ease and pageants entertained;
My hours my own, my pleasures unrestrained.
So bred, no wonder if I took the bent
That seemed e'en warrented by thy consent;   440
For, when the father is too fondly kind,
Such seed he sows, such harvest shall he find.
Blame then thyself, as reason's law requires,
(Since nature gave, and thou fomentst my fires;)
If still those appetites continue strong,
Thou mayst consider, I am yet but young:
Consider too, that having been a wife,
I must have tasted of a better life,

And am not to be blamed, if I renew,
By lawful means, the joys which then I knew.   450
Where was the crime, if pleasure I procured,
Young, and a woman, and to bliss inured?
That was my case, and this is my defence:
I pleased myself, I shunned incontinence,
And urged by strong desires, indulged my sense.

'Left to myself, I must avow, I strove
From public shame to screen my secret love,
And well acquainted with thy native pride,
Endeavoured, what I could not help, to hide;
For which, a woman's wit an easy way supplied.   460
How this, so well contrived, so closely laid,
Was known to thee, or by what chance betrayed,
Is not my care: to please thy pride alone,
I could have wished it had been still unknown.

'Nor took I Guiscard by blind fancy led,
Or hasty choice, as many women wed;
But with deliberate care, and ripened thought,
At leisure first designed, before I wrought:
On him I rested, after long debate,
And not without considering, fixed my fate: 470
His flame was equal, though by mine inspired;
(For so the difference of our birth required:)
Had he been born like me, like me his love
Had first begun what mine was forced to move:
But thus beginning, thus we persevere;
Our passions yet continue what they were,
Nor length of trial makes our joys the less sincere.

'At this my choice, though not by thine allowed,
(Thy judgment herding with the common crowd)
Thou takest unjust offence; and, led by them   480
Dost less the merit than the man esteem.
Too sharply, Tancred, by thy pride betrayed,
Hast thou against the laws of kind inveighed;
For all the offence is in opinion placed,
Which deems high birth by lowly choice debased:
This thought alone with fury fires thy breast,
(For holy marriage justifies the rest)
That I have sunk the glories of the state,
And mixed my blood with a plebeian mate:

In which I wonder thou shouldst oversee   490
Superior causes, or impute to me
The fault of fortune, or the fates' decree.
Or call it heaven's imperial power alone,
Which moves on springs of justice, though unknown;
Yet this we see, though ordered for the best,
The bad exalted, and the good oppressed;
Permitted laurels grace the lawless brow,
The unworthy raised, the worthy cast below.
   'But leaving that: search we the secret springs,
And backward trace the principles of things;   500
There shall we find, that when the world began,
One common mass composed the mould of man;
One paste of flesh on all degrees bestowed,
And kneaded up alike with moistening blood.
The same almighty power inspired the frame
With kindled life, and formed the souls the same:
The faculties of intellect, and will,
Dispensed with equal hand, disposed with equal skill,
Like liberty indulged with choice of good or ill.
Thus born alike, from virtue first began   510
The difference that distinguished man from man:
He claimed no title from descent of blood,
But that which made him noble made him good:
Warmed with more particles of heavenly flame,
He winged his upward flight, and soared to fame;
The rest remained below, a tribe without a name.
   'This law, though custom now diverts the course,
As nature's institute, is yet in force;
Uncancelled, though disused: and he whose mind
Is virtuous, is alone of noble kind.   520
Though poor in fortune, of celestial race;
And he commits the crime, who calls him base.
   'Now lay the line; and measure all thy court,
By inward virtue, not external port,
And find whom justly to prefer above
The man on whom my judgment placed my love:
So shalt thou see his parts, and person shine;
And thus compared, the rest a base degenerate line.
Nor took I, when I first surveyed thy court,
His valour, or his virtues on report;   530

But trusted what I ought to trust alone,
Relying on thy eyes, and not my own;
Thy praise (and thine was then the public voice)
First recommended Guiscard to my choice:
Directed thus by thee, I looked and found
A man I thought deserving to be crowned;
First by my father pointed to my sight,
Nor less conspicuous by his native light:
His mind, his mien, the features of his face,
Excelling all the rest of human race: 540
These were thy thoughts, and thou couldst judge aright,
Till interest made a jaundice in thy sight.
　'Or should I grant, thou didst not rightly see;
Then thou wert first deceived, and I deceived by thee.
But if thou shalt allege, through pride of mind,
Thy blood with one of base condition joined,
'Tis false; for 'tis not baseness to be poor;
His poverty augments thy crime the more;
Upbraids thy justice with the scant regard
Of worth: whom princes praise, they should reward.   550
Are these the kings entrusted by the crowd
With wealth to be dispensed for common good?
The people sweat not for their king's delight,
To enrich a pimp, or raise a parasite;
Theirs is the toil; and he who well has served
His country, has his country's wealth deserved.
　'E'en mighty monarchs oft are meanly born,
And kings by birth, to lowest rank return;
All subject to the power of giddy chance,
For fortune can depress, or can advance: 560
But true nobility is of the mind,
Not given by chance, and not to chance resigned.
　'For the remaining doubt of thy decree,
What to resolve, and how dispose of me,
Be warned to cast that useless care aside,
My self alone, will for myself provide:
If in thy doting, and decrepit age,
Thy soul, a stranger in the youth to rage,
Begins in cruel deeds to take delight,
Gorge with my blood thy barbarous appetite;   570
For I so little am disposed to pray

For life, I would not cast a wish away.
Such as it is, the offence is all my own;
And what to Guiscard is already done,
Or to be done, is doomed by thy decree,
That, if not executed first by thee,
Shall on my person be performed by me.
    'Away! with women weep, and leave me here,
Fixed, like a man to die, without a tear;
Or save, or slay us both this present hour,   580
'Tis all that fate has left within thy power.'
    She said; nor did her father fail to find,
In all she spoke, the greatness of her mind;
Yet thought she was not obstinate to die,
Nor deemed the death she promised was so nigh:
Secure in this belief, he left the dame,
Resolved to spare her life, and save her shame;
But that detested object to remove,
To wreak his vengeance, and to cure her love.
    Intent on this, a secret order signed,   590
The death of Guiscard to his guards enjoined:
Strangling was chosen, and the night the time,
A mute revenge, and blind as was the crime:
His faithful heart, a bloody sacrifice,
Torn from his breast, to glut the tyrant's eyes,
Closed the severe command: for, (slaves to pay)
What kings decree, the soldier must obey:
Waged against foes; and, when the wars are o'er
Fit only to maintain despotic power:
Dangerous to freedom, and desired alone   600
By kings, who seek an arbitrary throne:
Such were these guards; as ready to have slain
The prince himself, allured with greater gain:
So was the charge performed with better will,
By men enured to blood, and exercised in ill.
    Now, though the sullen sire had eased his mind,
The pomp of his revenge was yet behind,
A pomp prepared to grace the present he designed.
A goblet rich with gems, and rough with gold,
Of depth, and breadth, the precious pledge to hold,   610
With cruel care he chose: the hollow part
Enclosed; the lid concealed the lover's heart:

Then of his trusted mischiefs, one he sent,
And bade him with these words the gift present:
'Thy father sends thee this, to cheer thy breast,
And glad thy sight with what thou lovest the best;
As thou hast pleased his eyes, and joyed his mind,
With what he loved the most of human kind.'
    Ere this the royal dame, who well had weighed
The consequence of what her sire had said,   620
Fixed on her fate, against the expected hour,
Procured the means to have it in her power:
For this, she had distilled, with early care,
The juice of simples, friendly to despair,
A magazine of death; and thus prepared,
Secure to die, the fatal message heard:
Then smiled severe; nor with a troubled look,
Or trembling hand, the funeral present took;
E'en kept her countenance, when the lid removed,
Disclosed the heart unfortunately loved: 630
She needed not be told within whose breast
It lodged; the message had explained the rest.
Or not amazed, or hiding her surprise,
She sternly on the bearer fixed her eyes:
Then thus: 'Tell Tancred on his daughter's part,
The gold, though precious, equals not the heart:
But he did well to give his best; and I,
Who wished a worthier urn, forgive his poverty.'
    At this, she curbed a groan, that else had come,
And pausing, viewed the present in the tomb: 640
Then to the heart adored devoutly glued
Her lips, and raising it, her speech renewed:
'E'en from my day of birth, to this, the bound
Of my unhappy being, I have found
My father's care and tenderness expressed.
But this last act of love excels the rest:
For this so dear a present, bear him back
The best return that I can live to make.'
    The messenger dispatched, again she viewed
The loved remains and, sighing, thus pursued: 650
'Source of my life, and lord of my desires,
In whom I lived, with whom my soul expires;
Poor heart, no more the spring of vital heat,

Cursed be the hands that tore thee from thy seat!
The course is finished, which thy fates decreed,
And thou, from thy corporeal prison freed:
Soon hast thou reached the goal with mended pace,
A world of woes dispatched in little space:
Forced by the worth, thy foe in death become
Thy friend, has lodged thee in a costly tomb;   660
There yet remained thy funeral exequies,
The weeping tribute of thy widow's eyes,
And those, indulgent heaven has found the way
That I, before my death, have leave to pay.
My father e'en in cruelty is kind,
Or heaven has turned the malice of his mind
To better uses that his hate designed;
And made the insult which in his gift appears,
The means to mourn thee with my pious tears;
Which I will pay thee down, before I go,   670
And save myself the pains to weep below,
If souls can weep; thought once I meant to meet
My fate with face unmoved, and eyes unwet,
Yet since I have thee here in narrow room,
My tears shall set thee first afloat within thy tomb:
Then (as I know thy spirit hovers nigh)
Under thy friendly conduct will I fly
To regions unexplored, secure to share
Thy state; nor hell shall punishment appear,
And heaven is double heaven, if thou art there.'   680
    She said. Her brimful eyes, that ready stood,
And only wanted will to weep a flood,
Released their watery store, and poured amain,
Like clouds low hung, a sober shower of rain;
Mute solemn sorrow, free from female noise,
Such as the majesty of grief destroys:
For, bending o'er the cup, the tears she shed
Seemed by the posture to discharge her head,
O'erfilled before; and oft (her mouth applied
To the cold heart) she kissed at once and cried.   690
Her maids, who stood amazed, nor knew the cause
Of her complaining, nor whose heart it was;
Yet all due measures of her mourning kept,
Did office at the dirge, and by infection wept;

And oft inquired the occasion of her grief,
(Unanswered but by sighs) and offered vain relief.
At length, her stock of tears already shed,
She wiped her eyes, she raised her drooping head,
And thus pursued: 'O ever faithful heart,
I have performed the ceremonial part,   700
The decencies of grief. It rests behind,
That as our bodies were, our souls be joined:
To thy whate'er abode, my shade convey,
And as an elder ghost, direct the way.'
She said; and bade the vial to be brought,
Where she before had brewed the deadly draught,
First pouring out the medicinable bane,
The heart, her tears had rinsed, she bathed again;
Then down her throat the death securely throws,
And quaffs a long oblivion of her woes.   710
    This done, she mounts the genial bed, and there,
(Her body first composed with honest care,)
Attends the welcome rest. Her hands yet hold
Close to her heart, the monumental gold;
Nor further word she spoke, but closed her sight,
And quiet, sought the covert of the night.
    The damsels, who the while in silence mourned,
Not knowing, nor suspecting death suborned,
Yet, and their duty was, to Tancred sent,
Who, conscious of the occasion, feared the event.   720
Alarmed, and with presaging heart he came,
And drew the curtains, and exposed the dame
To loathsome light: then with a late relief
Made vain efforts to mitigate her grief.
She, what she could excluding day, her eyes
Kept firmly sealed, and sternly thus replies:
    'Tancred, restrain thy tears, unsought by me,
And sorrow, unavailing now to thee:
Did ever man before afflict his mind
To see the effect of what himself designed?   730
Yet, if thou hast remaining in thy heart
Some sense of love, some unextinguished part
Of former kindness, largely once professed,
Let me by that adjure thy hardened breast,
Not to deny thy daughter's last request:

The secret love, which I so long enjoyed,
And still concealed, to gratify thy pride,
Thou hast disjoined; but with my dying breath,
Seek not, I beg thee, to disjoin our death:
Where'er his corpse by thy command is laid,   740
Thither let mine in public be conveyed;
Exposed in open view, and side by side,
Acknowledged as a bridegroom, and a bride.'
    The prince's anguish hindered his reply;
And she, who felt her fate approaching nigh,
Seized the cold heart, and heaving to her breast,
'Here, precious pledge,' she said, 'securely rest.'
These accents were her last; the creeping death
Benumbed her senses first, then stopped her breath.
    Thus she for disobedience justly died;   750
The sire was justly punished for his pride:
The youth, least guilty, suffered for the offence
Of duty violated to his prince;
Who late repenting of his cruel deed,
One common sepulchre for both decreed;
Entombed the wretched pair in royal state,
And on their monument inscribed their fate.

Baucis and Philemon

Thus Achelous ends. His audience hear,
With admiration, and admiring, fear
The powers of heaven; except Ixion's son
Who laughed at all the gods, believed in none.
He shook his impious head, and thus replies,
'These legends are no more than pious lies:
You attribute too much to heavenly sway
To think they give us forms, and take away.'
    The rest, of better minds, their sense declared
Against this doctrine, and with horror heard.   10
Then Lelex rose, an old experienced man,
And thus with sober gravity began:
'Heaven's power is infinite: earth, air, and sea,
The manufacture mass, the making power obey:

By proof to clear your doubt: in Phrygian ground
Two neighbouring trees, with walls encompassed round,
Stand on a moderate rise, with wonder shown,
One a hard oak, a softer linden one:
I saw the place and them, by Pittheus sent
To Phrygian realms, my grandsire's government.   20
Not far from thence is seen a lake, the haunt
Of coots, and of the fishing cormorant.
Here Jove with Hermes came; but in disguise
Of mortal men concealed their deities.
One laid aside his thunder, one his rod;
And many toilsome steps together trod.
For harbour at a thousand doors they knocked,
Not one of all the thousand but was locked.
At last a hospitable house they found,
A homely shed; the roof not far from ground,   30
Was thatched with reeds and straw together bound.
There Baucis and Philemon lived, and there
Had lived long married, and a happy pair:
Now old in love; though little was their store,
Inured to want, their poverty they bore,
Nor aimed at wealth, professing to be poor.
For master or for servant here to call,
Was all alike, when only two were all.
Command was none, where equal love was paid,
Or rather both commanded, both obeyed.   40
  'From lofty roofs the gods repulsed before,
Now stooping, entered through the little door.
The man (their hearty welcome first expressed)
A common settle drew for either guest,
Inviting each his weary limbs to rest.
But ere they sat, officious Baucis lays
Two cushions stuffed with straw, the seat to raise;
Coarse, but the best she had; then rakes the load
Of ashes from the hearth, and spreads abroad
The living coals, and lest they should expire,   50
With leaves and barks she feeds her infant fire.
It smokes, and then with trembling breath she blows,
Till in a cheerful blaze the flames arose.
With brushwood and with chips she strengthens these,
And adds at last the boughs of rotten trees.

The fire thus formed, she sets the kettle on
(Like burnished gold the little seether shone)
Next took the coleworts which her husband got
From his own ground (a small well-watered spot)
She stripped the stalks of all their leaves, the best   60
She culled, and then with handy care she dressed.
High o'er the hearth a chine of bacon hung:
Good old Philemon seized it with a prong,
And from the sooty rafter drew it down;
Then cut a slice, but scarce enough for one;
Yet a large portion of a little store,
Which for their sakes alone he wished were more.
This in the pot he plunged without delay,
To tame the flesh and drain the salt away.
The time between, before the fire they sat,   70
And shortened the delay by pleasing chat.
    'A beam there was, on which a beechen pail
Hung by the handle on a driven nail:
This filled with water, gently warmed, they set
Before their guests; in this they bathed their feet,
And after with clean towels dried their sweat:
This done, the host produced the genial bed,
Sallow the feet, the borders, and the stead,
Which with no costly coverlet they spread,
But course old garments; yet such robes as these   80
They laid alone at feasts, on holidays.
The good old housewife, tacking up her gown,
The table sets; the invited gods lie down.
The trivet table of a foot was lame,
A blot which prudent Baucis overcame,
Who thrusts beneath the limping leg a shard;
So was the mended board exactly reared:
Then rubbed it o'er with newly gathered mint,
A wholesome herb, that breathed a grateful scent.
Pallas began the feast, where first was seen   90
The particoloured olive, black and green:
Autumnal cornels next in order served,
In lees of wine well pickled, and preserved.
A garden salad was the third supply,
Of endive, radishes and chicory;
Then curds and cream, the flower of country fare,

And new laid eggs, which Baucis' busy care
Turned by a gentle fire, and roasted rare.
All these in earthenware were served to board;
And next in place an earthen pitcher, stored 100
With liquor of the best the cottage could afford.
This was the table's ornament and pride,
With figures wrought: like pages at his side
Stood beechen bowls; and these were shining clean,
Varnished with wax without, and lined within.
By this the boiling kettle had prepared,
And to the table sent the smoking lard;
On which with eager appetite they dine,
A savoury bit, that served to relish wine.
The wine itself was suiting to the rest, 110
Still working in the must, and lately pressed.
The second course succeeds like that before,
Plums, apples, nuts, and of their wintry store,
Dry figs, and grapes, and wrinkled dates were set
In canisters, to enlarge the little treat.
All these a milk-white honeycomb surround,
Which in the midst the country banquet crowned.
But the kind hosts their entertainment grace
With hearty welcome, and an open face.
In all they did, you might discern with ease, 120
A willing mind, and a desire to please.
  'Meantime the beechen bowls went round, and still
Though often emptied, were observed to fill;
Filled without hands, and of their own accord
Ran without feet, and danced about the board.
Devotion seized the pair, to see the feast
With wine, and of no common grape, increased;
And up they held their hands, and fell to prayer,
Excusing as they could their country fare.
  'One goose they had, ('twas all they could allow) 130
A wakeful sentry, and on duty now,
Whom to the gods for sacrifice they vow:
Her, with malicious zeal, the couple viewed;
She ran for life, and limping they pursued:
Full well the fowl perceived their bad intent,
And would not make her masters' compliment;
But persecuted, to the powers she flies,

And close between the legs of Jove she lies.
He with a gracious ear the suppliant heard,
And saved her life; then what he was declared,   140
And owned the god. "The neighbourhood", said he,
"Shall justly perish for impiety:
You stand alone exempted; but obey
With speed, and follow where we lead the way;
Leave these accursed; and to the mountain's height
Ascend; nor once look backward in your flight."
   'They haste, and what their tardy feet denied,
The trusty staff (their better leg) supplied.
An arrow's flight they wanted to the top,
And there secure, but spent with travel, stop;   150
Then turn their now no more forbidden eyes:
Lost in a lake the floated level lies;
A watery desert covers all the plains,
Their cot alone, as in an isle, remains.
Wondering with weeping eyes, while they deplore
Their neighbours' fate, and country now no more,
Their little shed, scarce large enough for two,
Seems, from the ground increased, in height and bulk to grow.
A stately temple shoots within the skies;
The crotches of their cot in columns rise;   160
The pavement polished marble they behold,
The gates with sculpture graced, the spires and tiles of gold.
   'Then thus the sire of gods, with look serene,
"Speak thy desire, thou only just of men;
And thou, O woman, only worthy found
To be with such a man in marriage bound."
   'Awhile they whisper; then to Jove addressed,
Philemon thus prefers their joint request.
"We crave to serve before your sacred shrine,
And offer at your altars rites divine;   170
And since not any action of our life
Has been polluted with domestic strife,
We beg one hour of death; that neither she
With widow's tears may live to bury me,
Nor weeping I, with withered arms may bear
My breathless Baucis to the sepulcher."
   'The godheads sign their suit. They run their race
In the same tenor all the appointed space:

Then, when their hour was come, while they relate
These past adventures at the temple gate,   180
Old Baucis is by old Philemon seen
Sprouting with sudden leaves of sprightly green.
Old Baucis looked where old Philemon stood,
And saw his lengthened arms a sprouting wood.
New roots their fastened feet begin to bind,
Their bodies stiffen in a rising rind:
Then ere the bark above their shoulders grew,
They give and take at once their last adieu.
At once, "Farewell, O faithful spouse," they said;
At once the encroaching rinds their closing lips invade.   190
E'en yet, an ancient Tyanaean shows
A spreading oak, that near a linden grows;
The neighbourhood confirm the prodigy,
Grave men, not vain of tongue, or like to lie.
I saw myself the garlands on their boughs,
And tablets hung for gifts of granted vows;
And offering fresher up, with pious prayer,
"The good", said I, "are god's peculiar care,
And such as honour heaven, shall heavenly honour share."'

Pygmalion and the Statue

Pygmalion, loathing their lascivious life,
Abhorred all womankind, but most a wife;
So single chose to live, and shunned to wed,
Well pleased to want a consort of his bed.
Yet fearing idleness, the nurse of ill,
In sculpture exercised his happy skill;
And carved in ivory such a maid, so fair,
As nature could not with his art compare,
Were she to work; but in her own defence,
Must take her pattern here, and copy hence.   10
Pleased with his idol, he commends, admires,
Adores; and last, the thing adored desires.
A very virgin in her face was seen,
And, had she moved, a living maid had been;
One would have thought she could have stirred, but strove

With modesty, and was ashamed to move.
Art, hid with art, so well performed the cheat,
It caught the carver with his own deceit.
He knows 'tis madness, yet he must adore,
And still the more he knows it, loves the more;   20
The flesh, or what so seems, he touches oft,
Which feels so smooth, that he believes it soft.
Fired with this thought, at once he strained the breast,
And on the lips a burning kiss impressed.
'Tis true, the hardened breast resists the gripe,
And the cold lips return a kiss unripe;
But when, retiring back, he looked again,
To think it ivory was a thought too mean;
So would believe she kissed, and courting more,
Again embraced her naked body o'er;   30
And, straining hard the statue, was afraid
His hands had made a dint, and hurt his maid;
Explored her, limb by limb, and feared to find
So rude a grip had left a livid mark behind.
With flattery now he seeks her mind to move,
And now with gifts, the powerful bribes of love;
He furnishes her closet first; and fills
The crowded shelves with rarities of shells;
Adds orient pearls, which from the conchs he drew.
And all the sparkling stones of various hue;   40
And parrots, imitating human tongue,
And singing-birds in silver cages hung;
And every fragrant flower, and odorous green,
Were sorted well, with lumps of amber laid between;
Rich fashionable robes her person deck;
Pendants her ears, and pearls adorn her neck;
Her tapered fingers too with rings are graced,
And an embroidered zone surrounds her slender waist.
Thus like a queen arrayed, so richly dressed,
Beauteous she showed, but naked showed the best.   50
Then from the floor he raised a royal bed,
With coverings of Sidonian purple spread;
The solemn rites performed, he calls her bride,
With blandishments invites her to his side,
And as she were with vital sense possessed,
Her head did on a plumy pillow rest.

The feast of Venus came, a solemn day,
To which the Cypriots due devotion pay;
With gilded horns the milk-white heifers led,
Slaughtered before the sacred altars, bled;   60
Pygmalion, offering, first approached the shrine,
And then with prayers implored the powers divine;
'Almighty gods, if all we mortals want,
If all we can require, be yours to grant,
Make this fair statue mine,' he would have said,
But changed his words for shame, and only prayed,
'Give me the likeness of my ivory maid!'
     The golden goddess, present at the prayer,
Well knew he meant the inanimated fair,
And gave the sign of granting his desire;   70
For thrice in cheerful flames ascends the fire.
The youth, returning to his mistress hies,
And impudent in hope, with ardent eyes,
And beating breast, by the dear statue lies.
He kisses her white lips, renews the bliss,
And looks and thinks they redden at the kiss;
He thought them warm before: nor longer stays,
But next his hand on her hard bosom lays;
Hard as it was, beginning to relent,
It seemed the breast beneath his fingers bent;   80
He felt again, his fingers made a print,
'Twas flesh, but flesh so firm, it rose against the dint.
The pleasing task he fails not to renew;
Soft, and more soft at every touch it grew;
Like pliant wax, when chafing hands reduce
The former mass to form, and frame for use.
He would believe, but yet is still in pain,
And tries his argument of sense again,
Presses the pulse, and feels the leaping vein.
Convinced, o'erjoyed, his studied thanks and praise,   90
To her who made the miracle, he pays;
Then lips to lips he joined; now freed from fear,
He found the savour of the kiss sincere.
At this the wakened image oped her eyes,
And viewed at once the light and lover with surprise.
The goddess, present at the match she made,
So blessed the bed, such fruitfulness conveyed,

That ere ten moons had sharpened either horn,
To crown their bliss, a lovely boy was born;
Paphos his name, who, grown to manhood, walled   100
The city Paphos, from the founder called.

Cinyras and Myrrha

Nor him alone produced the fruitful queen;
But Cinyras, who like his sire had been
A happy prince, had he not been a sire.
Daughters and fathers, from my song retire!
I sing of horror; and, could I prevail,
You should not hear, or not believe my tale.
Yet if the pleasure of my song be such,
That you will hear, and credit me too much,
Attentive listen to the last event,
And with the sin believe the punishment: 10
Since nature could behold so dire a crime,
I gratulate at least my native clime.
That such a land, which such a monster bore,
So far is distant from our Thracian shore.
Let Araby extol her happy coast,
Her cinnamon and sweet amomum boast;
Her fragrant flowers, her trees with precious tears.
Her second harvests, and her double years;
How can the land be called so blessed that Myrrha bears?
Not all her odorous tears can cleanse her crime,   20
Her plant alone deforms the happy clime;
Cupid denies to have inflamed thy heart,
Disowns thy love, and vindicates his dart:
Some fury gave thee those infernal pains,
And shot her venomed vipers in thy veins.
To hate thy sire, had merited a curse;
But such an impious love deserved a worse.
The neighbouring monarchs, by thy beauty led,
Contend in crowds, ambitious of thy bed;
The world is at thy choice, except but one.   30
Except but him thou canst not choose alone.
She knew it too, the miserable maid,

Ere impious love her better thoughts betrayed,
And thus within her secret soul she said:
'Ah, Myrrha! whither would thy wishes tend?
Ye gods, ye sacred laws, my soul defend
From such a crime as all mankind detest,
And never lodged before in human breast!
But is it sin? Or makes my mind alone
The imagined sin? For nature makes it none.   40
What tyrant then these envious laws began,
Made not for any other beast but man!
The father-bull his daughter may bestride,
The horse may make his mother-mare a bride;
What piety forbids the lusty ram,
Or more salacious goat, to rut their dam?
The hen is free to wed the chick she bore,
And make a husband, whom she hatched before.
All creatures else are of a happier kind,
Whom nor ill-natured laws from pleasure bind,   50
Nor thoughts of sin disturb their peace of mind.
But man a slave of his own making lives;
The fool denies himself what nature gives;
Too busy senates, with an over-care
To make us better than our kind can bear,
Have dashed a spice of envy in the laws,
And, straining up too high, have spoiled the cause.
Yet some wise nations break their cruel chains,
And own no laws, but those which love ordains;
Where happy daughters with their sires are joined,   60
And piety is doubly paid in kind.
O that I had been born in such a clime,
Not here, where 'tis the country makes the crime!
But whither would my impious fancy stray?
Hence hopes, and ye forbidden thoughts, away!
His worth deserves to kindle my desires,
But with the love that daughters bear to sires.
Then had not Cinyras my father been,
What hindered Myrrha's hopes to be his queen?
But the perverseness of my fate is such,   70
That he's not mine, because he's mine too much:
Our kindred-blood debars a better tie;
He might be nearer, were he not so nigh.

Eyes and their objects never must unite,
Some distance is required to help the sight.
Fain would I travel to some foreign shore,
Never to see my native country more,
So might I to myself myself restore;
So might my mind these impious thoughts remove,
And, ceasing to behold, might cease to love.   80
But stay I must, to feed my famished sight,
To talk, to kiss; and more, if more I might:
More, impious maid! What more canst thou design?
To make a monstrous mixture in thy line,
And break all statues human and divine?
Canst thou be called (to save thy wretched life)
Thy mother's rival, and thy father's wife?
Confound so many sacred names in one,
Thy brother's mother! sister to thy son!
And fear'st thou not to see the infernal bands,   90
Their heads with snakes, with torches armed their hands,
Full at thy face the avenging brands to bear,
And shake the serpents from their hissing hair?
But thou in time the increasing ill control,
Nor first debauch the body by the soul;
Secure the sacred quiet of thy mind,
And keep the sanctions nature has designed,
Suppose I should attempt, the attempt were vain;
No thoughts like mine his sinless soul profane,
Observant of the right; and O, that he   100
Could cure my madness, or be mad like me!'
   Thus she; but Cinyras, who daily sees
A crowd of noble suitors at his knees,
Among so many, knew not whom to choose,
Irresolute to grant, or to refuse;
But, having told their names, inquired of her,
Who pleased her best, and whom she would prefer?
The blushing maid stood silent with surprise,
And on her father fixed her ardent eyes,
And, looking, sighed; and, as she sighed, began   110
Round tears to shed that scalded as they ran.
The tender sire, who saw her blush, and cry,
Ascribed it all to maiden modesty;
And dried the falling drops, and, yet more kind,

He stroked her cheeks, and holy kisses joined:
She felt a secret venom fire her blood.
And found more pleasure than a daughter should;
And, asked again, what lover of the crew
She liked the best she answered, 'One like you.'
Mistaking what she meant, her pious will   120
He praised, and bade her so continue still:
The word of 'pious' heard, she blushed with shame
Of secret guilt, and could not bear the name.
　'Twas now the mid of night, when slumbers close
Our eyes, and soothe our cares with soft repose;
But no repose could wretched Myrrha find,
Her body rolling, as she rolled her mind:
Mad with desire, she ruminates her sin,
And wishes all her wishes o'er again:
Now she despairs, and now resolves to try;   130
Would not, and would again, she knows not why;
Stops and returns, makes and retracts the vow;
Fain would begin, but understands not how:
As when a pine is hewn upon the plains,
And the last mortal stroke alone remains,
Labouring in pangs of death, and threatening all,
This way and that she nods, considering where to fall;
So Myrrha's mind, impelled on either side,
Takes every bent, but cannot long abide:
Irresolute on which she should rely,   140
At last, unfixed in all, is only fixed to die.
On that sad thought she rests; resolved on death,
She rises, and prepares to choke her breath;
Then while about the beam her zone she ties,
'Dear Cinyras, farewell,' she softly cries;
'For thee I die, and only wish to be
Not hated, when thou know'st I die for thee:
Pardon the crime in pity to the cause.'
This said, about her neck the noose she draws.
The nurse, who lay without, her faithful guard,   150
Though not the words, the murmurs overheard,
And sighs and hollow sounds; surprised with fright,
She starts, and leaves her bed, and springs a light;
Unlocks the door, and entering out of breath,
The dying saw and instruments of death.

She shrieks, she cuts the zone with trembling haste,
And in her arms her fainting charge embraced;
Next (for she now had leisure for her tears)
She weeping asked, in these her blooming years,
What unforeseen misfortune caused her care,   160
To loathe her life, and languish in despair?
The maid, with downcast eyes, and mute with grief,
For death unfinished, and ill-timed relief,
Stood sullen to her suit: the beldam pressed
The more to know, and bared her withered breast;
Adjured her, by the kindly food she drew
From those dry founts, her secret ill to show.
Sad Myrrha sighed, and turned her eyes aside;
The nurse still urged and would not be denied:
Nor only promised secrecy, but prayed   170
She might have leave to give her offered aid.
'Good will', she said, 'my want of strength supplies,
And diligence shall give what age denies.
If strong desires thy mind to fury move,
With charms and medicines I can cure thy love;
If envious eyes their hurtful rays have cast,
More powerful verse shall free thee from the blast;
If heaven, offended, sends thee this disease,
Offended heaven with prayers we can appease.
What then remains that can these cares procure?   180
Thy house is flourishing, thy fortune sure;
Thy careful mother yet in health survives.
And, to thy comfort, thy kind father lives.'
   The virgin started at her father's name,
And sighed profoundly, conscious of the shame;
Nor yet the nurse her impious love divined,
But yet surmised, that love disturbed her mind.
Thus thinking, she pursued her point, and laid
And lulled within her lap the mourning maid;
Then softly soothed her thus: 'I guess your grief;   190
You love, my child; your love shall find relief.
My long experienced age shall be your guide;
Rely on that, and lay distrust aside;
No breath of air shall on the secret blow,
Nor shall (what most you fear) your father know.'
Struck once again, as with a thunderclap,

The guilty virgin bounded from her lap,
And threw her body prostrate on the bed,
And, to conceal her blushes, hid her head:
There silent lay, and warned her with her hand   200
To go; but she received not the command;
Remaining still importunate to know.
Then Myrrha thus: 'Or ask no more, or go;
I prithee go, or, staying, spare my shame;
What thou wouldst hear, is impious e'en to name.'
At this, on high the beldam holds her hands,
And trembling, both with age and terror, stands;
Adjures, and, falling at her feet, intreats,
Soothes her with blandishments, and frights with threats,
To tell the crime intended, or disclose   210
What part of it she knew, if she no further knows;
And last, if conscious to her counsel made,
Confirms anew the promise of her aid.

Now Myrrha raised her head: but soon, oppressed
With shame, reclined it on her nurse's breast;
Bathed it with tears, and strove to have confessed:
Twice she began, and stopped; again she tried;
The faltering tongue its office still denied;
At last her veil before her face she spread.
And drew a long preluding sigh, and said,   220
'O happy mother, in thy marriage bed!'
Then groaned, and ceased. The good old woman shook,
Stiff were her eyes, and ghastly was her look:
Her hoary hair upright with horror stood.
Made (to her grief) more knowing than she would;
Much she reproached, and many things she said,
To cure the madness of the unhappy maid;
In vain; for Myrrha stood convict of ill;
Her reason vanquished, but unchanged her will;
Perverse of mind, unable to reply,   230
She stood resolved or to possess, or die.
At length the fondness of a nurse prevailed
Against her better sense, and virtue failed:
'Enjoy, my child, since such is thy desire,
Thy love,' she said; she durst not say, 'Thy sire.'
'Live, though unhappy, live on any terms;'
Then with a second oath her faith confirms.

The solemn feast of Ceres now was near,
When long white linen stoles the matrons wear;
Ranked in procession walk the pious train,   240
Offering first-fruits, and spikes of yellow grain;
For nine long nights the nuptial bed they shun,
And, sanctifying harvest, lie alone.
Mixed with the crowd, the queen forsook her lord,
And Ceres' power with secret rites adored.
The royal couch now vacant for a time,
The crafty crone, officious in her crime,
The cursed occasion took; the king she found
Easy with wine, and deep in pleasures drowned,
Prepared for love; the beldam blew the flame,   250
Confessed the passion, but concealed the name.
Her form she praised; the monarch asked her years,
And she replied, 'The same thy Myrrha bears.'
Wine and commended beauty fired his thought;
Impatient, he commands her to be brought.
Pleased with her charge performed, she hies her home,
And gratulates the nymph, the task was overcome.
Myrrha was joyed the welcome news to hear;
But, clogged with guilt, the joy was insincere.
So various, so discordant is the mind,   260
That in our will, a different will we find.
Ill she presaged, and yet pursued her lust;
For guilty pleasures give a double gust.
'Twas depth of night: Arctophylax had driven
His lazy wain half round the northern heaven,
When Myrrha hastened to the crime desired.
The moon beheld her first, and first retired;
The stars, amazed, ran backward from the sight,
And, shrunk within their sockets, lost their light.
Icarius first withdraws his holy flame;   270
The Virgin sign, in heaven the second name,
Slides down the belt, and from her station flies,
And night with sable clouds involves the skies.
Bold Myrrha still pursues her black intent;
She stumbled thrice, (an omen of the event;)
Thrice shrieked the funeral owl, yet on she went,
Secure of shame, because secure of sight;
E'en bashful sins are impudent by night.

Linked hand in hand, the accomplice and the dame,
Their way exploring, to the chamber came;   280
The door was ope, they blindly grope their way,
Where dark in bed the expecting monarch lay:
Thus far her courage held, but here forsakes;
Her faint knees knock at every step she makes.
The nearer to her crime, the more within
She feels remorse, and horror of her sin;
Repents too late her criminal desire,
And wishes, that unknown she could retire.
Her, lingering thus, the nurse, who feared delay
The fatal secret might at length betray,   290
Pulled forward, to complete the work begun,
And said to Cinyras, 'Receive thy own!'
Thus saying, she delivered kind to kind,
Accursed, and their devoted bodies joined.
The sire, unknowing of the crime, admits
His bowels, and profanes the hallowed sheets.
He found she trembled, but believed she strove
With maiden modesty, against her love:
And sought, with flattering words, vain fancies to remove.
Perhaps he said, 'My daughter, cease thy fears,'   300
Because the title suited with her years;
And, 'Father,' she might whisper him again,
That names might not be wanting to the sin.
Full of her sire, she left the incestuous bed,
And carried in her womb the crime she bred.
Another, and another night she came;
For frequent sin had left no sense of shame:
Till Cinyras desired to see her face,
Whose body he had held in close embrace,
And brought a taper; the revealer, light,   310
Exposed both crime, and criminal, to sight.
Grief, rage, amazement, could no speech afford,
But from the sheath he drew the avenging sword;
The guilty fled; the benefit of night,
That favoured first the sin, secured the flight.
Long wandering through the spacious fields, she bent
Her voyage to the Arabian continent;
Then passed the region which Panchaia joined,
And flying left the palmy plains behind.

Nine times the moon had mewed her horns; at length,   320
With travel weary, unsupplied with strength,
And with the burden of her womb oppressed,
Sabaean fields afford her needful rest;
There, loathing life, and yet of death afraid,
In anguish of her spirit, thus she prayed:
'Ye powers, if any so propitious are
To accept my penitence, and hear my prayer,
Your judgments, I confess, are justly sent;
Great sins deserve as great a punishment:
Yet, since my life the living will profane,   330
And since my death the happy dead will stain,
A middle state your mercy may bestow,
Betwixt the realms above, and those below;
Some other form to wretched Myrrha give,
Nor let her wholly die, nor wholly live.'
    The prayers of penitents are never vain;
At least, she did her last request obtain,
For, while she spoke, the ground began to rise,
And gathered round her feet, her legs, and thighs;
Her toes in roots descend, and, spreading wide,   340
A firm foundation for the trunk provide;
Her solid bones convert to solid wood,
To pith her marrow, and to sap her blood:
Her arms are boughs, her fingers change their kind,
Her tender skin is hardened into rind.
And now the rising tree her womb invests,
Now, shooting upwards still, invades her breasts,
And shades the neck; when, weary with delay,
She sunk her head within, and met it half the way.
And though with outward shape she lost her sense,   350
With bitter tears she wept her last offence;
And still she weeps, nor sheds her tears in vain;
For still the precious drops her name retain.
Meantime the misbegotten infant grows,
And, ripe for birth, distends with deadly throes
The swelling rind, with unavailing strife,
To leave the wooden womb, and pushes into life.
The mother-tree, as if oppressed with pain,
Writhes here and there, to break the bark, in vain;
And, like a labouring woman, would have prayed,   360

But wants a voice to call Lucina's aid;
The bending bole sends out a hollow sound,
And trickling tears fall thicker on the ground.
The mild Lucina came uncalled, and stood
Beside the struggling boughs, and heard the groaning wood;
Then reached her midwife-hand, to speed the throes,
And spoke the powerful spells that babes to birth disclose.
The bark divides, the living load to free,
And safe delivers the convulsive tree.
The ready nymphs receive the crying child,   370
And wash him in the tears the parent plant distilled.
They swathed him with their scarfs; beneath him spread
The ground with herbs; with roses raised his head.
The lovely babe was born with every grace;
E'en envy must have praised so fair a face:
Such was his form, as painters, when they show
Their utmost art, on naked loves bestow;
And that their arms no difference might betray,
Give him a bow, or his from Cupid take away.
Time glides along, with undiscovered haste,   380
The future but a length behind the past,
So swift are years; the babe, whom just before
His grandsire got, and whom his sister bore;
The drop, the thing which late the tree enclosed,
And late the yawning bark to life exposed;
A babe, a boy, a beauteous youth appears;
And lovelier than himself at riper years.
Now to the queen of love he gave desires,
And, with her pains, revenged his mother's fires.

The Cock and the Fox

There lived, as authors tell, in days of yore,
A widow, somewhat old, and very poor;
Deep in a dell her cottage lonely stood,
Well thatched, and under covert of a wood.
    This dowager, on whom my tale I found,
Since last she laid her husband in the ground,
A simple sober life in patience led,

And had but just enough to buy her bread;
But housewifing the little heaven had lent,
She duly paid a groat for quarter rent;   10
And pinched her belly, with her daughters two,
To bring the year about with much ado.
   The cattle in her homestead were three sows,
A ewe called Mally, and three brinded cows.
Her parlour-window stuck with herbs around,
Of savoury smell, and rushes strewed the ground.
A maple dresser in her hall she had,
On which full many a slender meal she made:
For no delicious morsel passed her throat;
According to her cloth she cut her coat.   20
No poignant sauce she knew, no costly treat,
Her hunger gave a relish to her meat.
A sparing diet did her health assure;
Or sick, a pepper posset was her cure.
Before the day was done, her work she sped,
And never went by candle-light to bed.
With exercise she sweat ill humours out;
Her dancing was not hindered by the gout.
Her poverty was glad, her heart content,
Nor knew she what the spleen or vapours meant.   30
Of wine she never tasted through the year,
But white and black was all her homely cheer;
Brown bread and milk, (but first she skimmed her bowls,)
And rashers of singed bacon on the coals;
On holidays an egg, or two at most;
But her ambition never reached to roast.
   A yard she had, with pales enclosed about,
Some high, some low, and a dry ditch without.
Within this homestead lived, without a peer
For crowing loud, the noble Chanticleer;   40
So hight her cock, whose singing did surpass
The merry notes of organs at the mass.
More certain was the crowing of a cock
To number hours, than is an abbey-clock;
And sooner than the matin-bell was rung,
He clapped his wings upon his roost, and sung:
For when degrees fifteen ascended right,
By sure instinct he knew 'twas one at night.

High was his comb, and coral-red withal,
In dents embattled like a castle wall;   50
His bill was raven-black, and shone like jet;
Blue were his legs, and orient were his feet;
White were his nails, like silver to behold,
His body glittering like the burnished gold.

   This gentle cock, for solace of his life,
Six misses had, beside his lawful wife;
Scandal, that spares no king, though ne'er so good,
Says, they were all of his own flesh and blood;
His sisters, both by sire and mother's side,
And sure their likeness showed them near allied.   60
But make the worst, the monarch did no more,
Than all the Ptolemies had done before:
When incest is for interest of a nation,
'Tis made no sin by holy dispensation.
Some lines have been maintained by this alone,
Which by their common ugliness are known.

   But passing this as from our tale apart,
Dame Partlet was the sovereign of his heart:
Ardent in love, outrageous in his play,
He feathered her a hundred times a day;   70
And she, that was not only passing fair,
But was withal discreet, and debonair,
Resolved the passive doctrine to fulfil,
Though loath, and let him work his wicked will:
At board and bed was affable and kind,
According as their marriage-vow did bind,
And as the church's precept had enjoined.
E'en since she was a se'nnight old, they say,
Was chaste and humble to her dying day,
Nor chick nor hen was known to disobey.   80

   By this her husband's heart she did obtain;
What cannot beauty, joined with virtue, gain?
She was his only joy, and he her pride,
She, when he walked, went pecking by his side;
If, spurning up the ground, he sprung a corn,
The tribute in his bill to her was borne.
But oh! what joy it was to hear him sing
In summer, when the day began to spring,
Stretching his neck, and warbling in his throat,

Solus cum sola, then was all his note.   90
For in the days of yore, the birds of parts
Were bred to speak, and sing, and learn the liberal arts.
   It happ'd that perching on the parlour-beam,
Amidst his wives, he had a deadly dream,
Just at the dawn; and sighed, and groaned so fast,
As every breath he drew would be his last.
Dame Partlet, ever nearest to his side,
Heard all his piteous moan, and how he cried
For help from gods and men; and sore aghast
She pecked and pulled, and wakened him at last.   100
   'Dear heart', said she, 'for love of heaven declare
Your pain, and make me partner of your care.
You groan, sir, ever since the morning light,
As something had disturbed your noble sprite.'
   'And, madam, well I might,' said Chanticleer,
'Never was shrovetide-cock in such a fear.
E'en still I run all over in a sweat,
My princely senses not recovered yet.
For such a dream I had of dire portent,
That much I fear my body will be shent: 110
It bodes I shall have wars and woeful strife,
Or in a loathsome dungeon end my life.
Know, dame, I dreamt within my troubled breast,
That in our yard I saw a murderous beast,
That on my body would have made arrest.
With waking eyes I ne'er beheld his fellow;
His colour was betwixt a red and yellow:
Tipped was his tail, and both his pricking ears,
With black, and much unlike his other hairs;
The rest, in shape a beagle's whelp throughout,   120
With broader forehead, and a sharper snout:
Deep in his front were sunk his glowing eyes,
That yet, methinks, I see him with surprise.
Reach out your hand, I drop with clammy sweat,
And lay it to my heart, and feel it beat.'
   'Now fie for shame!' quoth she: 'by heaven above,
Thou hast for ever lost thy lady's love.
No woman can endure a recreant knight;
He must be bold by day, and free by night:
Our sex desires a husband or a friend,   130

Who can our honour and his own defend;
Wise, hardy, secret, liberal of his purse;
A fool is nauseous, but a coward worse:
No bragging coxcomb, yet no baffled knight,
How dar'st thou talk of love, and dar'st not fight?
How dar'st thou tell thy dame thou art affeared?
Hast thou no manly heart, and hast a beard?
  'If aught from fearful dreams may be divined,
They signify a cock of dunghill kind.
All dreams, as in old Galen I have read,   140
Are from repletion and complexion bred;
From rising fumes of indigested food,
And noxious humours that infect the blood:
And sure, my lord, if I can read aright,
These foolish fancies, you have had tonight,
Are certain symptoms (in the canting style)
Of boiling choler, and abounding bile;
This yellow gall, that in your stomach floats,
Engenders all these visionary thoughts.
When choler overflows, then dreams are bred   150
Of flames, and all the family of red;
Red dragons, and red beasts in sleep we view,
For humours are distinguished by their hue.
From hence we dream of wars and warlike things,
And wasps and hornets with their double wings.
  'Choler adust congeals our blood with fear,
Then black bulls toss us, and black devils tear.
In sanguine airy dreams aloft we bound;
With rheums oppressed, we sink in rivers drowned.
  'More I could say, but thus conclude my theme,   160
The dominating humour makes the dream.
Cato was in his time accounted wise,
And he condemns them all for empty lies.
Take my advice, and when we fly to ground,
With laxatives preserve your body sound,
And purge the peccant humours that abound.
I should be loath to lay you on a bier;
And though there lives no 'pothecary near,
I dare for once prescribe for your disease,
And save long bills, and a damned doctor's fees.   170
  'Two sovereign herbs, which I by practice know,

And both at hand, (for in our yard they grow,)
On peril of my soul shall rid you wholly
Of yellow choler, and of melancholy:
You must both purge and vomit; but obey,
And for the love of heaven make no delay.
Since hot and dry in your complexion join,
Beware the sun when in a vernal sign;
For when he mounts exalted in the Ram,
If then he finds your body in a flame,   180
Replete with choler, I dare lay a groat,
A tertian ague is at least your lot.
Perhaps a fever (which the gods forefend)
May bring your youth to some untimely end:
And therefore, sir, as you desire to live,
A day or two before your laxative,
Take just three worms, nor over nor above,
Because the gods unequal numbers love.
These digestives prepare you for your purge;
Of fumetery, centaury, and spurge,   190
And of ground-ivy add a leaf, or two,
All which within our yard or garden grow.
Eat these, and be, my lord, of better cheer;
Your father's son was never born to fear.'
    'Madam,' quoth he, 'gramercy for your care,
But Cato, whom you quoted, you may spare.
'Tis true, a wise and worthy man he seems,
And (as you say) gave no belief to dreams;
But other men of more authority,
And, by the immortal powers, as wise as he,   200
Maintain, with sounder sense, that dreams forbode;
For Homer plainly says they come from God.
Nor Cato said it; but some modern fool
Imposed in Cato's name on boys at school.
    'Believe me, madam, morning dreams foreshow
The events of things, and future weal or woe:
Some truths are not by reason to be tried,
But we have sure experience for our guide.
An ancient author, equal with the best,
Relates this tale of dreams among the rest: 210
    'Two friends or brothers, with devout intent,
On some far pilgrimage together went.

It happened so, that when the sun was down,
They just arrived by twilight at a town;
That day had been the baiting of a bull,
'Twas at a feast, and every inn so full,
That no void room in chamber, or on ground,
And but one sorry bed was to be found;
And that so little it would hold but one,
Though till this hour they never lay alone.   220

　'So were they forced to part; one stayed behind,
His fellow sought what lodging he could find:
At last he found a stall where oxen stood,
And that he rather chose than lie abroad.
'Twas in a further yard without a door;
But, for his ease, well littered was the floor.

　'His fellow, who the narrow bed had kept,
Was weary, and without a rocker slept:
Supine he snored; but in dead of night,
He dreamt his friend appeared before his sight,   230
Who, with a ghastly look and doleful cry,
Said, "Help me, brother, or this night I die:
Arise, and help, before all help be vain,
Or in an ox's stall I shall be slain."

　'Roused from his rest, he wakened in a start,
Shivering with horror, and with aching heart;
At length to cure himself by reason tries;
'Twas but a dream, and what are dreams but lies?
So thinking changed his side, and closed his eyes.
His dream returns: his friend appears again: 240
"The murderers come, now help, or I am slain:"
'Twas but a vision still, and visions are but vain.

　'He dreamt the third; but now his friend appeared
Pale, naked, pierced with wounds, with blood besmeared:
"Thrice warned, awake," said he; "relief is late,
The deed is done; but thou revenge my fate:
Tardy of aid, unseal thy heavy eyes,
Awake, and with the dawning day arise:
Take to the western gate thy ready way,
For by that passage they my corpse convey: 250
My corpse is in a tumbrel laid, among
The filth and ordure, and enclosed with dung.
That cart arrest, and raise a common cry;

For sacred hunger of my gold I die:"
Then showed his grisly wounds; and last he drew
A piteous sigh, and took a long adieu.
  'The frightened friend arose by break of day,
And found the stall where late his fellow lay.
Then of his impious host inquiring more,
Was answered that his guest was gone before: 260
"Muttering he went," said he, "by morning light,
And much complained of his ill rest by night."
This raised suspicion in the pilgrim's mind;
Because all hosts are of an evil kind,
And oft to share the spoil with robbers joined.
  'His dream confirmed his thought; with troubled look
Straight to the western gate his way he took;
There, as his dream foretold, a cart he found,
That carried compost forth to dung the ground.
This when the pilgrim saw, he stretched his throat,   270
And cried out "murder" with a yelling note.
"My murdered fellow in this cart lies dead;
Vengeance and justice on the villain's head!
You, magistrates, who sacred laws dispense,
On you I call to punish this offence."
  'The word thus given, within a little space,
The mob came roaring out, and thronged the place.
All in a trice they cast the cart to ground,
And in the dung the murdered body found;
Though breathless, warm, and reeking from the wound.   280
Good heaven, whose darling attribute we find
Is boundless grace, and mercy to mankind,
Abhors the cruel; and the deeds of night
By wondrous ways reveals in open light:
Murder may pass unpunished for a time,
But tardy justice will o'ertake the crime.
And oft a speedier pain the guilty feels,
The hue and cry of heaven pursues him at the heels,
Fresh from the fact, as in the present case:
The criminals are seized upon the place;   290
Carter and host confronted face to face.
Stiff in denial, as the law appoints,
On engines they distend their tortured joints;
So was confession forced, the offence was known,

And public justice on the offenders done.
   'Here may you see that visions are to dread;
And in the page that follows this, I read
Of two young merchants, whom the hope of gain
Induced in partnership to cross the main;
Waiting till willing winds their sails supplied,   300
Within a trading-town they long abide,
Full fairly situate on a haven's side.
   'One evening it befell, that, looking out,
The wind they long had wished was come about;
Well pleased they went to rest; and if the gale
Till morn continued, both resolved to sail.
But as together in a bed they lay,
The younger had a dream at break of day.
A man, he thought, stood frowning at his side,
Who warned him for his safety to provide,   310
Not put to sea, but safe on shore abide.
"I come, thy genius, to command thy stay;
Trust not the winds, for fatal is the day,
And death unhoped attends the watery way."
   'The vision said, and vanished from his sight.
The dreamer wakened in a mortal fright;
Then pulled his drowsy neighbour, and declared,
What in his slumber he had seen and heard.
His friend smiled scornful, and with proud contempt
Rejects as idle what his fellow dreamt.   320
"Stay, who will stay; for me no fears restrain,
Who follow Mercury, the god of gain;
Let each man do as to his fancy seems,
I wait not, I, till you have better dreams.
Dreams are but interludes, which fancy makes;
When monarch reason sleeps, this mimic wakes;
Compounds a medley of disjointed things,
A mob of cobblers, and a court of kings:
Light fumes are merry, grosser fumes are sad;
Both are the reasonable soul run mad;   330
And many monstrous forms in sleep we see,
That neither were, nor are, nor e'er can be.
Sometimes, forgotten things long cast behind
Rush forward in the brain, and come to mind.
The nurse's legends are for truths received,

And the man dreams but what the boy believed.
'"Sometimes we but rehearse a former play,
The night restores our actions done by day,
As hounds in sleep will open for their prey.
In short, the farce of dreams is of a piece,   340
Chimeras all; and more absurd, or less.
You, who believe in tales, abide alone;
Whate'er I get this voyage is my own."
'Thus while he spoke, he heard the shouting crew
That called aboard, and took his last adieu.
The vessel went before a merry gale,
And for quick passage put on every sail;
But when least feared, and e'en in open day,
The mischief overtook her in the way:
Whether she sprung a leak, I cannot find,   350
Or whether she was overset with wind,
Or that some rock below her bottom rent,
But down at once with all the crew she went.
Her fellow-ships from far her loss descried;
But only she was sunk, and all were safe beside.
'By this example you are taught again,
That dreams and visions are not always vain;
But if, dear Partlet, you are yet in doubt,
Another tale shall make the former out.
'Kenelm, the son of Kenulph, Mercia's king,   360
Whose holy life the legends loudly sing,
Warned in a dream, his murder did foretell,
From point to point as after it befell:
All circumstances to his nurse he told,
(A wonder from a child of seven years old;)
The dream with horror heard, the good old wife
From treason counselled him to guard his life;
But close to keep the secret in his mind,
For a boy's vision small belief would find.
The pious child, by promise bound, obeyed,   370
Nor was the fatal murder long delayed;
By Quenda slain, he fell before his time,
Made a young martyr by his sister's crime.
The tale is told by venerable Bede,
Which, at your better leisure, you may read.
'Macrobius too relates the vision sent

To the great Scipio, with the famed event;
Objections makes, but after makes replies,
And adds, that dreams are often prophecies.

   'Of Daniel you may read in holy writ,   380
Who, when the king his vision did forget,
Could word for word the wondrous dream repeat.
Nor less of patriarch Joseph understand,
Who by a dream enslaved the Egyptian land,
The years of plenty and of dearth foretold,
When, for their bread, their liberty they sold.
Nor must the exalted butler be forgot,
Nor he whose dream presaged his hanging lot.

   'And did not Croesus the same death foresee,
Raised in his vision on a lofty tree?   390
The wife of Hector, in his utmost pride,
Dreamt of his death the night before he died:
Well was he warned from battle to refrain,
But men to death decreed are warned in vain;
He dared the dream, and by his fatal foe was slain.

   'Much more I know, which I forbear to speak,
For see the ruddy day begins to break:
Let this suffice, that plainly I foresee
My dream was bad, and bodes adversity;
But neither pills nor laxatives I like,   400
They only serve to make a well man sick;
Of these his gain the sharp physician makes,
And often gives a purge, but seldom takes;
They not correct, but poison all the blood,
And ne'er did any but the doctors good.
Their tribe, trade, trinkets, I defy them all,
With every work of 'Pothecaries' Hall.

   'These melancholy matters I forbear;
But let me tell thee, Partlet mine, and swear,
That when I view the beauties of thy face,   410
I fear not death, nor dangers, nor disgrace;
So may my soul have bliss, as when I spy
The scarlet red about thy partridge eye,
While thou art constant to thy own true knight,
While thou art mine, and I am thy delight,
All sorrows at thy presence take their flight.
For true it is, as *in principio*,

Mulier est hominis confusio.
Madam, the meaning of this Latin is,
That woman is to man his sovereign bliss.   420
For when by night I feel your tender side,
Though for the narrow perch I cannot ride,
Yet I have such a solace in my mind,
That all my boding cares are cast behind,
And e'en already I forget my dream.'
He said, and downward flew from off the beam,
For daylight now began apace to spring,
The thrush to whistle, and the lark to sing.
Then crowing, clapped his wings, the appointed call,
To chuck his wives together in the hall.   430
      By this the widow had unbarred the door,
And Chanticleer went strutting out before,
With royal courage, and with heart so light,
As showed he scorned the visions of the night.
Now roaming in the yard, he spurned the ground,
And gave to Partlet the first grain he found.
Then often feathered her with wanton play,
And trod her twenty times ere prime of day;
And took by turns and gave so much delight,
Her sisters pined with envy at the sight.   440
      He chucked again, when other corns he found,
And scarcely deigned to set a foot to ground;
But swaggered like a lord about his hall,
And his seven wives came running at his call.
      'Twas now the month in which the world began,
(If March beheld the first created man;)
And since the vernal equinox, the sun
In Aries twelve degrees, or more, had run;
When casting up his eyes against the light,
Both month, and day, and hour, he measured right,   450
And told more truly than the Ephemeris;
For art may err, but nature cannot miss.
      Thus numbering times and seasons in his breast,
His second crowing the third hour confessed.
Then turning, said to Partlet, 'See, my dear,
How lavish nature has adorned the year;
How the pale primrose and blue violet spring,
And birds essay their throats disused to sing:

All these are ours; and I with pleasure see,
Man strutting on two legs, and aping me; 460
An unfledged creature, of a lumpish frame,
Endued with fewer particles of flame:
Our dame sits cowering o'er a kitchen fire,
I draw fresh air, and nature's works admire;
And e'en this day in more delight abound,
Than, since I was an egg, I ever found.'
 The time shall come, when Chanticleer shall wish
His words unsaid, and hate his boasted bliss;
The crested bird shall be experience know,
Jove made not him his masterpiece below, 470
And learn the latter end of joy is woe.
The vessel of his bliss to dregs is run,
And heaven will have him taste his other tun.
 Ye wise! draw near and hearken to my tale,
Which proves that oft the proud by flattery fall;
The legend is as true I undertake
As Tristram is, and Launcelot of the lake;
Which all our ladies in such reverence hold,
As if in Book of Martyrs it were told.
 A fox, full-fraught with seeming sanctity, 480
That feared an oath, but, like the devil, would lie;
Who looked like Lent, and had the holy leer,
And durst not sin before he said his prayer;
This pious cheat, that never sucked the blood,
Nor chewed the flesh of lambs, but when he could,
Had passed three summers in the neighbouring wood;
And musing long, whom next to circumvent,
On Chanticleer his wicked fancy bent;
And in his high imagination cast,
By stratagem to gratify his taste. 490
 The plot contrived, before the break of day,
Saint Reynard through the hedge had made his way;
The pale was next, but proudly, with a bound,
He leapt the fence of the forbidden ground;
Yet fearing to be seen, within a bed
Of coleworts he concealed his wily head;
There skulked till afternoon, and watched his time,
(As murderers use,) to perpetrate his crime.
 O hypocrite, ingenious to destroy!

O traitor, worse than Sinon was to Troy!   500
O vile subverter of the Gallic reign,
More false than Gano was to Charlemagne!
O Chanticleer, in an unhappy hour
Didst thou forsake the safety of thy bower;
Better for thee thou hadst believed thy dream,
And not that day descended from the beam!
    But here the doctors eagerly dispute;
Some hold predestination absolute;
Some clerks maintain, that heaven at first foresees,
And in the virtue of foresight decrees.   510
If this be so, then prescience binds the will,
And mortals are not free to good or ill;
For what he first foresaw, he must ordain,
Or its eternal prescience may be vain;
As bad for us as prescience had not been;
For first, or last, he's author of the sin.
And who says that, let the blaspheming man
Say worse e'en of the devil, if he can.
For how can that eternal power be just
To punish man, who sins because he must?   520
Or, how can he reward a virtuous deed,
Which is not done by us, but first decreed?
    I cannot bolt this matter to the bran,
As Bradwardine and holy Austin can:
If prescience can determine actions so,
That we must do, because he did foreknow,
Or that foreknowing, yet our choice is free.
Not forced to sin by strict necessity;
This strict necessity they simple call,
Another sort there is conditional.   530
The first so binds the will, that things foreknown
By spontaneity, not choice, are done.
Thus galley-slaves tug willing at their oar,
Consent to work, in prospect of the shore;
But would not work at all, if not constrained before.
That other does not liberty constrain,
But man may either act, or may refrain.
Heaven made us agents free to good or ill,
And forced it not, though he foresaw the will.
Freedom was first bestowed on human race,   540

And prescience only held the second place.
   If he could make such agents wholly free,
I not dispute; the point's too high for me:
For heaven's unfathomed power what man can sound,
Or put to his omnipotence a bound?
He made us to his image, all agree;
That image is the soul, and that must be,
Or not the maker's image, or be free.
But whether it were better man had been
By nature bound to good, not free to sin,   550
I waive, for fear of splitting on a rock;
The tale I tell is only of a cock;
Who had not run the hazard of his life,
Had he believed his dream, and not his wife:
For women, with a mischief to their kind,
Pervert, with bad advice, our better mind.
A woman's counsel brought us first to woe,
And made her man his paradise forego,
Where at heart's ease he lived; and might have been
As free from sorrow as he was from sin.   560
For what the devil had their sex to do,
That, born to folly, they presumed to know,
And could not see the serpent in the grass?
But I myself presume, and let it pass.
   Silence in times of suffering is the best,
'Tis dangerous to disturb a hornet's nest.
In other authors you may find enough,
But all they say of dames is idle stuff.
Legends of lying wits together bound,
The wife of Bath would throw them to the ground: 570
These are the words of Chanticleer, not mine,
I honour dames, and think their sex divine.
   Now to continue what my tale begun.
Lay madam Partlet basking in the sun,
Breast-high in sand; her sisters, in a row,
Enjoyed the beams above, the warmth below.
The cock, that of his flesh was ever free,
Sung merrier than the mermaid in the sea;
And so befell, that as he cast his eye,
Among the coleworts, on a butterfly,   580
He saw false Reynard where he lay full low;

I need not swear he had no list to crow;
But cried, *Cock, cock*, and gave a sudden start,
As sore dismayed and frighted at his heart.
For birds and beasts, informed by nature, know
Kinds opposite to theirs, and fly their foe.
So Chanticleer, who never saw a fox,
Yet shunned him, as a sailor shuns the rocks.
   But the false loon, who could not work his will
By open force, employed his flattering skill: 590
'I hope, my lord,' said he, 'I not offend;
Are you afraid of me, that am your friend?
I were a beast indeed to do you wrong,
I, who have loved and honoured you so long:
Stay, gentle sir, nor take a false alarm,
For, on my soul, I never meant you harm!
I come no spy, nor as a traitor press,
To learn the secrets of your soft recess:
Far be from Reynard so profane a thought,
But by the sweetness of your voice was brought: 600
For, as I bid my beads, by chance I heard
The song as of an angel in the yard;
A song that would have charmed the infernal gods,
And banished horror from the dark abodes:
Had Orpheus sung it in the nether sphere,
So much the hymn had pleased the tyrant's ear,
The wife had been detained, to keep the husband there.
   'My lord, your sire familiarly I knew,
A peer deserving such a son as you:
He, with your lady-mother, (whom heaven rest!)   610
Has often graced my house, and been my guest:
To view his living features does me good,
For I am your poor neighbour in the wood;
And in my cottage should be proud to see
The worthy heir of my friend's family.
   'But since I speak of singing, let me say,
As with an upright heart I safely may,
That, save yourself, there breathes not on the ground
One like your father for a silver sound.
So sweetly would he wake the winter-day,   620
That matrons to the church mistook their way,
And thought they heard the merry organ play.

And he to raise his voice with artful care,
(What will not beaux attempt to please the fair?)
On tiptoe stood to sing with greater strength,
And stretched his comely neck at all the length:
And while he pained his voice to pierce the skies,
As saints in raptures use, would shut his eyes,
That the sound striving through the narrow throat,
His winking might avail to mend the note.   630
By this, in song, he never had his peer,
From sweet Cecilia down to Chanticleer;
Not Maro's muse, who sung the mighty man,
Nor Pindar's heavenly lyre, nor Horace when a swan.
Your ancestors proceed from race divine:
From Brennus and Belinus is your line;
Who gave to sovereign Rome such loud alarms,
That e'en the priests were not excused from arms.
    'Besides, a famous monk of modern times
Has left of cocks recorded in his rhymes,   640
That of a parish priest the son and heir,
(When sons of priests were from the proverb clear,)
Affronted once a cock of noble kind,
And either lamed his legs, or struck him blind;
For which the clerk his father was disgraced,
And in his benefice another placed.
Now sing, my lord, if not for love of me,
Yet for the sake of sweet saint charity;
Make hills and dales, and earth and heaven, rejoice,
And emulate your father's angel-voice.'   650
    The cock was pleased to hear him speak so fair,
And proud beside, as solar people are;
Nor could the treason from the truth descry,
So was he ravished with this flattery:
So much the more, as from a little elf,
He had a high opinion of himself;
Though sickly, slender, and not large of limb,
Concluding all the world was made for him.
    Ye princes, raised by poets to the gods,
And Alexandered up in lying odes,   660
Believe not every flattering knave's report,
There's many a Reynard lurking in the court;
And he shall be received with more regard,

And listened to, than modest truth is heard.
　　This Chanticleer, of whom the story sings,
Stood high upon his toes, and clapped his wings;
Then stretched his neck, and winked with both his eyes,
Ambitious, as he sought the Olympic prize.
But while he pained himself to raise his note,
False Reynard rushed, and caught him by the throat.　　670
Then on his back he laid the precious load,
And sought his wonted shelter of the wood;
Swiftly he made his way, the mischief done,
Of all unheeded, and pursued by none.
　　Alas! what stay is there in human state,
Or who can shun inevitable fate?
The doom was written, the decree was passed,
Ere the foundations of the world were cast!
In Aries though the sun exalted stood,
His patron-planet to procure his good;　　680
Yet Saturn was his mortal foe, and he,
In Libra raised, opposed the same degree:
The rays both good and bad, of equal power,
Each thwarting other, made a mingled hour.
　　On Friday-morn he dreamt his direful dream,
Cross to the worthy native, in his scheme.
Ah, blissful Venus! goddess of delight!
How couldst thou suffer thy devoted knight,
On thy own day, to fall by foe oppressed,
The wight of all the world who served thee best?　　690
Who, true to love, was all for recreation,
And minded not the work of propagation?
Gaufride, who couldst so well in rhyme complain
The death of Richard with an arrow slain,
Why had not I thy muse, or thou my heart,
To sing this heavy dirge with equal art!
That I like thee on Friday might complain;
For on that day was Coeur de Lion slain.
　　Not louder cries, when Ilium was in flames,
Were sent to heaven by woeful Trojan dames,　　700
When Pyrrhus tossed on high his burnished blade,
And offered Priam to his father's shade,
Than for the cock the widowed poultry made.
Fair Partlet first, when he was borne from sight,

With sovereign shrieks bewailed her captive knight;
Far louder than the Carthaginian wife,
When Asdrubal her husband lost his life,
When she beheld the smouldering flames ascend,
And all the Punic glories at an end:
Willing into the fires she plunged her head,   710
With greater ease than others seek their bed.
Not more aghast the matrons of renown,
When tyrant Nero burned the imperial town,
Shrieked for the downfall in a doleful cry,
For which their guiltless lords were doomed to die.
    Now to my story I return again:
The trembling widow, and her daughters twain,
This woeful cackling cry with horror heard,
Of those distracted damsels in the yard;
And starting up, beheld the heavy sight,   720
How Reynard to the forest took his flight,
And cross his back, as in triumphant scorn,
The hope and pillar of the house was borne.
    'The fox, the wicked fox,' was all the cry;
Out from his house ran every neighbour nigh:
The vicar first, and after him the crew,
With forks and staves the felon to pursue.
Ran Coll our dog, and Talbot with the band,
And Malkin, with her distaff in her hand:
Ran cow and calf, and family of hogs,   730
In panic horror of pursuing dogs;
With many a deadly grunt and doleful squeak,
Poor swine, as if their pretty hearts would break.
The shouts of men, the women in dismay,
With shrieks augment the terror of the day,
The ducks, that heard the proclamation cried,
And feared a persecution might betide,
Full twenty miles from town their voyage take,
Obscure in rushes of the liquid lake.
The geese fly o'er the barn; the bees, in arms,   740
Drive headlong from their waxen cells in swarms.
Jack Straw at London-stone, with all his rout,
Struck not the city with so loud a shout;
Not when with English hate they did pursue
A Frenchman, or an unbelieving Jew;

Not when the welkin rung with *One and all*,
And echoes bounded back from Fox's hall;
Earth seemed to sink beneath, and heaven above to fall.
With might and main they chased the murderous fox,
With brazen trumpets, and inflated box,   750
To kindle Mars with military sounds,
Nor wanted horns to inspire sagacious hounds.
  But see how fortune can confound the wise,
And when they least expect it, turn the dice.
The captive-cock, who scarce could draw his breath,
And lay within the very jaws of death;
Yet in this agony his fancy wrought,
And fear supplied him with this happy thought:
'Yours is the prize, victorious prince,' said he,
'The vicar my defeat, and all the village see.   760
Enjoy your friendly fortune while you may,
And bid the churls that envy you the prey
Call back their mongrel curs, and cease their cry:
See fools, the shelter of the wood is nigh,
And Chanticleer in your despite shall die;
He shall be plucked and eaten to the bone.'
  ''Tis well advised, in faith it shall be done;'
This Reynard said: but as the word he spoke,
The prisoner with a spring from prison broke;
Then stretched his feathered fans with all his might,   770
And to the neighbouring maple winged his flight.
  Whom, when the traitor safe on tree beheld,
He cursed the gods, with shame and sorrow filled:
Shame for his folly; sorrow out of time,
For plotting an unprofitable crime:
Yet, mastering both, the artificer of lies,
Renews the assault, and his last battery tries.
  'Though I,' said he, 'did ne'er in thought offend,
How justly may my lord suspect his friend?
The appearance is against me, I confess,   780
Who seemingly have put you in distress.
You, if your goodness does not plead my cause,
May think I broke all hospitable laws,
To bear you from your palace-yard by might,
And put your noble person in a fright.
This, since you take it ill, I must repent,

Though heaven can witness, with no bad intent
I practised it, to make you taste your cheer
With double pleasure, first prepared by fear.
So loyal subjects often seize their prince,   790
Forced (for his good) to seeming violence,
Yet mean his sacred person not the least offence.
Descend; so help me, Jove, as you shall find,
That Reynard comes of no dissembling kind.'
'Nay,' quoth the cock; 'but I beshrew us both,
If I believe a saint upon his oath:
An honest man may take a knave's advice,
But idiots only will be cozened twice:
Once warned is well bewared; no flattering lies
Shall soothe me more to sing with winking eyes,   800
And open mouth, for fear of catching flies.
Who blindfold walks upon a river's brim,
When he should see, has he deserved to swim?'
    'Better, Sir Cock, let all contention cease;
Come down,' said Reynard, 'let us treat of peace.'
    'A peace with all my soul,' said Chanticleer;
'But, with your favour, I will treat it here:
And lest the truce with treason should be mixed,
'Tis my concern to have the tree betwixt.'

THE MORAL

In this plain fable you the effect may see   810
Of negligence, and fond credulity:
And learn besides of flatterers to beware,
Then most pernicious when they speak too fair.
The cock and fox, the fool and knave imply;
The truth is moral, though the tale a lie.
Who spoke in parables, I dare not say;
But sure he knew it was a pleasing way,
Sound sense, by plain example, to convey.
And in a heathen author we may find,
That pleasure with instruction should be joined;   820
So take the corn, and leave the chaff behind.

Ceyx and Alcyone

These prodigies afflict the pious prince;
But, more perplexed with those that happened since,
He purposes to seek the Clarian god,
Avoiding Delphos, his more famed abode;
Since Phlegian robbers made unsafe the road.
Yet could not he from her he loved so well,
The fatal voyage, he resolved, conceal;
But when she saw her lord prepared to part,
A deadly cold ran shivering to her heart;
Her faded cheeks are changed to boxen hue,   10
And in her eyes the tears are ever new;
She thrice essayed to speak; her accents hung,
And, faltering, died unfinished on her tongue,
Or vanished into sighs; with long delay
Her voice returned; and found the wonted way.
'Tell me, my lord,' she said, 'what fault unknown
Thy once beloved Alcyone has done?
Whither, ah whither is thy kindness gone!
Can Ceyx then sustain to leave his wife,
And unconcerned forsake the sweets of life?   20
What can thy mind to this long journey move,
Or need'st thou absence to renew thy love?
Yet, if thou goest by land, though grief possess
My soul e'en then, my fears will be the less.
But ah! be warned to shun the watery way,
The face is frightful of the stormy sea.
For late I saw adrift disjointed planks,
And empty tombs erected on the banks.
Nor let false hopes to trust betray thy mind,
Because my sire in caves constrains the wind,   30
Can with a breath their clamorous rage appease,
They fear his whistle, and forsake the seas:
Not so; for once indulged, they sweep the main,
Deaf to the call, or, hearing, hear in vain;
But bent on mischief, bear the waves before,
And not content with seas insult the shore;
When ocean, air, and earth, at once engage,
And rooted forests fly before their rage;

At once the clashing clouds to battle move,
And lightnings run across the fields above: 40
I know them well, and marked their rude comport,
While yet a child within my father's court;
In times of tempest they command alone,
And he but sits precarious on the throne;
The more I know, the more my fears augment,
And fears are oft prophetic of the event.
But if not fears, or reasons will prevail,
If fate has fixed thee obstinate to sail,
Go not without thy wife, but let me bear
My part of danger with an equal share, 50
And present what I suffer only fear;
Then o'er the bounding billows shall we fly,
Secure to live together, or to die.'

These reasons moved her starlike husband's heart,
But still he held his purpose to depart;
For as he loved her equal to his life,
He would not to the seas expose his wife;
Nor could be wrought his voyage to refrain,
But sought by arguments to soothe her pain:
Nor these availed; at length he lights on one, 60
With which so difficult a cause he won:
'My love, so short an absence cease to fear,
For by my father's holy flame I swear,
Before two moons their orb with light adorn,
If heaven allow me life, I will return.'

This promise of so short a stay prevails;
He soon equips the ship, supplies the sails,
And gives the word to launch; she trembling views
This pomp of death, and parting tears renews;
Last with a kiss, she took a long farewell, 70
Sighed with a sad presage, and swooning fell.
While Ceyx seeks delays, the lusty crew,
Raised on their banks, their oars in order drew
To their broad breasts,—the ship with fury flew.

The queen, recovered, rears her humid eyes,
And first her husband on the poop espies,
Shaking his hand at distance on the main;
She took the sign, and shook her hand again.
Still as the ground recedes, contracts her view

With sharpened sight, till she no longer knew 80
The much-loved face; that comfort lost, supplies
With less, and with the galley feeds her eyes;
The galley borne from view by rising gales,
She followed with her sight the flying sails;
When e'en the flying sails were seen no more.
Forsaken of all sight, she left the shore.
Then on her bridal bed her body throws,
And sought in sleep her wearied eyes to close;
Her husband's pillow, and the widowed part
Which once he pressed, renewed the former smart. 90

And now a breeze from shore began to blow;
The sailors ship their oars, and cease to row;
Then hoist their yards atrip, and all their sails
Let fall, to court the wind and catch the gales.
By this the vessel half her course had run,
And as much rested till the rising sun;
Both shores were lost to sight, when at the close
Of day, a stiffer gale at east arose;
The sea grew white, the rolling waves from far,
Like heralds, first denounce the watery war. 100

This seen, the master soon began to cry,
'Strike, strike the top-sail; let the main sheet fly,
And furl your sails.' The winds repel the sound,
And in the speaker's mouth the speech is drowned.
Yet of their own accord, as danger taught,
Each in his way, officiously they wrought;
Some stow their oars, or stop the leaky sides;
Another, bolder yet, the yard bestrides,
And folds the sails; a fourth, with labour, laves
The intruding seas, and waves ejects on waves. 110

In this confusion while their work they ply,
The winds augment the winter of the sky,
And wage intestine wars; the suffering seas
Are tossed, and mingled as their tyrants please.
The master would command, but in despair
Of safety, stands amazed with stupid care,
Nor what to bid, or what forbid, he knows,
The ungoverned tempest to such fury grows;
Vain is his force, and vainer is his skill,
With such a concourse comes the flood of ill; 120

The cries of men are mixed with rattling shrouds;
Seas dash on seas, and clouds encounter clouds;
At once from east to west, from pole to pole,
The forky lightnings flash, the roaring thunders roll.
    Now waves on waves ascending scale the skies,
And in the fires above, the water fries;
When yellow sands are sifted from below,
The glittering billows give a golden show;
And when the fouler bottom spews the black,
The Stygian dye the tainted waters take;   130
Then frothy white appear the flatted seas,
And change their colour, changing their disease.
Like various fits the Trachin vessel finds,
And now sublime she rides upon the winds;
As from a lofty summit looks from high,
And from the clouds beholds the nether sky;
Now from the depth of hell they lift their sight,
And at a distance see superior light;
The lashing billows make a loud report,
And beat her sides, as battering rams a fort;   140
Or as a lion, bounding in his way,
With force augmented bears against his prey,
Sidelong to seize; or, unappalled with fear,
Springs on the toils, and rushes on the spear;
So seas impelled by winds, with added power,
Assault the sides, and o'er the hatches tower.
    The planks, their pitchy covering washed away,
Now yield; and now a yawning breach display;
The roaring waters with a hostile tide
Rush through the ruins of her gaping side.   150
Meantime, in sheets of rain the sky descends,
And ocean, swelled with waters, upwards tends,
One rising, falling one; the heavens and sea
Meet at their confines, in the middle way;
The sails are drunk with showers, and drop with rain,
Sweet waters mingle with the briny main.
No star appears to lend his friendly light;
Darkness and tempest make a double night;
But flashing fires disclose the deep by turns,
And while the lightnings blaze, the water burns.   160
    Now all the waves their scattered force unite;

And as a soldier, foremost in the fight,
Makes way for others, and, a host alone,
Still presses on, and, urging, gains the town;
So while the invading billows come abreast,
The hero tenth, advanced before the rest,
Sweeps all before him with impetuous sway,
And from the walls descends upon the prey;
Part following enter, part remain without,
With envy hear their fellows' conquering shout,   170
And mount on others' backs, in hope to share
The city, thus become the seat of war.

   A universal cry resounds aloud,
The sailors run in heaps, a helpless crowd;
Art fails, and courage falls, no succour near;
As many waves, as many deaths appear.
One weeps, and yet despairs of late relief;
One cannot weep, his fears congeal his grief;
But, stupid, with dry eyes expects his fate.
One with loud shrieks laments his lost estate,   180
And calls those happy whom their funerals wait.
This wretch with prayers and vows the gods implores,
And e'en the skies he cannot see, adores.
That other on his friends his thoughts bestows,
His careful father and his faithful spouse.
The covetous worldling in his anxious mind
Thinks only on the wealth he left behind.

   All Ceyx his Alcyone employs,
For her he grieves, yet in her absence joys;
His wife he wishes, and would still be near,   190
Not her with him, but wishes him with her:
Now with last looks he seeks his native shore,
Which fate has destined him to see no more;
He sought, but in the dark tempestuous night
He knew not whither to direct his sight.
So whirl the seas, such darkness blinds the sky,
That the black night receives a deeper dye.

   The giddy ship ran round; the tempest tore
Her mast, and overboard the rudder bore.
One billow mounts; and with a scornful brow,   200
Proud of her conquest gained, insults the waves below;
Nor lighter falls, than if some giant tore

Pindus and Athos, with the freight they bore,
And tossed on seas; pressed with the ponderous blow,
Down sinks the ship within the abyss below;
Down with the vessel sink into the main
The many, never more to rise again.
Some few on scattered planks with fruitless care
Lay hold, and swim; but, while they swim, despair.
E'en he who late a sceptre did command,　　　　　　210
Now grasps a floating fragment in his hand;
And while he struggles on the stormy main,
Invokes his father, and his wife's, in vain:
But yet his consort is his greatest care;
Alcyone he names amidst his prayer;
Names as a charm against the waves and wind,
Most in his mouth, and ever in his mind.
Tired with his toil, all hopes of safety past,
From prayers to wishes he descends at last:
That his dead body, wafted to the sands,　　　　　　220
Might have its burial from her friendly hands.
As oft as he can catch a gulp of air,
And peep above the seas, he names the fair;
And, e'en when plunged beneath, on her he raves,
Murmuring Alcyone below the waves:
At last a falling billow stops his breath,
Breaks o'er his head, and whelms him underneath.
Bright Lucifer unlike himself appears
That night, his heavenly form obscured with tears;
And since he was forbid to leave the skies,　　　　　　230
He muffled with a cloud his mournful eyes.
　Meantime Alcyone (his fate unknown)
Computes how many nights he had been gone,
Observes the waning moon with hourly view,
Numbers her age, and wishes for a new;
Against the promised time provides with care,
And hastens in the woof the robes he was to wear;
And for herself employs another loom,
New-dressed to meet her lord returning home,
Flattering her heart with joys that never were to come.　　240
She fumed the temples with an odorous flame,
And oft before the sacred altars came
To pray for him, who was an empty name;

All powers implored, but far above the rest,
To Juno she her pious vows addressed,
Her much-loved lord from perils to protect,
And safe o'er seas his voyage to direct;
Then prayed that she might still possess his heart,
And no pretending rival share a part.
This last petition heard, of all her prayer;   250
The rest, dispersed by winds, were lost in air.

   But she, the goddess of the nuptial bed,
Tired with her vain devotions for the dead,
Resolved the tainted hand should be repelled,
Which incense offered, and her altar held:
Then Iris thus bespoke, 'Thou faithful maid,
By whom thy queen's commands are well conveyed,
Haste to the house of Sleep, and bid the god,
Who rules the night by visions with a nod,
Prepare a dream, in figure and in form   260
Resembling him who perished in the storm:
This form before Alcyone present,
To make her certain of the sad event.'

   Endued with robes of various hue she flies,
And flying draws an arch, a segment of the skies;
Then leaves her bending bow, and from the steep
Descends to search the silent house of Sleep.

   Near the Cimmerians, in his dark abode,
Deep in a cavern, dwells the drowsy god;
Whose gloomy mansion nor the rising sun,   270
Nor setting, visits, nor the lightsome noon;
But lazy vapours round the region fly,
Perpetual twilight, and a doubtful sky;
No crowing cock does there his wings display,
Nor with his horny bill provoke the day;
Nor watchful dogs, nor the more wakeful geese,
Disturb with nightly noise the sacred peace;
Nor beast of nature, nor the tame, are nigh,
Nor trees with tempests rocked, nor human cry;
But safe repose, without an air of breath,   280
Dwells here, and a dumb quiet next to death.

   An arm of Lethe, with a gentle flow,
Arising upwards from the rock below,
The palace moats, and o'er the pebbles creeps,

And with soft murmurs calls the coming sleeps;
Around its entry nodding poppies grow,
And all cool simples that sweet rest bestow;
Night from the plants their sleepy virtue drains,
And passing sheds it on the silent plains:
No door there was the unguarded house to keep, 290
On creaking hinges turned, to break his sleep.

But in the gloomy court was raised a bed,
Stuffed with black plumes, and on an ebon stead;
Black was the covering too, where lay the god,
And slept supine, his limbs displayed abroad;
About his head fantastic visions fly,
Which various images of things supply,
And mock their forms; the leaves on trees not more,
Nor bearded ears in fields, nor sands upon the shore.

The virgin, entering bright, indulged the day 300
To the brown cave, and brushed the dreams away;
The god, disturbed with this new glare of light
Cast sudden on his face, unsealed his sight,
And raised his tardy head, which sunk again,
And sinking on his bosom, knocked his chin;
At length shook off himself, and asked the dame
(And asking yawned), for what intent she came?

To whom the goddess thus: 'O sacred rest,
Sweet pleasing sleep, of all the powers the best!
O peace of mind, repairer of decay, 310
Whose balm renews the limbs to labours of the day,
Care shuns thy soft approach, and sullen flies away!
Adorn a dream, expressing human form,
The shape of him who suffered in the storm,
And send it flitting to the Trachin court,
The wreck of wretched Ceyx to report:
Before his queen bid the pale spectre stand,
Who begs a vain relief at Juno's hand.'
She said, and scarce awake her eyes could keep,
Unable to support the fumes of sleep;
But fled, returning by the way she went, 320
And swerved along her bow with swift ascent.

The god, uneasy till he slept again,
Resolved at once to rid himself of pain;
And though against his custom, called aloud,

Exciting Morpheus from the sleepy crowd;
Morpheus, of all his numerous train, expressed
The shape of man, and imitated best;
The walk, the words, the gesture could supply,
The habit mimic, and the mien belie;   330
Plays well, but all his action is confined;
Extending not beyond our human kind.
Another birds, and beasts, and dragons apes,
And dreadful images, and monster shapes:
This daemon, Icelos, in heaven's high hall
The gods have named; but men Phobetor call:
A third is Phantasus, whose actions roll
On meaner thoughts, and things devoid of soul;
Earth, fruits, and flowers, he represents in dreams,
And solid rocks unmoved, and running streams.   340
These three to kings and chiefs their scenes display,
The rest before the ignoble commons play:
Of these the chosen Morpheus is dispatched;
Which done, the lazy monarch overwatched,
Down from his propping elbow drops his head,
Dissolved in sleep, and shrinks within his bed.

  Darkling the demon glides, for flight prepared,
So soft that scarce his fanning wings are heard.
To Trachin, swift as thought, the flitting shade
Through air his momentary journey made: 350
Then lays aside the steerage of his wings,
Forsakes his proper form, assumes the king's;
And pale as death, despoiled of his array,
Into the queen's apartment takes his way,
And stands before the bed at dawn of day:
Unmoved his eyes, and wet his beard appears,
And shedding vain, but seeming real tears;
The briny water dropping from his hairs;
Then staring on her, with a ghastly look
And hollow voice, he thus the queen bespoke: 360
  'Knowest thou not me? Not yet, unhappy wife?
Or are my features perished with my life?
Look once again, and for thy husband lost,
Lo! all that's left of him, thy husband's ghost!
Thy vows for my return were all in vain;
The stormy south o'ertook us in the main;

And never shalt thou see thy living lord again.
Bear witness, heaven, I called on thee in death,
And, while I called, a billow stopped my breath.
Think not that flying fame reports my fate; 370
I present, I appear, and my own wreck relate.
Rise, wretched widow, rise, nor undeplored
Permit my ghost to pass the Stygian ford;
But rise, prepared in black to mourn thy perished lord.'
　Thus said the player god; and adding art
Of voice and gesture, so performed his part,
She thought (so like her love the shade appears)
That Ceyx spake the words, and Ceyx shed the tears.
She groaned, her inward soul with grief oppressed,
She sighed, she wept, and sleeping beat her breast: 380
Then stretched her arms to embrace his body bare,
Her clasping arms enclose but empty air:
At this, not yet awake, she cried, 'Oh stay,
One is our fate, and common is our way!'
So dreadful was the dream, so loud she spoke,
That, starting sudden up, the slumber broke;
Then cast her eyes around in hope to view
Her vanished lord, and find the vision true;
For now the maids, who waited her commands,
Ran in with lighted tapers in their hands. 390
Tired with the search, not finding what she seeks,
With cruel blows she pounds her blubbered cheeks;
Then from her beaten breast the linen tare,
And cut the golden caul that bound her hair.
Her nurse demands the cause; with louder cries
She prosecutes her griefs, and thus replies:
　'No more Alcyone; she suffered death
With her loved lord, when Ceyx lost his breath:
No flattery, no false comfort, give me none,
My shipwrecked Ceyx is for ever gone; 400
I saw, I saw him manifest in view,
His voice, his figure, and his gestures knew:
His lustre lost, and every living grace,
Yet I retained the features of his face:
Though with pale cheeks, wet beard, and dropping hair,
None but my Ceyx could appear so fair;
I would have strained him with a strict embrace,

But through my arms he slipped, and vanished from the place;
There, e'en just there he stood;' and as she spoke,
Where last the spectre was, she cast her look;   410
Fain would she hope, and gazed upon the ground,
If any printed footsteps might be found;
Then sighed, and said, 'This I too well foreknew,
And my prophetic fear presaged too true;
'Twas what I begged, when with a bleeding heart
I took my leave, and suffered thee to part,
Or I to go along, or thou to stay,
Never, ah never to divide our way!
Happier for me, that, all our hours assigned,
Together we had lived, e'en not in death disjoined!   420
So had my Ceyx still been living here,
Or with my Ceyx I had perished there;
Now I die absent, in the vast profound,
And me without myself the seas have drowned:
The storms were not so cruel; should I strive
To lengthen life, and such a grief survive;
But neither will I strive, nor wretched thee
In death forsake, but keep thee company.
If not one common sepulchre contains
Our bodies, or one urn our last remains,   430
Yet Ceyx and Alcyone shall join,
Their names remembered in one common line.'
   No further voice her mighty grief affords,
For sighs come rushing in betwixt her words,
And stopped her tongue; but what her tongue denied,
Soft tears, and groans, and dumb complaints supplied.
   'Twas morning; to the port she takes her way,
And stands upon the margin of the sea;
That place, that very spot of ground she sought,
Or thither by her destiny was brought,   440
Where last he stood; and while she sadly said,
''Twas here he left me, lingering here, delayed
His parting kiss, and there his anchors weighed.'
Thus speaking, while her thoughts past actions trace,
And call to mind, admonished by the place,
Sharp at her utmost ken she cast her eyes,
And somewhat floating from afar descries;
It seemed a corpse adrift, to distant sight,

But at a distance who could judge aright?
It wafted nearer yet, and then she knew   450
That what before she but surmised was true;
A corpse it was, but whose it was, unknown,
Yet moved, howe'er, she made the case her own;
Took the bad omen of a shipwrecked man,
As for a stranger wept, and thus began:
  'Poor wretch, on stormy seas to lose thy life,
Unhappy thou, but more thy widowed wife!'
At this she paused; for now the flowing tide
Had brought the body nearer to the side:
The more she looks, the more her fears increase   460
At nearer sight, and she's herself the less:
Now driven ashore, and at her feet it lies;
She knows too much, in knowing whom she sees,—
Her husband's corpse; at this she loudly shrieks,
''Tis he, 'tis he,' she cries, and tears her cheeks,
Her hair, her vest; and stooping to the sands,
About his neck she cast her trembling hands.
  'And is it thus, O dearer than my life,
Thus, thus return'st thou to thy longing wife!'
She said, and to the neighbouring mole she strode,   470
Raised there to break the incursions of the flood;
Headlong from hence to plunge herself she springs,
But shoots along supported on her wings;
A bird new-made about the banks she plies,
Not far from shore, and short excursions tries;
Nor seeks in air her humble flight to raise,
Content to skim the surface of the seas;
Her bill, though slender, sends a creaking noise,
And imitates a lamentable voice;
Now lighting where the bloodless body lies,   480
She with a funeral note renews her cries.
At all her stretch her little wings she spread,
And with her feathered arms embraced the dead;
Then flickering to his pallid lips, she strove
To print a kiss, the last essay of love;
Whether the vital touch revived the dead,
Or that the moving waters raised his head
To meet the kiss, the vulgar doubt alone,
For sure a present miracle was shown.

The gods their shapes to winter birds translate,   490
But both obnoxious to their former fate.
Their conjugal affection still is tied,
And still the mournful race is multiplied;
They bill, they tread; Alcyone compressed,
Seven days sits brooding on her floating nest,
A wintry queen: her sire at length is kind,
Calms every storm, and hushes every wind;
Prepares his empire for his daughter's ease,
And for his hatching nephews smooths the seas.

The Twelfth Book of Ovid's Metamorphoses

Priam, to whom the story was unknown,
As dead, deplored his metamorphosed son;
A cenotaph his name and title kept,
And Hector round the tomb, with all his brothers, wept.
This pious office Paris did not share;
Absent alone, and author of the war,
Which, for the Spartan queen, the Grecians drew
To avenge the rape, and Asia to subdue.
   A thousand ships were manned, to sail the sea;
Nor had their just resentments found delay,   10
Had not the winds and waves opposed their way.
At Aulis, with united powers, they meet,
But there, cross winds or calms detained the fleet.
Now, while they raise an altar on the shore,
And Jove with solemn sacrifice adore,
A boding sign the priests and people see:
A snake of size immense ascends a tree,
And in the leafy summit spied a nest,
Which, o'er her callow young, a sparrow pressed.
Eight were the birds unfledged; their mother flew,   20
And hovered round her care, but still in view;
Till the fierce reptile first devoured the brood,
Then seized the fluttering dam, and drank her blood.
This dire ostent the fearful people view;
Calchas alone, by Phoebus taught, foreknew
What heaven decreed; and, with a smiling glance,

Thus gratulates to Greece her happy chance.
'O Argives, we shall conquer; Troy is ours,
But long delays shall first afflict our powers;
Nine years of labour the nine birds portend,   30
The tenth shall in the town's destruction end.'

The serpent, who his maw obscene had filled,
The branches in his curled embraces held;
But as in spires he stood, he turned to stone;
The stony snake retained the figure still his own.

Yet not for this the windbound navy weighed;
Slack were their sails, and Neptune disobeyed.
Some thought him loath the town should be destroyed,
Whose building had his hands divine employed;
Not so the seer, who knew, and known foreshowed,   40
The virgin Phoebe, with a virgin's blood,
Must first be reconciled; the common cause
Prevailed; and pity yielding to the laws,
Fair Iphigenia, the devoted maid,
Was, by the weeping priests, in linen robes arrayed.
All mourn her fate, but no relief appeared;
The royal victim bound, the knife already reared;
When that offended power, who caused their woe,
Relenting ceased her wrath, and stopped the coming blow.
A mist before the ministers she cast,   50
And in the virgin's room a hind she placed.
The oblation slain, and Phoebe reconciled,
The storm was hushed, and dimpled ocean smiled;
A favourable gale arose from shore,
Which to the port desired the Grecian galleys bore.

Full in the midst of this created space,
Betwixt heaven, earth, and skies, there stands a place
Confining on all three, with triple bound;
Whence all things, though remote, are viewed around,
And thither bring their undulating sound;   60
The palace of loud Fame; her seat of power,
Placed on the summit of a lofty tower.
A thousand winding entries, long and wide,
Receive of fresh reports a flowing tide;
A thousand crannies in the walls are made;
Nor gate nor bars exclude the busy trade.
'Tis built of brass, the better to diffuse

The spreading sounds, and multiply the news;
Where echoes in repeated echoes play:
A mart for ever full, and open night and day.   70
Nor silence is within, nor voice express,
But a deaf noise of sounds that never cease;
Confused, and chiding, like the hollow roar
Of tides, receding from the insulted shore.
Or like the broken thunder, heard from far,
When Jove to distance drives the rolling war.
The courts are filled with a tumultuous din
Of crowds, or issuing forth, or entering in;
A thoroughfare of news; where some devise
Things never heard; some mingle truth with lies;   80
The troubled air with empty sounds they beat;
Intent to hear, and eager to repeat.
Error sits brooding there; with added train
Of vain credulity, and joys as vain;
Suspicion, with sedition joined, are near;
And rumours raised, and murmurs mixed, and panic fear.
Fame sits aloft, and sees the subject ground,
And seas about, and skies above, inquiring all around.
    The goddess gives the alarm; and soon is known
The Grecian fleet, descending on the town.   90
Fixed on defence, the Trojans are not slow
To guard their shore from an expected foe.
They meet in fight; by Hector's fatal hand
Protesilaus falls, and bites the strand;
Which with expense of blood the Grecians won,
And proved the strength unknown of Priam's son;
And to their cost the Trojan leaders felt
The Grecian heroes, and what deaths they dealt.
From these first onsets, the Sigaean shore
Was strewed with carcases, and stained with gore.   100
Neptunian Cygnus troops of Greeks had slain;
Achilles in his car had scoured the plain,
And cleared the Trojan ranks; where'er he fought,
Cygnus, or Hector, through the fields he sought:
Cygnus he found; on him his force essayed;
For Hector was to the tenth year delayed.
His white-maned steeds, that bowed beneath the yoke,
He cheered to courage, with a gentle stroke;

Then urged his fiery chariot on the foe,
And rising shook his lance, in act to throw.   110
But first he cried, 'O youth, be proud to bear
Thy death, ennobled by Pelides' spear.'
The lance pursued the voice without delay;
Nor did the whizzing weapon miss the way,
But pierced his cuirass, with such fury sent,
And signed his bosom with a purple dint.
At this the seed of Neptune: 'Goddess-born,
For ornament, not use, these arms are worn;
This helm, and heavy buckler, I can spare,
As only decorations of the war;   120
So Mars is armed, for glory, not for need.
'Tis somewhat more from Neptune to proceed,
Than from a daughter of the sea to spring;
Thy sire is mortal; mine is ocean's king.
Secure of death, I should contemn thy dart,
Though naked, and impassible depart.'
He said, and threw; the trembling weapon passed
Through nine bull-hides, each under other placed
On his broad shield, and stuck within the last.
Achilles wrenched it out; and sent again   130
The hostile gift; the hostile gift was vain.
He tried a third, a tough well-chosen spear;
The inviolable body stood sincere,
Though Cygnus then did no defence provide,
But scornful offered his unshielded side.

  Not otherwise the impatient hero fared,
Than as a bull, encompassed with a guard,
Amid the circus roars; provoked from far
By sight of scarlet, and a sanguine war.
They quit their ground, his bended horns elude,   140
In vain pursuing, and in vain pursued.

  Before to further fight he would advance,
He stood considering, and surveyed his lance.
Doubts if he wielded not a wooden spear
Without a point; he looked, the point was there.
'This is my hand, and this my lance,' he said,
'By which so many thousand foes are dead,
O whither is their usual virtue fled!
I had it once; and the Lyrnessian wall,

And Tenedos, confessed it in their fall.   150
Thy streams, Caicus, rolled a crimson flood;
And Thebes ran red with her own natives' blood.
Twice Telephus employed this piercing steel,
To wound him first, and afterward to heal.
The vigour of this arm was never vain;
And that my wonted prowess I retain,
Witness these heaps of slaughter on the plain.'
He said, and, doubtful of his former deeds,
To some new trial of his force proceeds.
He chose Menoetes from among the rest;   160
At him he lanced his spear, and pierced his breast;
On the hard earth the Lycian knocked his head,
And lay supine; and forth the spirit fled.

Then thus the hero: 'Neither can I blame
The hand, or javelin; both are still the same.
The same I will employ against this foe,
And wish but with the same success to throw.'
So spoke the chief, and while he spoke he threw;
The weapon with unerring fury flew,
At his left shoulder aimed; nor entrance found;   170
But back, as from a rock, with swift rebound
Harmless returned; a bloody mark appeared,
Which with false joy the flattered hero cheered.
Wound there was none; the blood that was in view,
The lance before from slain Menoetes drew.

Headlong he leaps from off his lofty car,
And in close fight on foot renews the war;
Raging with high disdain, repeats his blows;
Nor shield nor armour can their force oppose;
Huge cantlets of his buckler strew the ground,   180
And no defence in his bored arms is found.
But on his flesh no wound or blood is seen;
The sword itself is blunted on the skin.

This vain attempt the chief no longer bears;
But round his hollow temples and his ears,
His buckler beats; the son of Neptune, stunned
With these repeated buffets, quits his ground;
A sickly sweat succeeds, and shades of night;
Inverted nature swims before his sight:
The insulting victor presses on the more,   190

And treads the steps the vanquished trod before,
Nor rest, nor respite gives. A stone there lay
Behind his trembling foe, and stopped his way;
Achilles took the advantage which he found,
O'erturned, and pushed him backward on the ground.
His buckler held him under, while he pressed,
With both his knees above, his panting breast;
Unlaced his helm; about his chin the twist
He tied, and soon the strangled soul dismissed.

    With eager haste he went to strip the dead;   200
The vanquished body from his arms was fled.
His sea-god sire, to immortalise his fame,
Had turned it to the bird that bears his name.

    A truce succeeds the labours of this day,
And arms suspended with a long delay.
While Trojan walls are kept with watch and ward,
The Greeks before their trenches mount the guard.
The feast approached; when to the blue-eyed maid,
His vows for Cygnus slain the victor paid,
And a white heifer on her altar laid.   210
The reeking entrails on the fire they threw,
And to the gods the grateful odour flew;
Heaven had its part in sacrifice; the rest
Was broiled and roasted for the future feast.
The chief invited guests were set around;
And hunger first assuaged, the bowls were crowned,
Which in deep draughts their cares and labours drowned.
The mellow harp did not their ears employ,
And mute was all the warlike symphony;
Discourse, the food of souls, was their delight,   220
And pleasing chat prolonged the summer's night.
The subject, deeds of arms and valour shown,
Or on the Trojan side, or on their own.
Of dangers undertaken, fame achieved,
They talked by turns, the talk by turns relieved.
What things but these could fierce Achilles tell,
Or what could fierce Achilles hear so well?
The last great act performed, of Cygnus slain,
Did most the martial audience entertain;
Wondering to find a body, free by fate   230
From steel, and which could e'en that steel rebate.

Amazed, their admiration they renew;
And scarce Pelides could believe it true.
   Then Nestor thus: 'What once this age has known,
In fated Cygnus, and in him alone,
These eyes have seen in Caeneus long before,
Whose body not a thousand swords could bore.
Caeneus in courage and in strength excelled,
And still his Othrys with his fame is filled;
But what did most his martial deeds adorn,   240
(Though, since, he changed his sex,) a woman born.'
   A novelty so strange and full of fate
His listening audience asked him to relate.
Achilles thus commends their common suit:
'O father, first for prudence in repute,
Tell, with that eloquence so much thy own,
What thou hast heard, or what of Caeneus known;
What was he, whence his change of sex begun,
What trophies, joined in wars with thee, he won?
Who conquered him, and in what fatal strife   250
The youth, without a wound, could lose his life?'
   Neleides then: 'Though tardy age, and time,
Have shrunk my sinews, and decayed my prime;
Though much I have forgotten of my store,
Yet, not exhausted, I remember more.
Of all that arms achieved, or peace designed,
That action still is fresher in my mind
Than aught beside. If reverend age can give
To faith a sanction, in my third I live.
   ''Twas in my second century, I surveyed   260
Young Caenis, then a fair Thessalian maid.
Caenis the bright was born to high command;
A princess, and a native of thy land,
Divine Achilles; every tongue proclaimed
Her beauty, and her eyes all hearts inflamed.
Peleus, thy sire, perhaps had sought her bed,
Among the rest; but he had either led
Thy mother then, or was by promise tied;
But she to him, and all, alike her love denied.
   'It was her fortune once, to take her way   270
Along the sandy margin of the sea;
The power of ocean viewed her as she passed,

And, loved as soon as seen, by force embraced.
So fame reports. Her virgin treasure seized,
And his new joys the ravisher so pleased,
That thus, transported, to the nymph he cried,
"Ask what thou wilt, no prayer shall be denied."
This also fame relates; the haughty fair,
Who not the rape e'en of a god could bear,
This answer, proud, returned: "To mighty wrongs,   280
A mighty recompense, of right, belongs.
Give me no more to suffer such a shame;
But change the woman for a better name,
One gift for all." She said, and, while she spoke,
A stern, majestic, manly tone she took.
A man she was; and, as the godhead swore,
To Caeneus turned, who Caenis was before.
   'To this the lover adds, without request,
No force of steel should violate his breast.
Glad of the gift, the new-made warrior goes,   290
And arms among the Greeks, and longs for equal foes.
   'Now brave Pirithous, bold Ixion's son,
The love of fair Hippodame had won.
The cloud-begotten race, half men, half beast,
Invited, came to grace the nuptial feast.
In a cool cave's recess the treat was made,
Whose entrance trees with spreading boughs o'ershade.
They sat: and summoned by the bridegroom, came,
To mix with those, the Lapithaean name:
Nor wanted I; the roofs with joy resound;   300
And "Hymen, Iö Hymen", rung around.
Raised altars shone with holy fires; the bride,
Lovely herself (and lovely by her side
A bevy of bright nymphs, with sober grace,)
Came glittering like a star, and took her place,
Her heavenly form beheld, all wished her joy,
And little wanted, but in vain their wishes all employ.
   'For one, most brutal of the brutal brood,
Or whether wine or beauty fired his blood,
Or both at once, beheld with lustful eyes   310
The bride; at once resolved to make his prize.
Down went the board, and fastening on her hair,
He seized with sudden force the frighted fair.

'Twas Eurytus began; his bestial kind
His crime pursued; and each as pleased his mind,
Or her, whom chance presented, took; the feast
An image of a taken town expressed.
 'The cave resounds with female shrieks: we rise,
Mad with revenge, to make a swift reprise:
And Theseus first: "What frenzy has possessed,   320
O Eurytus", he cried, "thy brutal breast,
To wrong Pirithous, and not him alone,
But while I live, two friends conjoined in one?"
 'To justify his threat, he thrusts aside
The crowd of centaurs, and redeems the bride.
The monster naught replied; for words were vain,
And deeds could only deeds unjust maintain;
But answers with his hand, and forward pressed,
With blows redoubled, on his face and breast.
An ample goblet stood, of antique mould,   330
And rough with figures of the rising gold;
The hero snatched it up, and tossed in air
Full at the front of the foul ravisher.
He falls, and falling vomits forth a flood
Of wine, and foam, and brains, and mingled blood.
Half roaring, and half neighing through the hall,
"Arms, arms!" the double-formed with fury call,
To wreak their brother's death. A medley flight
Of bowls and jars, at first supply the fight.
Once instruments of feasts, but now of fate;   340
Wine animates their rage, and arms their hate.
 'Bold Amycus from the robbed vestry brings
The chalices of heaven, and holy things
Of precious weight; a sconce, that hung on high,
With tapers filled, to light the sacristy,
Torn from the cord, with his unhallowed hand
He threw amid the Lapithaean band.
On Celadon the ruin fell, and left
His face of feature and of form bereft;
So, when some brawny sacrificer knocks   350
Before an alter led, an offered ox,
His eyeballs, rooted out, are thrown to ground,
His nose dismantled in his mouth is found,
His jaws, cheeks, front, one undistinguished wound.

'This, Pelates, the avenger, could not brook;
But, by the foot, a maple-board he took,
And hurled at Amycus; his chin it bent
Against his chest, and down the centaur sent,
Whom, sputtering bloody teeth, the second blow
Of his drawn sword dispatched to shades below.   360

'Grineus was near; and cast a furious look
On the side-altar, censed with sacred smoke,
And bright with flaming fires; "The gods," he cried,
"Have with their holy trade our hands supplied:
Why use we not their gifts?" Then from the floor
An altar-stone he heaved, with all the load it bore;
Altar and altar's freight together flew,
Where thickest thronged the Lapithaean crew,
And, Broteas and at once Oryus slew.
Oryus' mother, Mycale, was known   370
Down from her sphere to draw the labouring moon.

'Exadius cried: "Unpunished shall not go
This fact, if arms are found against the foe."
He looked about, where on a pine were spread
The votive horns of a stag's branching head:
At Grineus these he throws; so just they fly,
That the sharp antlers stuck in either eye.
Breathless and blind he fell; with blood besmeared,
His eyeballs beaten out hung dangling on his beard.
Fierce Rhoetus from the hearth a burning brand   380
Selects, and whirling waves, till from his hand
The fire took flame; then dashed it from the right,
On fair Charaxus' temples, near the sight:
The whistling pest came on, and pierced the bone,
And caught the yellow hair, that shrivelled while it shone;
Caught, like dry stubble fired, or like sear wood;
Yet from the wound ensued no purple flood,
But looked a bubbling mass of frying blood.
His blazing locks sent forth a crackling sound,
And hissed, like red-hot iron within the smithy drowned. 390
The wounded warrior shook his flaming hair,
Then (what a team of horse could hardly rear,)
He heaves the threshold stone, but could not throw;
The weight itself forbade the threatened blow,
Which dropping from his lifted arms, came down

Full on Cometes' head, and crushed his crown.
Nor Rhoetus then retained his joy; but said,
"So by their fellows may our foes be sped."
Then with redoubled strokes he plies his head:
The burning lever not deludes his pains,   400
But drives the battered skull within the brains.
    'Thus flushed, the conqueror, with force renewed,
Evagrus, Dryas, Corythus, pursued.
First, Corythus, with downy cheeks, he slew;
Whose fall when fierce Evagrus had in view,
He cried, "What palm is from a beardless prey?"
Rhoetus prevents what more he had to say;
And drove within his mouth the fiery death,
Which entered hissing in, and choked his breath.
At Dryas next he flew; but weary chance   410
No longer would the same success advance;
For while he whirled in fiery circles round
The brand, a sharpened stake strong Dryas found,
And in the shoulder's joint inflicts the wound.
The weapon struck; which, roaring out with pain,
He drew; nor longer durst the fight maintain,
But turned his back for fear, and fled amain.
With him fled Orneus, with like dread possessed;
Thaumas and Medon, wounded in the breast,
And Mermeros, in the late race renowned,   420
Now limping ran, and tardy with his wound.
Pholus and Melaneus from fight withdrew,
And Abas maimed, who boars encountering slew;
And augur Astylos, whose art in vain
From fight dissuaded the four-footed train,
Now beat the hoof with Nessus on the plain;
But to his fellow cried, "Be safely slow;
Thy death deferred is due to great Alcides' bow."
    'Meantime strong Dryas urged his chance so well,
That Lycidas, Areos, Imbreus fell;   430
All, one by one, and fighting face to face:
Crenaeus fled, to fall with more disgrace;
For, fearful while he looked behind, he bore,
Betwixt his nose and front, the blow before.
Amid the noise and tumult of the fray,
Snoring and drunk with wine, Aphidas lay.

E'en then the bowl within his hand he kept,
And on a bear's rough hide securely slept.
Him Phorbas with his flying dart transfixed;
"Take thy next draught with Stygian waters mixed,   440
And sleep thy fill," the insulting victor cried;
Surprised with death unfelt, the centaur died:
The ruddy vomit, as he breathed his soul,
Repassed his throat, and filled his empty bowl.

 'I saw Petraeus' arms employed around
A well-grown oak, to root it from the ground.
This way, and that, he wrenched the fibrous bands;
The trunk was like a sapling in his hands,
And still obeyed the bent: while thus he stood,
Pirithous' dart drove on, and nailed him to the wood.   450
Lycus and Chromis fell, by him oppressed:
Helops and Dictys added to the rest
A nobler palm: Helops, through either ear
Transfixed, received the penetrating spear.
This Dictys saw; and seized with sudden fright,
Leapt headlong from the hill of steepy height,
And crushed an ash beneath, that could not bear his weight.
The shattered tree receives his fall, and strikes,
Within his full-blown paunch, the sharpened spikes.
Strong Aphareus had heaved a mighty stone,   460
The fragment of a rock, and would have thrown;
But Theseus, with a club of hardened oak,
The cubit-bone of the bold centaur broke,
And left him maimed, nor seconded the stroke;
Then leapt on tall Bienor's back; (who bore
No mortal burden but his own, before,)
Pressed with his knees his sides; the double man,
His speed with spurs increased, unwilling ran.
One hand the hero fastened on his locks;
His other plied him with repeated strokes.   470
The club rung round his ears, and battered brows;
He falls; and, lashing up his heels, his rider throws.

 'The same Herculean arms Nedymnus wound,
And lay by him Lycopes on the ground;
And Hippasus, whose beard his breast invades;
And Ripheus, haunter of the woodland shades;
And Tereus, used with mountain bears to strive,

And from their dens to draw the indignant beasts alive.
'Demoleon could not bear this hateful sight,
Or the long fortune of the Athenian knight;   480
But pulled with all his force to disengage
From earth a pine, the product of an age.
The root stuck fast: the broken trunk he sent
At Theseus: Theseus frustrates his intent,
And leaps aside, by Pallas warned, the blow
To shun: (for so he said; and we believed it so.)
Yet not in vain the enormous weight was cast,
Which Crantor's body sundered at the waist:
Thy father's squire, Achilles, and his care;
Whom, conquered in the Dolopeian war,   490
Their king, his present ruin to prevent,
A pledge of peace implored, to Peleus sent.
'Thy sire, with grieving eyes, beheld his fate;
And cried, "not long, loved Crantor, shalt thou wait
Thy vowed revenge." At once he said, and threw
His ashen-spear, which quivered as it flew,
With all his force and all his soul applied;
The sharp point entered in the centaur's side:
Both hands, to wrench it out, the monster joined,
And wrenched it out, but left the steel behind.   500
Stuck in his lungs it stood; enraged he rears
His hoofs, and down to ground thy father bears.
Thus trampled under foot, his shield defends
His head; his other hand the lance protends.
E'en while he lay extended on the dust,
He sped the centaur, with one single thrust.
Two more his lance before transfixed from far,
And two his sword had slain in closer war.
To these was added Dorylas; who spread
A bull's two goring horns around his head.   510
With these he pushed; in blood already dyed,
Him, fearless, I approached, and thus defied:
"Now, monster, now, by proof it shall appear,
Whether thy horns are sharper, or my spear."
At this, I threw; for want of other ward,
He lifted up his hand, his front to guard.
His hand it passed, and fixed it to his brow.
Loud shouts of ours attend the lucky blow:

Him Peleus finished, with a second wound,
Which through the navel pierced; he reeled around,   520
And dragged his dangling bowels on the ground;
Trod what he dragged, and what he trod he crushed;
And to his mother earth, with empty belly, rushed.
   'Nor could thy form, O Cyllarus, foreslow
Thy fate, if form to monsters men allow:
Just bloomed thy beard, thy beard of golden hue;
Thy locks, in golden waves about thy shoulders flew.
Sprightly thy look; thy shapes in every part
So clean, as might instruct the sculptor's art,
As far as man extended; where began   530
The beast, the beast was equal to the man.
Add but a horse's head and neck, and he,
O Castor, was a courser worthy thee.
So was his back proportioned for the seat;
So rose his brawny chest; so swiftly moved his feet.
Coal-black his colour, but like jet it shone;
His legs and flowing tail were white alone.
Beloved by many maidens of his kind,
But fair Hylonome possessed his mind;
Hylonome, for features, and for face,   540
Excelling all the nymphs of double race.
Nor less her blandishments, than beauty move;
At once both loving, and confessing love.
For him she dressed; for him with female care
She combed and set in curls her auburn hair.
Of roses, violets, and lilies mixed,
And sprigs of flowing rosemary betwixt,
She formed the chaplet, that adorned her front;
In waters of the Pegasaean fount,
And in the streams that from the fountain play,   550
She washed her face, and bathed her twice a day.
The scarf of furs, that hung below her side,
Was ermine, or the panther's spotted pride;
Spoils of no common beast. With equal flame
They loved; their sylvan pleasures were the same:
All day they hunted; and when day expired,
Together to some shady cave retired.
Invited to the nuptials both repair;
And side by side they both engage in war.

'Uncertain from what hand, a flying dart   560
At Cyllarus was sent, which pierced his heart.
The javelin drawn from out the mortal wound,
He faints with staggering steps, and seeks the ground:
The fair within her arms received his fall,
And strove his wandering spirits to recall;
And while her hand the streaming blood opposed,
Joined face to face, his lips with hers she closed.
Stifled with kisses, a sweet death he dies;
She fills the fields with undistinguished cries;
At least her words were in her clamour drowned;   570
For my stunned ears received no vocal sound.
In madness of her grief, she seized the dart
New-drawn, and reeking from her lover's heart;
To her bare bosom the sharp point applied,
And wounded fell; and falling by his side,
Embraced him in her arms, and thus embracing died.
     'E'en still, methinks, I see Phaeocomes;
Strange was his habit, and as odd his dress.
Six lions' hides, with thongs together fast,
His upper part defended to his waist;   580
And where man ended, the continued vest,
Spread on his back, the house and trappings of a beast.
A stump too heavy for a team to draw,
(It seems a fable, though the fact I saw,)
He threw at Pholon; the descending blow
Divides the skull, and cleaves his head in two.
The brains, from nose and mouth, and either ear,
Came issuing out, as through a colander
The curdled milk; or from the press the whey,
Driven down by weights above, is drained away.   590
     'But him, while stooping down to spoil the slain,
Pierced through the paunch, I tumbled on the plain.
Then Chthonius and Teleboas I slew;
A fork the former armed; a dart his fellow threw:
The javelin wounded me; behold the scar.
Then was my time to seek the Trojan war;
Then I was Hector's match in open field;
But he was then unborn, at least a child;
Now, I am nothing. I forbear to tell
By Periphantes how Pyretus fell,   600

The centaur by the knight; nor will I stay
On Ampyx, or what deaths he dealt that day;
What honour, with a pointless lance, he won,
Stuck in the front of a four-footed man;
What fame young Macareus obtained in fight,
Or dwell on Nessus, now returned from flight.
How prophet Mopsus not alone divined,
Whose valour equalled his foreseeing mind.

   'Already Caeneus, with his conquering hand,
Had slaughtered five, the boldest of their band;   610
Pyracmus, Elymus, Antimachus,
Bromus the brave, and stronger Stiphelus;
Their names I numbered, and remember well,
No trace remaining, by what wounds they fell.

   'Latreus, the bulkiest of the double race,
Whom the spoiled arms of slain Halesus grace,
In years retaining still his youthful might,
Though his black hairs were interspersed with white,
Betwixt the embattled ranks began to prance,
Proud of his helm, and Macedonian lance;   620
And rode the ring around, that either host
Might hear him, while he made this empty boast:
"And from a strumpet shall we suffer shame?
For Caenis still, not Caeneus, is thy name;
And still the native softness of thy kind
Prevails, and leaves the woman in thy mind.
Remember what thou wert; what price was paid
To change thy sex, to make thee not a maid;
And but a man in show; go card and spin,
And leave the business of the war to men."   630

   'While thus the boaster exercised his pride,
The fatal spear of Caeneus reached his side;
Just in the mixture of the kinds it ran,
Betwixt the nether beast and upper man.
The monster, mad with rage, and stung with smart,
His lance directed at the hero's heart:
It struck; but bounded from his hardened breast,
Like hail from tiles, which the safe house invest;
Nor seemed the stroke with more effect to come,
Than a small pebble falling on a drum.   640
He next his falchion tried in closer fight;

But the keen falchion had no power to bite.
He thrust; the blunted point returned again:
"Since downright blows", he cried, "and thrusts are vain,
I'll prove his side;"—in strong embraces held,
He proved his side; his side the sword repelled;
His hollow belly echoed to the stroke:
Untouched his body, as a solid rock;
Aimed at his neck at last, the blade in shivers broke.

   'The impassive knight stood idle, to deride   650
His rage, and offered oft his naked side;
At length, "Now, monster, in thy turn," he cried,
"Try thou the strength of Caeneus:" at the word
He thrust; and in his shoulder plunged the sword.
Then writhed his hand; and as he drove it down
Deep in his breast, made many wounds in one.

   'The centaurs saw, enraged, the unhoped success,
And rushing on in crowds, together press.
At him, and him alone, their darts they threw;
Repulsed they from his fated body flew.   660
Amazed they stood; till Monychus began,
"O shame, a nation conquered by a man!
A woman-man; yet more a man is he,
Than all our race; and what he was, are we.
Now, what avail our nerves? the united force
Of two the strongest creatures, man and horse?
Nor goddess-born, nor of Ixion's seed
We seem, (a lover built for Juno's bed,)
Mastered by this half man. Whole mountains throw
With woods at once, and bury him below.   670
This only way remains. Nor need we doubt
To choke the soul within, though not to force it out.
Heap weights, instead of wounds:" he chanced to see
Where southern storms had rooted up a tree;
This, raised from earth, against the foe he threw;
The example shown, his fellow brutes pursue.
With forest-loads the warrior they invade;
Othrys and Pelion soon were void of shade,
And spreading groves were naked mountains made.
Pressed with the burden, Caeneus pants for breath,   680
And on his shoulders bears the wooden death.
To heave the intolerable weight he tries;

At length it rose above his mouth and eyes.
Yet still he heaves; and, struggling with despair,
Shakes all aside, and gains a gulp of air;
A short relief, which but prolongs his pain:
He faints by fits, and then respires again.
At last, the burden only nods above,
As when an earthquake stirs the Idaean grove.
Doubtful his death; he suffocated seemed   690
To most; but otherwise our Mopsus deemed,
Who said he saw a yellow bird arise
From out the pile, and cleave the liquid skies.
I saw it too, with golden feathers bright,
Nor e'er before beheld so strange a sight;
Whom Mopsus viewing as it soared around
Our troop and heard the pinions' rattling sound,
"All hail," he cried, "thy country's grace and love;
Once first of men below, now first of birds above!"
Its author to the story gave belief;   700
For us, our courage was increased by grief:
Ashamed to see a single man, pursued
With odds, to sink beneath a multitude,
We pushed the foe, and forced to shameful flight:
Part fell, and part escaped by favour of the night.'
    This tale, by Nestor told, did much displease
Tlepolemus, the seed of Hercules;
For often he had heard his father say,
That he himself was present at the fray,
And more than shared the glories of the day.   710
    'Old Chronicle,' he said, 'among the rest,
You might have named Alcides at the least;
Is he not worth your praise?' The Pylian prince
Sighed ere he spoke, then made this proud defence:
'My former woes, in long oblivion drowned,
I would have lost, but you renew the wound;
Better to pass him o'er, than to relate
The cause I have your mighty sire to hate.
His fame has filled the world, and reached the sky;
Which, oh, I wish with truth I could deny!   720
We praise not Hector, though his name we know
Is great in arms; 'tis hard to praise a foe.
He, your great father, levelled to the ground

Messenia's towers; nor better fortune found
Elis, and Pylas; that, a neighbouring state,
And this, my own; both guiltless of their fate.
To pass the rest, twelve, wanting one, he slew,
My brethren, who their birth from Neleus drew;
All youths of early promise, had they lived;
By him they perished; I alone survived.   730
The rest were easy conquest; but the fate
Of Periclymenos is wondrous to relate.
To him our common grandsire of the main
Had given to change his form, and, changed, resume again.
Varied at pleasure, every shape he tried,
And in all beasts Alcides still defied;
Vanquished on earth, at length he soared above,
Changed to the bird, that bears the bolt of Jove.
The new dissembled eagle, now endued
With beak and pounces, Hercules pursued,   740
And cuffed his manly cheeks, and tore his face,
Then, safe retired, and towered in empty space.
Alcides bore not long his flying foe,
But bending his inevitable bow,
Reached him in air, suspended as he stood,
And in his pinion fixed the feathered wood.
Light was the wound; but in the sinew hung
The point, and his disabled wing unstrung.
He wheeled in air, and stretched his fans in vain;
His fans no longer could his flight sustain;   750
For while one gathered wind, one unsupplied
Hung drooping down, nor poised his other side.
He fell; the shaft, that slightly was impressed,
Now from his heavy fall with weight increased,
Drove through his neck aslant; he spurns the ground,
And the soul issues through the weasand's wound.
      'Now, brave commander of the Rhodian seas,
What praise is due from me to Hercules?
Silence is all the vengeance I decree
For my slain brothers; but 'tis peace with thee.'   760
      Thus with a flowing tongue old Nestor spoke;
Then, to full bowls each other they provoke;
At length, with weariness and wine oppressed,
They rise from table, and withdraw to rest.

The sire of Cygnus, monarch of the main,
Meantime laments his son in battle slain;
And vows the victor's death, nor vows in vain.
For nine long years the smothered pain he bore;
Achilles was not ripe for fate before;
Then when he saw the promised hour was near,   770
He thus bespoke the god, that guides the year:
'Immortal offspring of my brother Jove,
My brightest nephew, and whom best I love,
Whose hands were joined with mine, to raise the wall
Of tottering Troy, now nodding to her fall;
Dost thou not mourn our power employed in vain,
And the defenders of our city slain?
To pass the rest, could noble Hector lie
Unpitied, dragged around his native Troy?
And yet the murderer lives; himself by far   780
A greater plague, than all the wasteful war.
He lives; the proud Pelides lives, to boast
Our town destroyed, our common labour lost.
O could I meet him! But I wish too late,
To prove my trident is not in his fate.
But let him try (for that's allowed) thy dart,
And pierce his only penetrable part.'
    Apollo bows to the superior throne,
And to his uncle's anger adds his own;
Then in a cloud involved, he takes his flight,   790
Where Greeks and Trojans mixed in mortal fight;
And found out Paris, lurking where he stood,
And stained his arrows with plebeian blood.
Phoebus to him alone the god confessed,
Then to the recreant knight he thus addressed:
'Dost thou not blush, to spend thy shafts in vain
On a degenerate and ignoble train?
If fame, or better vengeance, be thy care,
There aim, and with one arrow end the war.'
    He said; and showed from far the blazing shield   800
And sword which but Achilles none could wield;
And how he moved a god, and mowed the standing field.
The deity himself directs aright
The envenomed shaft, and wings the fatal flight.
    Thus fell the foremost of the Grecian name,

And he, the base adulterer, boasts the fame;
A spectacle to glad the Trojan train,
And please old Priam, after Hector slain.
If by a female hand he had foreseen
He was to die, his wish had rather been   810
The lance and double axe of the fair warrior queen.
And now, the terror of the Trojan field,
The Grecian honour, ornament, and shield,
High on a pile, the unconquered chief is placed;
The god, that armed him first, consumed at last.
Of all the mighty man, the small remains
A little urn, and scarcely filled, contains,
Yet, great in Homer, still Achilles lives,
And, equal to himself, himself survives.

  His buckler owns its former lord, and brings   820
New cause of strife betwixt contending kings;
Who worthiest, after him, his sword to wield,
Or wear his armour, or sustain his shield.
E'en Diomede sat mute, with downcast eyes,
Conscious of wanted worth to win the prize;
Nor Menelaus presumed these arms to claim,
Nor he the king of men, a greater name.
Two rivals only rose; Laertes' son,
And the vast bulk of Ajax Telamon.
The king, who cherished each with equal love,   830
And from himself all envy would remove,
Left both to be determined by the laws,
And to the Grecian chiefs transferred the cause.

The Speeches of Ajax and Ulysses

The chiefs were set, the soldiers crowned the field;
To these the master of the sevenfold shield
Upstarted fierce; and kindled with disdain,
Eager to speak, unable to contain
His boiling rage, he rolled his eyes around
The shore, and Grecian galleys hauled aground.
Then stretching out his hands, 'O Jove,' he cried,
'Must then our cause before the fleet be tried?

And dares Ulysses for the prize contend
In sight of what he durst not once defend   10
But basely fled, that memorable day,
When I from Hector's hands redeemed the flaming prey?
So much 'tis safer at the noisy bar
With words to flourish, than engage in war.
By different methods we maintain our right,
Nor am I made to talk, nor he to fight.
In bloody fields I labour to be great;
His arms are a smooth tongue and soft deceit.
Nor need I speak my deeds, for those you see;
The sun and day are witnesses for me.   20
Let him who fights unseen relate his own,
And vouch the silent stars, and conscious moon.
Great is the prize demanded, I confess,
But such an abject rival makes it less.
That gift, those honours, he but hoped to gain,
Can leave no room for Ajax to be vain;
Losing he wins, because his name will be
Ennobled by defeat, who durst contend with me.
Were my known valour questioned, yet my blood
Without that plea would make my title good;   30
My sire was Telamon whose arms, employed
With Hercules, these Trojan walls destroyed;
And who before, with Jason, sent from Greece,
In the first ship brought home the golden fleece:
Great Telamon from Aeacus derives
His birth: (the inquisitor of guilty lives
In shades below; where Sisyphus, whose son
This thief is thought, rolls up the restless heavy stone.)
Just Aeacus the king of gods above
Begot; thus Ajax is the third from Jove.   40
Nor should I seek advantage from my line,
Unless, Achilles, it were mixed with thine:
As next of kin Achilles' arms I claim;
This fellow would ingraft a foreign name
Upon our stock, and the Sisyphian seed
By fraud and theft asserts his father's breed.
Then must I lose these arms, because I came
To fight uncalled, a voluntary name?
Nor shunned the cause, but offered you my aid,

While he long lurking was to war betrayed: 50
Forced to the field he came, but in the rear,
And feigned distraction, to conceal his fear;
Till one more cunning caught him in the snare,
Ill for himself, and dragged him into war.
Now let a hero's arms a coward vest,
And he who shunned all honours gain the best;
And let me stand excluded from my right,
Robbed of my kinsman's arms who first appeared in fight.
Better for us at home he had remained,
Had it been true the madness which he feigned,   60
Or so believed; the less had been our shame,
The less his counselled crime which brands the Grecian name;
Nor Philocetes had been left enclosed
In a bare isle to wants and pains exposed;
Where to the rocks, with solitary groans,
His sufferings and our baseness he bemoans,
And wishes (so may heaven his wish fulfil!)
The due reward to him who caused his ill.
Now he with us to Troy's destruction sworn,
Our brother of the war, by whom are borne   70
Alcides' arrows, pent in narrow bounds,
With cold and hunger pinched, and pained with wounds,
To find him food and clothing, must employ
Against the birds the shafts due to the fate of Troy:
Yet still he lives, and lives from treason free,
Because he left Ulysses' company;
Poor Palamede might wish, so void of aid,
Rather to have been left, than so to death betrayed.
The coward bore the man immortal spite,
Who shamed him out of madness into fight;   80
Nor daring otherwise to vent his hate,
Accused him first of treason to the state;
And then for proof produced the golden store
Himself had hidden in his tent before.
Thus of two champions he deprived our host,
By exile one, and one by treason lost.
Thus fights Ulysses, thus his fame extends,
A formidable man but to his friends;
Great, for what greatness is in words and sound;
E'en faithful Nestor less in both is found;   90

But that he might without a rival reign,
He left this faithful Nestor on the plain,
Forsook his friend e'en at his utmost need,
Who, tired, and tardy with his wounded steed,
Cried out for aid, and called him by his name;
But cowardice has neither ears nor shame.
Thus fled the good old man, bereft of aid,
And, for as much as lay in him, betrayed.
That this is not a fable forged by me,
Like one of his, a Ulyssean lie,   100
I vouch e'en Diomede, who though his friend,
Cannot that act excuse, much less defend:
He called him back aloud, and taxed his fear;
And sure enough he heard, but durst not hear.
    'The gods with equal eyes on mortals look;
He justly was forsaken, who forsook;
Wanted that succour he refused to lend,
Found every fellow such another friend.
No wonder if he roared that all might hear,
His elocution was increased by fear;   110
I heard, I ran, I found him out of breath,
Pale, trembling, and half-dead with fear of death.
Though he had judged himself by his own laws,
And stood condemned, I helped the common cause:
With my broad buckler hid him from the foe,
(E'en the shield trembled as he lay below,)
And from impending fate the coward freed;
Good heaven forgive me for so bad a deed!
If still he will persist and urge the strife,
First let him give me back his forfeit life;   120
Let him return to that opprobrious field,
Again creep under my protecting shield;
Let him lie wounded, let the foe be near,
And let his quivering heart confess his fear;
There put him in the very jaws of fate,
And let him plead his cause in that estate;
And yet, when snatched from death, when from below
My lifted shield I loosed, and let him go:
Good heavens, how light he rose! with what a bound
He sprung from earth, forgetful of his wound!   130
How fresh, how eager then his feet to ply!

Who had not strength to stand, had speed to fly!
  'Hector came on, and brought the gods along;
Fear seized alike the feeble and the strong;
Each Greek was a Ulysses; such a dread
The approach, and e'en the sound, of Hector bred;
Him, fleshed with slaughter, and with conquest crowned,
I met, and overturned him to the ground.
When after, matchless as he deemed in might,
He challenged all our host to single fight,   140
All eyes were fixed on me; the lots were thrown,
But for your champion I was wished alone.
Your vows were heard; we fought, and neither yield;
Yet I returned unvanquished from the field.
With Jove to friend, the insulting Trojan came.
And menaced us with force, our fleet with flame;
Was it the strength of this tongue-valiant lord,
In that black hour, that saved you from the sword?
Or was my breast exposed alone, to brave
A thousand swords, a thousand ships to save,   150
The hopes of your return? and can you yield,
For a saved fleet, less than a single shield?
Think it no boast, O Grecians, if I deem
These arms want Ajax, more than Ajax them:
Or I with them an equal honour share;
They, honoured to be worn, and I, to wear.
Will he compare my courage with his sleight?
As well he may compare the day with night.
Night is indeed the province of his reign;
Yet all his dark exploits no more contain   160
Than a spy taken, and a sleeper slain,
A priest made prisoner, Pallas made a prey,
But none of all these actions done by day;
Nor aught of these was done, and Diomede away.
If on such petty merits you confer
So vast a prize, let each his portion share;
Make a just dividend; and, if not all,
The greater part to Diomede will fall.
But why for Ithacus such arms as those,
Who naked, and by night, invades his foes?   170
The glittering helm by moonlight will proclaim
The latent robber, and prevent his game;

Nor could he hold his tottering head upright
Beneath that motion, or sustain the weight;
Nor that right arm could toss the beamy lance,
Much less the left that ampler shield advance;
Ponderous with precious weight, and rough with cost
Of the round world in rising gold embossed.
That orb would ill become his hand to wield
And look as for the gold he stole the shield;   180
Which should your error on the wretch bestow,
It would not frighten, but allure the foe.
Why asks he what avails him not in fight,
And would but cumber and retard his flight,
In which his only excellence is placed?
You give him death, that intercept his haste.
Add, that his own is yet a maiden-shield,
Nor the least dint has suffered in the field,
Guiltless of fight; mine, battered, hewed, and bored,
Worn out of service, must forsake his lord.   190
What further need of words our right to scan?
My arguments are deeds, let action speak the man.
Since from a champion's arms the strife arose,
So cast the glorious prize amid the foes;
Then send us to redeem both arms and shield,
And let him wear, who wins them in the field.'
    He said: A murmur from the multitude,
Or somewhat like a stifled shout, ensued;
Till from his seat arose Laertes' son,
Looked down a while, and paused ere he begun;   200
Then to the expecting audience raised his look,
And not without prepared attention spoke;
Soft was his tone, and sober was his face,
Action his words, and words his action grace.
    'If heaven, my lords, had heard our common prayer,
These arms had caused no quarrel for an heir;
Still great Achilles had his own possessed,
And we with great Achilles had been blessed:
But since hard fate, and heaven's severe decree,
Have ravished him away from you and me,'   210
(At this he sighed, and wiped his eyes, and drew,
Or seemed to draw, some drops of kindly dew,)
'Who better can succeed Achilles lost,

Than he who gave Achilles to your host?
This only I request, that neither he
May gain, by being what he seems to be,
A stupid thing, nor I may lose the prize,
By having sense, which heaven to him denies;
Since, great or small, the talent I enjoyed
Was ever in the common cause employed: 220
Nor let my wit, and wonted eloquence,
Which often has been used in your defence
And in my own, this only time be brought
To bear against myself, and deemed a fault.
Make not a crime, where nature made it none;
For every man may freely use his own.
The deeds of long descended ancestors
Are but by grace of imputation ours,
Theirs in effect; but since he draws his line
From Jove, and seems to plead a right divine,   230
From Jove, like him, I claim my pedigree,
And am descended in the same degree.
My sire, Laertes, was Arcesius' heir,
Arcesius was the son of Jupiter;
No parricide, no banished man, is known
In all my line; let him excuse his own.
Hermes ennobles too my mother's side,
By both my parents to the gods allied.
But not because that on the female part
My blood is better, dare I claim desert,   240
Or that my sire from parricide is free;
But judge by merit betwixt him and me.
The prize be to the best; provided yet
That Ajax for a while his kin forget,
And his great sire, and greater uncle's name,
To fortify by them his feeble claim.
Be kindred and relation laid aside,
And honour's cause by laws of honour tried.
For, if he plead proximity of blood,
That empty title is with ease withstood.   250
Peleus, the hero's sire, more nigh than he,
And Pyrrhus, his undoubted progeny,
Inherit first these trophies of the field;
To Scyros, or to Phthia, send the shield:

And Teucer has an uncle's right, yet he
Waives his pretensions, nor contends with me.
    'Then, since the cause on pure desert is placed,
Whence shall I take my rise, what reckon last?
I not presume on every act to dwell,
But take these few, in order as they fell.   260
    'Thetis, who knew the fates, applied her care
To keep Achilles in disguise from war;
And till the threatening influence were past,
A woman's habit on the hero cast:
All eyes were cozened by the borrowed vest,
And Ajax (never wiser than the rest)
Found no Pelides there. At length I came
With proffered wares to this pretended dame;
She, not discovered by her mien or voice,
Betrayed her manhood by her manly choice;   270
And, while on female toys her fellows look,
Grasped in her warlike hand, a javelin shook;
Whom by this act revealed, I thus bespoke:
"O goddess born! resist not heaven's decree,
The fall of Ilium is reserved for thee;"
Then seized him, and, produced in open light,
Sent blushing to the field the fatal knight.
Mine then are all his actions of the war;
Great Telephus was conquered by my spear,
And after cured; to me the Thebans owe   280
Lesbos and Tenedos, their overthrow;
Scyros and Cylla; Not on all to dwell,
By me Lyrnessus and strong Chrysa fell;
And, since I sent the man who Hector slew,
To me the noble Hector's death is due.
Those arms I put into his living hand;
Those arms, Pelides dead, I now demand.
    'When Greece was injured in the Spartan prince,
And met at Aulis to revenge the offence,
'Twas a dead calm, or adverse blasts, that reigned,   290
And in the port the windbound fleet detained:
Bad signs were seen, and oracles severe
Were daily thundered in our general's ear,
That by his daughter's blood we must appease
Diana's kindled wrath, and free the seas.

Affection, interest, fame, his heart assailed,
But soon the father o'er the king prevailed;
Bold, on himself he took the pious crime,
As angry with the gods as they with him.
No subject could sustain their sovereign's look,   300
Till this hard enterprise I undertook;
I only durst the imperial power control,
And undermined the parent in his soul;
Forced him to exert the king for common good,
And pay our ransom with his daughter's blood.
Never was cause more difficult to plead,
Than where the judge against himself decreed;
Yet this I won by dint of argument.
The wrongs his injured brother underwent;
And his own office, shamed him to consent.   310

  ''Twas harder yet to move the mother's mind,
And to this heavy task was I designed:
Reasons against her love I knew were vain;
I circumvented whom I could not gain.
Had Ajax been employed, our slackened sails
Had still at Aulis waited happy gales.

  'Arrived at Troy, your choice was fixed on me,
A fearless envoy, fit for a bold embassy.
Secure, I entered through the hostile court,
Glittering with steel, and crowded with resort: 320
There in the midst of arms I plead our cause,
Urge the foul rape, and violated laws;
Accuse the foes as authors of the strife,
Reproach the ravisher, demand the wife.
Priam, Antenor, and the wiser few
I moved; but Paris and his lawless crew
Scarce held their hands, and lifted swords; but stood
In act to quench their impious thirst of blood.
This Menelaus knows; exposed to share
With me the rough preludium of the war.   330

  'Endless it were to tell what I have done,
In arms, or counsel, since the siege begun.
The first encounters past, the foe repelled,
They skulked within the town, we kept the field.
War seemed asleep for nine long years; at length,
Both sides resolved to push, we tried our strength.

Now what did Ajax while our arms took breath,
Versed only in the gross mechanic trade of death?
If you require my deeds, with ambushed arms
I trapped the foe, or tired with false alarms;   340
Secured the ships, drew lines along the plain,
The fainting cheered, chastised the rebel-train,
Provided forage, our spent arms renewed;
Employed at home, or sent abroad, the common cause pursued.
   'The king, deluded in a dream by Jove,
Despaired to take the town, and ordered to remove.
What subject durst arraign the power supreme,
Producing Jove to justify his dream?
Ajax might wish the soldiers to retain
From shameful flight, but wishes were in vain;   350
As wanting of effect had been his words,
Such as of course his thundering tongue affords.
But did this boaster threaten, did he pray,
Or by his own example urge their stay?
None, none of these, but ran himself away.
I saw him run, and was ashamed to see;
Who plied his feet so fast to get aboard as he?
Then speeding through the place, I made a stand,
And loudly cried, "O base degenerate band,
To leave a town already in your hand!   360
After so long expense of blood for fame,
To bring home nothing but perpetual shame!"
These words, or what I have forgotten since,
For grief inspired me then with eloquence,
Reduced their minds; they leave the crowded port,
And to their late forsaken camp resort.
Dismayed the council met; this man was there,
But mute, and not recovered of his fear.
Thersites taxed the king, and loudly railed,
But his wide opening mouth with blows I sealed.   370
Then, rising, I excite their souls to fame
And kindle sleeping virtue into flame.
From thence, whatever he performed in fight
Is justly mine, who drew him back from flight.
   'Which of the Grecian chiefs consorts with thee?
But Diomede desires my company,
And still communicates his praise with me.

As guided by a god, secure he goes,
Armed with my fellowship, amid the foes;
And sure no little merit I may boast,   380
Whom such a man selects from such an host.
Unforced by lots, I went without affright,
To dare with him the dangers of the night;
On the same errand sent, we met the spy
Of Hector, double-tongued, and used to lie;
Him I dispatched, but not till, undermined,
I drew him first to tell what treacherous Troy designed.
My task performed, with praise I had retired,
But not content with this, to greater praise aspired.
Invaded Rhesus, and his Thracian crew,   390
And him, and his, in their own strength I slew:
Returned a victor, all my vows complete,
With the king's chariot, in his royal seat.
Refuse me now his arms, whose fiery steeds
Were promised to the spy for his nocturnal deeds;
And let dull Ajax bear away my right,
When all his days outbalance this one night.
   'Nor fought I darkling still; the sun beheld
With slaughtered Lycians when I strewed the field:
You saw, and counted as I passed along,   400
Alaster, Cromius, Ceranos the strong,
Alcander, Prytanis, and Halius,
Noemon, Charopes, and Ennomus,
Choon, Chersidamas, and five beside,
Men of obscure descent, but courage tried;
All these this hand laid breathless on the ground.
Nor want I proofs of many a manly wound;
All honest, all before; believe not me,
Words may deceive, but credit what you see.'
   At this he bared his breast and showed his scars,   410
As of a furrowed field, well ploughed with wars;
'Nor is this part unexercised,' said he;
'That giant bulk of his from wounds is free;
Safe in his shield he fears no foe to try,
And better manages his blood than I.
But this avails me not; our boaster strove
Not with our foes alone, but partial Jove,
To save the fleet. This I confess is true,

Nor will I take from any man his due;
But, thus assuming all, he robs from you.
Some part of honour to your share will fall;
He did the best indeed, but did not all.
Patroclus in Achilles' arms, and thought
The chief he seemed, with equal ardour fought;
Preserved the fleet, repelled the raging fire,
And forced the fearful Trojans to retire.

'But Ajax boasts, that he was only thought
A match for Hector, who the combat sought:
Sure he forgets the king, the chiefs, and me,
All were as eager for the fight as he;
He but the ninth, and not by public voice,
Or ours preferred, was only fortune's choice:
They fought; nor can our hero boast the event,
For Hector from the field unwounded went.

'Why am I forced to name that fatal day,
That snatched the prop and pride of Greece away?
I saw Pelides sink, with pious grief,
And ran in vain, alas! to his relief,
For the brave soul was fled; full of my friend,
I rushed amid the war, his relics to defend;
Nor ceased my toil till I redeemed the prey,
And loaded with Achilles marched away.
Those arms, which on these shoulders then I bore,
'Tis just you to these shoulders should restore.
You see I want not nerves, who could sustain
The ponderous ruins of so great a man;
Or if in others equal force you find,
None is endued with a more grateful mind.

'Did Thetis then, ambitious in her care,
These arms thus laboured for her son prepare,
That Ajax after him the heavenly gift should wear?
For that dull soul to stare with stupid eyes
On the learned unintelligible prize?
What are to him the sculptures of the shield,
Heaven's planets, earth, and ocean's watery field?
The Pleiads, Hyads; Less and Greater Bear,
Undipped in seas; Orion's angry star;
Two differing cities, graved on either hand?
Would he wear arms he cannot understand?

'Beside, what wise objections he prepares   460
Against my late accession to the wars!
Does not the fool perceive his argument
Is with more force against Achilles bent?
For if dissembling be so great a crime,
The fault is common, and the same in him;
And if he taxes both of long delay,
My guilt is less, who sooner came away.
His pious mother, anxious for his life,
Detained her son; and me, my pious wife.
To them the blossoms of our youth were due;   470
Our riper manhood we reserved for you.
But grant me guilty, 'tis not much my care,
When with so great a man my guilt I share;
My wit to war the matchless hero brought,
But by this fool I never had been caught.

   'Nor need I wonder that on me he threw
Such foul aspersions, when he spares not you:
If Palamede unjustly fell by me,
Your honour suffered in the unjust decree.
I but accused, you doomed; and yet he died,   480
Convinced of treason, and was fairly tried.
You heard not he was false; your eyes beheld
The traitor manifest, the bribe revealed.

   'That Philoctetes is on Lemnos left
Wounded, forlorn, of human aid bereft,
Is not my crime, or not my crime alone;
Defend your justice, for the fact's your own.
'Tis true, the advice was mine; that, staying there,
He might his weary limbs with rest repair,
From a long voyage free, and from a longer war.   490
He took the counsel, and he lives at least;
The event declares I counselled for the best;
Though faith is all in ministers of state,
For who can promise to be fortunate?
Now since his arrows are the fate of Troy,
Do not my wit, or weak address, employ;
Send Ajax there, with his persuasive sense,
To mollify the man, and draw him thence:
But Xanthus shall run backward; Ida stand
A leafless mountain; and the Grecian band   500

Shall fight for Troy; if when my counsels fail,
The wit of heavy Ajax can prevail.

'Hard Philoctetes, exercise thy spleen
Against thy fellows, and the king of men;
Curse my devoted head, above the rest,
And wish in arms to meet me, breast to breast;
Yet I the dangerous task will undertake,
And either die myself, or bring thee back.

'Nor doubt the same success, as when, before,
The Phrygian prophet to these tents I bore,   510
Surprised by night, and forced him to declare
In what was placed the fortune of the war;
Heaven's dark decrees and answers to display,
And how to take the town, and where the secret lay.
Yet this I compassed, and from Troy conveyed
The fatal image of their guardian maid.
That work was mine; for Pallas, though our friend,
Yet while she was in Troy, did Troy defend.
Now what has Ajax done, or what designed?
A noisy nothing, and an empty wind.   520
If he be what he promises in show,
What was I sent, and why feared he to go?
Our boasting champion thought the task not light
To pass the guards, commit himself to night;
Not only through a hostile town to pass,
But scale, with steep ascent, the sacred place;
With wandering steps to search the citadel,
And from the priests their patroness to steal;
Then through surrounding foes to force my way,
And bear in triumph home the heavenly prey;   530
Which had I not, Ajax in vain had held
Before that monstrous bulk his seven-fold shield,
That night to conquer Troy I might be said,
When Troy was liable to conquest made.

Why point'st thou to my partner of the war?
Tydides had indeed a worthy share
In all my toil and praise; but when thy might
Our ships protected, didst thou singly fight?
All joined, and thou of many wert but one;
I asked no friend, nor had, but him alone;   540
Who, had he not been well assured, that art

And conduct were of war the better part,
And more availed than strength, my valiant friend
Had urged a better right, than Ajax can pretend;
As good at least Eurypylus may claim,
And the more moderate Ajax of the name;
The Cretan king, and his brave charioteer,
And Menelaus, bold with sword and spear:
All these had been my rivals in the shield,
And yet all these to my pretensions yield.   550
Thy boisterous hands are then of use, when I
With this directing head those hands apply.
Brawn without brain is thine; my prudent care
Foresees, provides, administers the war:
Thy province is to fight; but when shall be
The time to fight, the king consults with me.
No dram of judgment with thy force is joined,
Thy body is of profit, and my mind.
But how much more the ship her safety owes
To him who steers, than him that only rows;   560
By how much more the captain merits praise
Than he who fights, and fighting, but obeys;
By so much greater is my worth than thine,
Who canst but execute what I design.
What gain'st thou, brutal man, if I confess
Thy strength superior, when thy wit is less?
Mind is the man; I claim my whole desert
From the mind's vigour, and the immortal part.
   'But you, O Grecian chiefs, reward my care,
Be grateful to your watchman of the war;   570
For all my labours in so long a space,
Sure I may plead a title to your grace.
Enter the town; I then unbarred the gates,
When I removed their tutelary fates.
By all our common hopes, if hopes they be,
Which I have now reduced to certainty;
By falling Troy, by yonder tottering towers,
And by their taken gods, which now are ours;
Or if there yet a further task remains
To be performed by prudence or by pains;   580
If yet some desperate action rests behind,
That asks high conduct, and a dauntless mind:

If aught be wanting to the Trojan doom,
Which none but I can manage and o'ercome;
Award those arms I ask by your decree;
Or give to this what you refuse to me.'
  He ceased, and, ceasing, with respect he bowed,
And with his hand at once the fatal statue showed.
Heaven, air, and ocean rung, with loud applause,
And by the general vote he gained his cause.   590
Thus conduct won the prize, when courage failed,
And eloquence o'er brutal force prevailed.

THE DEATH OF AJAX

He who could often, and alone, withstand
The foe, the fire, and Jove's own partial hand,
Now cannot his unmastered grief sustain,
But yields to rage, to madness, and disdain;
Then snatching out his falchion, 'Thou,' said he,
'Art mine; Ulysses lays no claim to thee.
O often tried, and ever trusty sword,
Now do thy last kind office to thy lord!   600
'Tis Ajax who requests thy aid to show
None but himself, himself could overthrow.'
He said, and with so good a will to die,
Did to his breast the fatal point apply,
It found his heart, a way till then unknown,
Where never weapon entered but his own.
No hands could force it thence, so fixed it stood,
Till out it rushed, expelled by streams of spouting blood.
The fruitful blood produced a flower, which grew
On a green stem, and of a purple hue;   610
Like his, whom unaware Apollo slew.
Inscribed in both, the letters are the same,
But those express the grief, and these the name.

Of the Pythagorean Philosophy

A king is sought to guide the growing state,
One able to support the public weight,
And fill the throne where Romulus had sate.
Renown, which oft bespeaks the public voice,

Had recommended Numa to their choice:
A peaceful, pious prince; who not content
To know the Sabine rites his study bent
To cultivate his mind; to learn the laws
Of nature, and explore their hidden cause.
Urged by this care his country he forsook,   10
And to Crotona thence, his journey took.
Arrived, he first enquired the founder's name
Of this new colony, and whence he came.
Then thus a senior of the place replies,
Well read, and curious of antiquities:
''Tis said Alcides hither took his way
From Spain, and drove along his conquered prey;
Then leaving in the fields his grazing cows,
He sought himself some hospitable house:
Good Croton entertained his godlike guest;   20
While he repaired his weary limbs with rest.
The hero, thence departing, blessed the place;
"And here," he said, "in time's revolving race
A rising town shall take his name from thee."
Revolving time fulfilled the prophecy:
For Myscelos, the justest man of earth,
Alemon's son, at Argos had his birth.
Him Hercules, armed with his club of oak
O'ershadowed in a dream and thus bespoke,
"Go, leave thy native soil, and make abode   30
Where Aesaris rolls down his rapid flood;"
He said; and sleep forsook him, and the god.
Trembling he waked, and rose with anxious heart;
His country laws forbade him to depart;
What should he do? 'Twas death to go away,
And the god menaced if he dared to stay:
All day he doubted, and when night came on,
Sleep, and the same forewarning dream began:
Once more the god stood threatening o'er his head,
With added curses if he disobeyed.   40
Twice warned, he studied flight; but would convey
At once his person, and his wealth away;
Thus while he lingered, his design was heard;
A speedy process formed, and death declared.
Witness there needed none of his offence,

Against himself the wretch was evidence;
Condemned, and destitute of human aid,
To him, for whom he suffered, thus he prayed.
   '"O power who has deserved in heaven a throne
Not given, but by the labours made thy own,   50
Pity thy suppliant, and protect his cause,
Whom thou hast made obnoxious to the laws."
   'A custom was of old, and still remains,
Which life or death by suffrages ordains;
White stones and black within an urn are cast,
The first absolve, but fate is in the last.
The judges to the common urn bequeath
Their votes, and drop the sable signs of death;
The box receives all black, but poured from thence
The stones came candid forth: the hue of innocence.   60
Thus Alemonides his safety won,
Preserved from death by Alcumena's son.
Then to his kinsman god his vows he pays,
And cuts with prosperous gale the Ionian seas;
He leaves Tarentum favoured by the wind,
And Thurine bays, and Temises behind,
Soft Sybaris, and all the capes that stand
Along the shore, he makes in sight of land;
Still doubling and still coasting till he found
The mouth of Aesaris, and promised ground,   70
Then saw where on the margin of the flood
The tomb that held the bones of Croton stood;
Here, by the god's command, he built and walled
The place predicted, and Crotona called.'
Thus fame from time to time delivers down
The sure tradition of the Italian town.
   Here dwelt the man divine whom Samos bore,
But now self-banished from his native shore,
Because he hated tyrants, nor could bear
The chains which none but servile souls will wear.   80
He, though from heaven remote, to heaven could move,
With strength of mind, and tread the abyss above;
And penetrate with his interior light
Those upper depths which nature hid from sight;
And what he had observed, and learned from thence,
Loved in familiar language to dispense.

The crowd with silent admiration stand
And heard him, as they heard their god's command;
While he discoursed of heaven's mysterious laws,
The world's original, and nature's cause;   90
And what was god, and why the fleecy snows
In silence fell, and rattling winds arose;
What shook the steadfast earth, and whence begun
The dance of planets round the radiant sun;
If thunder was the voice of angry Jove,
Or clouds with nitre pregnant burst above:
Of these, and things beyond the common reach
He spoke, and charmed his audience with his speech.
   He first the taste of flesh from tables drove,
And argued well, if arguments could move.   100
'O mortals! from your fellows' blood abstain,
Nor taint your bodies with a food profane;
While corn and pulse by nature are bestowed,
And planted orchards bend their willing load;
While laboured gardens wholesome herbs produce,
And teeming vines afford their generous juice;
Nor tardier fruits of cruder kind are lost,
But tamed with fire, or mellowed by the frost;
While kine to pails distended udders bring,
And bees their honey redolent of spring;   110
While earth not only can your needs supply,
But lavish of her store, provides for luxury;
A guiltless feast administers with ease,
And without blood is prodigal to please.
Wild beasts their maws with their slain brethren fill,
And yet not all, for some refuse to kill;
Sheep, goats, and oxen, and the nobler steed
On browse and corn and flowery meadows feed.
Bears, tigers, wolves, the lion's angry brood,
Whom heaven endued with principles of blood,   120
He wisely sundered from the rest, to yell
In forests, and in lonely cave to dwell,
Where stronger beasts oppress the weak by might,
And all in prey, and purple feasts delight.
   'O impious use! to nature's laws opposed,
Where bowels are in other bowels closed;
Where fattened by their fellows' fat they thrive;

Maintained by murder, and by death they live.
'Tis then for naught that mother earth provides
The stores of all she shows, and all she hides,   130
If men with fleshy morsels must be fed,
And chew with bloody teeth the breathing bread:
What else is this but to devour our guests,
And barbarously renew cyclopean feasts!
We, by destroying life, our life sustain,
And gorge the ungodly maw with meats obscene.
    'Not so the golden age, who fed on fruit,
Nor durst with bloody meals their mouths pollute.
Then birds in airy space might safely move,
And timorous hares on heaths securely rove;   140
Nor needed fish the guileful hooks to fear,
For all was peaceful, and that peace sincere.
Whoever was the wretch (and cursed be he)
That envied first our food's simplicity,
The essay of bloody feasts on brutes began,
And after forged the sword to murder man.
Had he the sharpened steel alone employed
On beasts of prey that other beasts destroyed,
Or man invaded with their fangs and paws,
This had been justified by nature's laws,   150
And self-defence; but who did feasts begin
Of flesh, he stretched necessity to sin.
To kill man-killers, man has lawful power,
But not the extended licence to devour.
    'Ill habits gather by unseen degrees,
As brooks make rivers, rivers run to seas.
The sow, with her broad snout for rooting up
The entrusted seed, was judged to spoil the crop,
And intercept the sweating farmer's hope;
The covetous churl of unforgiving kind,   160
The offender to the bloody priest resigned:
Her hunger was no plea; for that she died.
The goat came next in order to be tried;
The goat had cropped the tendrils of the vine;
In vengeance laity and clergy join,
Where one had lost his profit, one his wine.
Here was at least some shadow of offence;
The sheep was sacrificed on no pretence,

But meek and unresisting innocence.
A patient, useful creature, born to bear   170
The warm and woolly fleece, that cloathed her murderer,
And daily to give down the milk she bred,
A tribute for the grass on which she fed.
Living, both food and raiment she supplies,
And is of least advantage when she dies.

   'How did the toiling ox his death deserve,
A downright simple drudge, and born to serve?
O tyrant! with what justice canst thou hope
The promise of the year, a plenteous crop,
When thou destroy'st thy labouring steer, who tilled,   180
And ploughed with pains, thy else ungrateful field?
From his yet reeking neck to draw the yoke,
(That neck with which the surly clods he broke)
And to the hatchet yield thy husband-man,
Who finished autumn and the spring began.

   'Nor this alone! but heaven itself to bribe,
We to the gods our impious acts ascribe;
First recompense with death their creatures' toil,
Then call the blest above to share the spoil:
The fairest victim must the powers appease,   190
(So fatal 'tis sometimes too much to please!)
A purple fillet his broad brows adorns,
With flowery garlands crowned, and gilded horns:
He hears the murderous prayer the priest prefers,
But understands not, 'tis his doom he hears;
Beholds the meal betwixt his temples cast,
The fruit and product of his labours past;
And in the water views perhaps the knife
Uplifted, to deprive him of his life;
Then, broken up alive, his entrails sees,   200
Torn out for priests to inspect the god's decrees.

   'From whence, O mortal men, this gust of blood
Have you derived, and interdicted food?
Be taught by me this dire delight to shun,
Warned by my precepts, by my practice won;
And when you eat the well deserving beast,
Think, on the labourer of your field you feast!

   'Now since the god inspires me to proceed,
Be that whate'er inspiring power obeyed.

For I will sing of mighty mysteries,   210
Of truths concealed before from human eyes,
Dark oracles unveil, and open all the skies.
Pleased as I am to walk along the sphere
Of shining stars, and travel with the year,
To leave the heavy earth, and scale the height
Of Atlas, who supports the heavenly weight;
To look from upper light, and thence survey
Mistaken mortals wandering from the way,
And wanting wisdom, fearful for the state
Of future things, and trembling at their fate!   220
  'Those I would teach; and by right reason bring
To think of death, as but an idle thing.
Why thus affrighted at an empty name,
A dream of darkness, and fictitious flame?
Vain themes of wit, which but in poems pass,
And fables of a world that never was!
What feels the body when the soul expires,
By time corrupted, or consumed by fires?
Nor dies the spirit, but new life repeats
In other forms, and only changes seats.   230
  'E'en I, who these mysterious truths declare,
Was once Euphorbus in the Trojan war;
My name and lineage I remember well,
And how in flight by Sparta's king I fell.
In Argive Juno's fane I late beheld
My buckler hung on high, and owned my former shield.
  'Then death, so called, is but old matter dressed
In some new figure, and a varied vest;
Thus all things are but altered, nothing dies,
And here and there the unbodied spirit flies,   240
By time, or force, or sickness dispossessed,
And lodges where it lights, in man or beast;
Or hunts without, till ready limbs it find,
And actuates those according to their kind;
From tenement to tenement is tossed;
The soul is still the same, the figure only lost.
And as the softened wax new seals receives,
This face assumes, and that impression leaves;
Now called by one, now by another name,
The form is only changed, the wax is still the same: 250

So death, so called, can but the form deface,
The immortal soul flies out in empty space
To seek her fortune in some other place.
    'Then let not piety be put to flight
To please the taste of glutton appetite;
But suffer inmate souls secure to dwell,
Lest from their seats your parents you expel;
With rabid hunger feed upon your kind,
Or from a beast dislodge a brother's mind.
    'And since, like Tiphys parting from the shore,   260
In ample seas I sail, and depths untried before,
This let me further add, that nature knows
No steadfast station, but, or ebbs or flows:
Ever in motion; she destroys her old,
And casts new figures in another mould.
E'en times are in perpetual flux, and run
Like rivers from their fountain rolling on;
For time no more than streams is at a stay:
The flying hour is ever on her way;
And as the fountain still supplies her store,   270
The wave behind impels the wave before,
Thus in successive course the minutes run,
And urge their predecessor minutes on,
Still moving, ever new; for former things
Are set aside, like abdicated kings;
And every moment alters what is done,
And innovates some act till then unknown.
    'Darkness we see emerges into light,
And shining suns descend to sable night;
E'en heaven itself receives another dye,   280
When wearied animals in slumbers lie
Of midnight ease; another when the grey
Of morn preludes the splendour of the day.
The disk of Phoebus when he climbs on high,
Appears at first but as a bloodshot eye;
And when his chariot downwards drives to bed,
His ball is with the same suffusion red;
But mounted high in his meridian race
All bright he shines, and with a better face;
For there, pure particles of ether flow   290
Far from the infection of the world below.

'Nor equal light the unequal moon adorns,
Or in her waxing or her waning horns.
For every day she wanes, her face is less,
But gathering into globe, she fattens at increase.

'Perceiv'st thou not the process of the year,
How the four seasons in four forms appear,
Resembling human life in every shape they wear?
Spring first, like infancy, shoots out her head,
With milky juice requiring to be fed: 300
Helpless, though fresh, and wanting to be led.
The green stem grows in stature and in size,
But only feeds with hope the farmer's eyes;
Then laughs the childish year, with flowerets crowned,
And lavishly perfumes the fields around,
But no substantial nourishment receives,
Infirm the stalks, unsolid are the leaves.

'Proceeding onward whence the year began
The summer grows adult, and ripens into man.

This season, as in men, is most replete   310
With kindly moisture, and prolific heat.

'Autumn succeeds, a sober tepid age,
Not froze with fear, nor boiling into rage;
More than mature, and tending to decay,
When our brown locks repine to mix with odious grey.

'Last, winter creeps along with tardy pace,
Sour is his front, and furrowed is his face;
His scalp if not dishonoured quite of hair,
The ragged fleece is thin, and thin is worse than bare.

E'en our own bodies daily change receive,   320
Some part of what was theirs before they leave;
Nor are today what yesterday they were;
Nor the whole same tomorrow will appear.

'Time was, when we were sowed, and just began,
From some few fruitful drops, the promise of a man;
Then nature's hand (fermented as it was)
Moulded to shape the soft, coagulated mass;
And when the little man was fully formed,
The breathless embryo with a spirit warmed;
But when the mother's throes begin to come,   330
The creature, pent within the narrow room,
Breaks his blind prison, pushing to repair

His stifled breath, and draw the living air;
Cast on the margin of the world he lies,
A helpless babe, but by instinct he cries.
He next essays to walk, but, downward pressed
On four feet imitates his brother beast:
By slow degrees he gathers from the ground
His legs, and to the rolling chair is bound;
Then walks alone; a horseman now become,   340
He rides a stick, and travels round the room:
In time he vaunts among his youthful peers,
Strong-boned, and strung with nerves, in pride of years,
He runs with mettle his first merry stage,
Maintains the next, abated of his rage,
But manages his strength, and spares his age.
Heavy the third, and stiff, he sinks apace,
And though 'tis downhill all, but creeps along the race.
Now sapless on the verge of death he stands,
Contemplating his former feet, and hands;   350
And Milo-like, his slackened sinews sees,
And withered arms, once fit to cope with Hercules,
Unable now to shake, much less to tear the trees.
    'So Helen wept when her too faithful glass
Reflected to her eyes the ruins of her face;
Wondering what charms her ravishers could spy,
To force her twice, or e'en but once enjoy!
    'Thy teeth, devouring time, thine, envious age,
On things below still exercise your rage:
With venomed grinders you corrupt your meat,   360
And then at lingering meals, the morsels eat.
    'Nor those, which elements we call, abide,
Nor to this figure, nor to that are tied:
For this eternal world is said of old
But four prolific principles to hold,
Four different bodies; two to heaven ascend,
And other two down to the centre tend.
Fire first with wings expanded mounts on high,
Pure, void of weight, and dwells in upper sky;
Then air, because unclogged in empty space   370
Flies after fire, and claims the second place;
But weighty water as her nature guides,
Lies on the lap of earth; and mother earth subsides.

'All things are mixed of these, which all contain,
And into these are all resolved again:
Earth rarefies to dew; expanded more,
The subtle dew in air begins to soar;
Spreads as she flies, and weary of her name
Extenuates still, and changes into flame;
Thus having by degrees perfection won,   380
Restless they soon untwist the web they spun,
And fire begins to lose her radiant hue,
Mixed with gross air, and air descends to dew;
And dew condensing, does her form forego,
And sinks, a heavy lump of earth below.
    'Thus are their figures never at a stand,
But changed by nature's innovating hand;
All things are altered, nothing is destroyed,
The shifted scene, for some new show employed.
    'Then to be born, is to begin to be   390
Some other thing we were not formerly:
And what we call to die, is not to appear,
Or be the thing that formerly we were.
Those very elements which we partake
Alive, when dead some other bodies make:
Translated grow, have sense, or can discourse,
But death on deathless substance has no force.
    'That forms are changed I grant, that nothing can
Continue in the figure it began:
The golden age, to silver was debased;   400
To copper that; our metal came at last.
    'The face of places and their forms decay,
And that is solid earth, that once was sea;
Seas in their turn retreating from the shore,
Make solid land, what ocean was before;
And far from strands are shells of fishes found,
And rusty anchors fixed on mountain ground;
And what were fields before, now washed and worn
By falling floods from high, to valleys turn,
And crumbling still descend to level lands;   410
And lakes, and trembling bogs are barren sands:
And the parched desert floats in streams unknown;
Wondering to drink of waters not her own.
    'Here nature living fountains opes; and there

Seals up the wombs where living fountains were;
Or earthquakes stop their ancient course, and bring
Diverted streams to feed a distant spring.
So Lycus, swallowed up, is seen no more,
But far from thence knocks out another door.
Thus Erasinus dives; and blind in earth   420
Runs on, and gropes his way to second birth,
Starts up in Argos meads, and shakes his locks
Around the fields, and fattens all the flocks.
So Mysus by another way is led,
And grown a river now disdains his head;
Forgets his humble birth, his name forsakes,
And the proud title of Caicus takes.
Large Amenane, impure with yellow sands,
Runs rapid often, and as often stands,
And here he threats the drunken fields to drown;   430
And there his dugs deny to give their liquor down.
    'Anigrus once did wholesome draughts afford,
But now his deadly waters are abhorred:
Since, hurt by Hercules, as fame resounds,
The centaurs, in his current washed their wounds.
The streams of Hypanis are sweet no more,
But brackish lose the taste they had before.
Antissa, Pharos, Tyre, in seas were pent,
Once isles, but now increase the continent;
While the Leucadian coast, mainland before,   440
By rushing seas is severed from the shore.
So Zancle to the Italian earth was tied,
And men once walked where ships at anchor ride.
Till Neptune overlooked the narrow way,
And in disdain poured in the conquering sea.
    'Two cities that adorned the Achaian ground,
Buris and Helice, no more are found,
But whelmed beneath a lake are sunk and drowned;
And boatsmen through the chrystal water show
To wondering passengers the walls below.   450
    'Near Troezen stands a hill, exposed in air
To winter winds, of leafy shadows bare:
This once was level ground; but (strange to tell)
The included vapours, that in caverns dwell,
Labouring with cholic pangs, and close confined,

In vain sought issue for the rumbling wind:
Yet still they heaved for vent, and heaving still
Enlarged the concave, and shot up the hill;
As breath extends a bladder, or the skins
Of goats are blown to enclose the hoarded wines.   460
The mountain yet retains a mountain's face,
And gathered rubbish heals the hollow space.
    'Of many wonders, which I heard or knew,
Retrenching most, I will relate but few.
What, are not springs with qualities opposed,
Endued at seasons, and at seasons lost?
Thrice in a day thine, Ammon, change their form,
Cold at high noon, at morn and evening warm:
Thine, Athaman, will kindle wood if thrown
On the piled earth, and in the waning moon.   470
The Thracians have a stream, if any try
The taste, his hardened bowels petrify;
Whate'er it touches it converts to stones,
And makes a marble pavement where it runs.
    'Crathis, and Sybaris her sister flood,
That slide through our Calabrian neighbour wood,
With gold and amber dye the shining hair,
And thither youth resort; for who would not be fair?
    'But stranger virtues yet in streams we find,
Some change not only bodies, but the mind.   480
Who has not heard of Salmacis obscene,
Whose waters into women soften men?
Or Ethiopian lakes which turn the brain
To madness, or in heavy sleep constrain?
Clytorian streams the love of wine expel,
(Such is the virtue of the abstemious well,)
Whether the colder nymph that rules the flood
Extinguishes, and balks the drunken god;
Or that Melampus (so have some assured)
When the mad Proetides with charms he cured;   490
And powerful herbs, both charms and simples cast
Into the sober spring, where still their virtues last.
    'Unlike effects Lyncestis will produce;
Who drinks his waters, though with moderate use,
Reels as with wine, and sees with double sight:
His heels too heavy, and his head too light.

Ladon, once Pheneos, an Arcadian stream,
(Ambiguous in the effects, as in the name)
By day is wholesome beverage; but is thought
By night infected, and a deadly draught.   500
    'Thus running rivers, and the standing lake
Now of these virtues, now of those partake:
Time was (and all things time and fate obey)
When fast Ortygia floated on the sea:
Such were Cyanean isles, when Typhis steered
Betwixt their straits, and their collision feared;
They swam where now they sit; and firmly joined
Secure of rooting up, resist the wind.
Nor Etna vomiting sulphureous fire
Will ever belch; for sulphur will expire,   510
The veins exhausted of the liquid store;
Time was she cast no flames; in time will cast no more.
    'For whether earth's an animal, and air
Imbibes, her lungs with coolness to repair,
And what she sucks remits; she still requires
Inlets for air, and outlets for her fires;
When tortured with convulsive fits she shakes,
That motion chokes the vent till other vent she makes:
Or when the winds in hollow caves are closed,
And subtle spirits find that way opposed,   520
They toss up flints in air; the flints that hide
The seeds of fire, thus tossed in air, collide,
Kindling the sulphur, till the fuel spent,
The cave is cooled, and the fierce winds relent.
Or whether sulphur, catching fire, feeds on
Its unctuous parts, till all the matter gone
The flames no more ascend; for earth supplies
The fat that feeds them; and when earth denies
That food, by length of time consumed, the fire
Famished for want of fuel must expire.   530
    'A race of men there are, as fame has told,
Who shivering suffer hyperborean cold,
Till nine times bathing in Minerva's lake,
Soft feathers, to defend their naked sides, they take.
'Tis said, the Scythian wives (believe who will)
Transform themselves to birds by magic skill;
Smeared over with an oil of wonderous might,

That adds new pinions to their airy flight.
   'But this by sure experiment we know
That living creatures from corruption grow: 540
Hide in a hollow pit a slaughtered steer,
Bees from his putrid bowels will appear;
Who like their parents haunt the fields, and bring
Their honey harvest home, and hope another spring.
The warlike steed is multiplied we find,
To wasps and hornets of the warrior kind.
Cut from a crab his crooked claws and hide
The rest in earth, a scorpion thence will glide
And shoot his sting, his tail in circles tossed
Refers the limbs his backward father lost.   550
And worms, that stretch on leaves their filmy loom,
Crawl from their bags, and butterflies become.
E'en slime begets the frog's loquacious race:
Short of their feet at first, in little space
With arms and legs endued, long leaps they take,
Raised on their hinder part, and swim the lake,
And waves repel: for nature gives their kind
To that intent, a length of legs behind.
   'The cubs of bears, a living lump appear,
When whelped, and no determined figure wear.   560
Their mother licks them into shape, and gives
As much of form, as she herself receives.
   'The grubs from their sexangular abode
Crawl out unfinished, like the maggot's brood,
Trunks without limbs; till time at leisure brings
The thighs they wanted, and their tardy wings.
   'The bird who draws the car of Juno, vain
Of her crowned head, and of her starry train;
And he that bears the artillery of Jove,
The strong-pounced eagle, and the billing dove;   570
And all the feathered kind, who could suppose
(But that from sight, the surest sense he knows)
They from the included yolk, not ambient white, arose.
   'There are who think the marrow of a man,
Which in the spine, while he was living, ran;
When dead, the pith corrupted will become
A snake, and hiss within the hollow tomb.
   'All these receive their birth from other things;

But from himself the phoenix only springs:
Self-born, begotten by the parent flame   580
In which he burned, another and the same;
Who not by corn or herbs his life sustains,
But the sweet essence of amomum drains,
And watches the rich gums Arabia bears,
While yet in tender dew they drop their tears.
He (his five centuries of life fulfilled)
His nest on oaken boughs begins to build,
Or trembling tops of palm, and first he draws
The plan with his broad bill, and crooked claws,
Nature's artificers; on this the pile   590
Is formed, and rises round, then with the spoil
Of cassia, cinnamon, and stems of nard,
(For softness strewed beneath,) his funeral bed is reared:
Funeral and bridal both; and all around
The borders with corruptless myrrh are crowned,
On this incumbent; till etherial flame
First catches, then consumes the costly frame:
Consumes him too, as on the pile he lies;
He lived on odours, and in odours dies.

  'An infant phoenix from the former springs   600
His father's heir, and from his tender wings
Shakes off his parent dust, his method he pursues,
And the same lease of life on the same terms renews.
When grown to manhood he begins his reign,
And with stiff pinions can his flight sustain,
He lightens of its load the tree that bore
His father's royal sepulchre before,
And his own cradle: (this with pious care
Placed on his back) he cuts the buxom air,
Seeks the sun's city, and his sacred church,   610
And decently lays down his burden in the porch.

  'A wonder more amazing would we find?
The hyena shows it, of a double kind,
Varying the sexes in alternate years,
In one begets, and in another bears.
The thin chameleon fed with air, receives
The colour of the thing to which he cleaves.

  'India when conquered, on the conquering god
For planted vines the sharp-eyed lynx bestowed,

Whose urine shed, before it touches earth,   620
Congeals in air, and gives to gems their birth.
So coral soft, and white in ocean's bed,
Comes hardened up in air, and glows with red.
   'All changing species should my song recite,
Before I ceased, would change the day to night.
Nations and empires flourish and decay,
By turns command, and in their turns obey;
Time softens hardy people, time again
Hardens to war a soft, unwarlike train.
Thus Troy for ten long years her foes withstood,   630
And daily bleeding bore the expense of blood;
Now for thick streets it shows an empty space,
Or only filled with tombs of her own perished race,
Herself becomes the sepulchre of what she was.
   'Mycene, Sparta, Thebes of mighty fame,
Are vanished out of substance into name,
And Dardan Rome that just begins to rise,
On Tiber's banks, in time shall mate the skies;
Widening her bounds, and working on her way;
E'en now she mediates imperial sway: 640
Yet this is change, but she by changing thrives,
Like moons new-born, and in her cradle strives
To fill her infant-horns; an hour shall come
When the round world shall be contained in Rome.
   'For thus old saws foretell, and Helenus
Anchises' drooping son enlivened thus;
When Ilium was now in a sinking state,
And he was doubtful of his future fate.
"O goddess-born, with thy hard fortune strive,
Troy never can be lost, and thou alive.   650
Thy passage thou shalt free through fire and sword,
And Troy in foreign lands shall be restored.
In happier fields a rising town I see,
Greater than what e'er was, or is, or e'er shall be;
And heaven yet owes the world a race derived from thee.
Sages, and chiefs of other lineage born
The city shall extend, extended shall adorn:
But from Julus he must draw his birth,
By whom thy Rome shall rule the conquered earth:
Whom heaven will lend mankind on earth to reign,   660

And late require the precious pledge again."
This Helenus to great Aeneas told,
Which I retain, e'er since in other mould:
My soul was clothed; and now rejoice to view
My country walls rebuilt, and Troy revived anew,
Raised by the fall: decreed by loss to gain;
Enslaved but to be free, and conquered but to reign.
  ''Tis time my hard-mouthed coursers to control,
Apt to run riot, and transgress the goal:
And therefore I conclude; whatever lies   670
In earth, or flits in air, or fills the skies,
All suffer change, and we, that are of soul
And body mixed, are members of the whole.
Then, when our sires, or grandsires, shall forsake
The forms of men, and brutal figures take,
Thus housed, securely let their spirits rest,
Nor violate thy father in the beast.
Thy friend, thy brother, any of thy kin,
Is none of these, yet there's a man within:
O spare to make a Thyestean meal,   680
To enclose his body, and his soul expel.
  'Ill customs by degrees to habits rise,
Ill habits soon become exalted vice:
What more advance can mortals make in sin
So near perfection, who with blood begin?
Deaf to the calf that lies beneath the knife,
Looks up, and from her butcher begs her life;
Deaf to the harmless kid, that ere he dies
All methods to procure thy mercy tries,
And imitates in vain thy children's cries.   690
Where will he stop, who feeds with household bread,
Then eats the poultry which before he fed?
Let plough thy steers; that when they lose their breath
To nature, not to thee, they may impute their death.
Let goats for food their loaded udders lend,
And sheep from winter-cold thy sides defend;
But neither springes, nets, nor snares employ,
And be no more ingenious to destroy.
Free as in air, let birds on earth remain,
Nor let insidious glue their wings constrain;   700
Nor opening hounds the trembling stag affright,

Nor purple feathers intercept his flight:
Nor hooks concealed in baits for fish prepare,
Nor lines to heave them twinkling up in air.
   'Take not away the life you cannot give;
For all things have an equal right to live.
Kill noxious creatures, where 'tis sin to save;
This only just prerogative we have:
But nourish life with vegetable food,
And shun the sacrilegious taste of blood.'   710
   These precepts by the Samian sage were taught,
Which godlike Numa to the Sabines brought,
And thence transferred to Rome, by gift his own,
A willing people, and an offered throne.
O happy monarch, sent by heaven to bless
A savage nation with soft arts of peace,
To teach religion, rapine to restrain,
Give laws to lust, and sacrifice ordain:
Himself a saint, a goddess was his bride,
And all the muses o'er his acts preside.   720

Aesacus Transformed into a Cormorant

These some old man sees wanton in the air,
And praises the unhappy constant pair.
Then to his friend the long-necked Cormorant shows,
The former tale reviving others' woes:
'That sable bird,' he cries, 'which cuts the flood
With slender legs, was once of royal blood;
His ancestors from mighty Tros proceed,
The brave Laomedon and Ganymede,
Whose beauty tempted Jove to steal the boy,
And Priam, hapless prince! who fell with Troy.   10
Himself was Hector's brother, and, had fate
But given this hopeful youth a longer date,
Perhaps had rivalled warlike Hector's worth,
Though on the mother's side of meaner birth;
Fair Alexiroë, a country maid,
Bore Aesacus by stealth in Ida's shade.
He fled the noisy town and pompous court,

Loved the lone hills and simple rural sport,
And seldom to the city would resort.
Yet he no rustic clownishness professed,   20
Nor was soft love a stranger to his breast;
The youth had long the nymph Hesperie wooed,
Oft through the thicket or the mead pursued.
Her haply on her father's bank he spied,
While fearless she her silver tresses dried;
Away she fled; not stags with half such speed,
Before the prowling wolf, scud o'er the mead;
Not ducks, when they the safer flood forsake,
Pursued by hawks, so swift regain the lake.
As fast he followed in the hot career;   30
Desire the lover winged, the virgin fear.
A snake unseen now pierced her heedless foot,
Quick through the veins the venomed juices shoot;
She fell, and scaped by death his fierce pursuit.
Her lifeless body, frighted, he embraced,
And cried, "Not this I dreaded, but thy haste;
O had my love been less, or less thy fear!
The victory thus bought is far too dear.
Accursed snake! yet I more cursed than he!
He gave the wound; the cause was given by me.   40
Yet none shall say that unrevenged you died."
He spoke; then climbed a cliff's o'erhanging side,
And, resolute, leaped on the foaming tide.
Tethys received him gently on the wave;
The death he sought, denied, and feathers gave.
Debarred the surest remedy of grief,
And forced to live, he cursed the unasked relief;
Then on his airy pinions upward flies,
And at a second fall successless tries,
The downy plume a quick descent denies.   50
Enraged, he often dives beneath the wave,
And there in vain expects to find a grave.
His ceaseless sorrow for the unhappy maid
Meagred his look, and on his spirits preyed.
Still near the sounding deep he lives; his name
From frequent diving and emerging came.'

Notes

I have used the following abbreviations (the place of publication is London unless otherwise specified):

C   *The Works of John Dryden*, ed. E. N. Hooker *et al.* (Berkeley and Los Angeles, 1956–). In progress ('The California edition').

D   Dryden.

Hopkins and *The Beauties of Dryden*, by David Hopkins and Tom Mason
Mason   (Bristol, 1982).

J   *A Dictionary of the English Language*, by Samuel Johnson (1755).

Kinsley   *The Poems of John Dryden*, ed. by James Kinsley (4 vols., Oxford, 1958).

Noyes   *The Poetical Works of Dryden*, ed. by George R. Noyes (2nd edn., Boston, 1950).

1 *MacFlecknoe*. First published in a pirated version in 1682, and published in an authorized version in *Miscellany Poems* in 1684. There is strong evidence that it was written in substantially the form given by *1684* in 1676. During this long period (unusual for Dryden) between writing and publication, the poem had a limited circulation in manuscript form. At least 12 manuscript copies are extant, none of them in Dryden's hand. Readings in the manuscripts do not substantially alter the text as given by *1684*, the version given here.

The poem enacts a series of ironical parallels between the handing on of the empire of Rome from Aeneas to Ascanius (Julus), and the handing on of the empire of dulness from Flecknoe to Shadwell.

The occasion of *MacFlecknoe* was a prolonged debate on the nature of drama, on plagiarism, and on wit and humour, between Dryden and Thomas Shadwell, a playwright at the rival Duke's House. The debate was sharpened when, in the dedication to *The Virtuoso* (1676), a satire on the new science of the Royal Society, of which Dryden had been a member, Shadwell went over the old ground and included an offensive and gratuitous swipe at Dryden's pension as Laureate and Historiographer Royal.

title. MacFlecknoe: son of Flecknoe.

l. 3. *Flecknoe*: Richard Flecknoe (d. 1678?), poetaster and Catholic priest. He was not Irish, as is often assumed. *like Augustus, young.* Octavius Caesar became emperor at the age of 32.

l. 15. *Shadwell*: spelt '*Sh—*' in *1684*. Proponents for the idea of a faecal innuendo get no support from the manuscripts. For Thomas Shadwell (?1642–92), playwright, see headnote above.

l. 25. *goodly fabric*: great bulk.

l. 29. *Heywood . . . Shirley*. Thomas Heywood (?1570–1641) and James Shirley (1596–1666), dramatists.

l. 32. *sent before but to prepare thy way*: Matt. 3: 3–4.

l. 33. *Norwich drugget*: drugget is coarse stuff of wool and linen. Shadwell came from Norfolk.

l. 35. *warbling lute*: in 'Flecknoe, an English Priest at Rome' Andrew Marvell tells how Flecknoe tried 'to allure me with his lute' (l. 36).

l. 36. *King John of Portugal*: Flecknoe had boasted of being patronized by the king.

2 l. 42. *Epsom blankets*: Sir Samuel Hearty in *The Virtuoso* was tossed in blankets. There is also a glance at a recent affray at Epsom, in which Rochester and some friends tossed some fiddlers. Later a man was murdered. l. 47. *Pissing Alley*: near the Strand.

l. 48. *Ashton Hall*: not satisfactorily explained. Perhaps the town house of Edmund Ashton, a friend of Thomas Shadwell. *1682* reads '*Aston-Hall*'; *1684* '*A—Hall*'. l. 50. *toast*: waste.

l. 53. *St. André's*: St André was a French dancing master who choreographed the dances in Shadwell's *Psyche* (1675).

l. 54. *Psyche's*: *Psyche*, an opera by Shadwell (1675).

l. 57. *Singleton*: James Singleton (d. 1686), one of the king's musicians.

l. 59. *Villerius*: a character in Davenant's *The Siege of Rhodes* (1656).

l. 64. *Augusta*: 'The old name of London' (Dryden's note to *Annus Mirabilis* 1177).

l. 67. *Barbican*: a barbican is an outer defence, especially a double tower over a gate.

ll. 72–3. *Where . . . sleep*: parodying Abraham Cowley's *Davideis* (1656) 1. 79–80:

> Where their vast court the mother-waters keep,
> And undisturbed by moons in silence sleep.

ll. 76–7. *Where . . . try*: parodying *Davideis* 1. 75–6:

> Beneath the dens where unfledged tempests lie,
> And infant winds their tender voices try.

l. 78. *Maximins*: Maximin is the ranting hero of Dryden's *Tyrannic Love* (1670).

l. 79. *Fletcher*: John Fletcher (1579–1625), dramatist. *buskins*: the high boots of Greek tragic actors; 'treads in buskins' means to write tragedy.

3 l. 80. *Jonson . . . socks*: Jonson as writer of comedy; socks are the light shoes of Greek comic actors.

l. 81. *Simkin*: simpleton. l. 84. *Panton*: apparently, a character in farce.

l. 87. *Dekker*: Thomas Dekker (1572–1632), city playwright.

ll. 91–2. *Misers . . . Hypocrites*: alluding to early plays of Shadwell: *The Miser* (1672), *The Humourists* (1671), and *The Hypocrite* (lost).

l. 93. *Raymond . . . Bruce*: men of wit in *The Humourists* and *The Virtuoso* (1676) respectively.

l. 97. *From . . . Street*: from one end of the town to the other; Bunhill was in the City of London; Watling Street, the Roman road which extends across England.

l. 101. *pies . . . bum*: unsold unbound printed sheets were used to line baking-dishes, or to furnish privies.

l. 102. *Ogilby*: John Ogilby (1600–76), translator of Virgil and Homer.

l. 104. *Bilked stationers*: booksellers ruined by the failure of their authors.

l. 105. *Herringman*: publisher of both Dryden and Shadwell.

l. 107. *High on a throne of his own labours reared*: alluding to Milton's Satan, 'High on a throne of royal state' (*Paradise Lost* 2. 1).

l. 109. *Rome's other hope*: translating *Aeneid* 12. 168.

ll. 110–11. *His brows . . . face*: parodying *Aeneid* 2. 682–4, which Dryden later rendered (*The Works of Virgil*, *Aeneid* 2. 930–2):

> from young Julus' head
> A lambent flame arose, which gently spread
> Around his brows, and on his temples fed.

4 l. 122. *Love's Kingdom*: a tragicomedy by Flecknoe (1664).

l. 126. *poppies*: soporifics instead of the expected laurels. Shadwell took opium. l. 129. *owls*: apparent wisdom masking real stupidity.

l. 131. *Presage . . . took*. Plutarch tells how Romulus won his argument about the site of Rome with Remus by seeing twelve vultures to Remus' six.

l. 151. *gentle George*: George Etherege (?1635–91), poet and playwright.

l. 152. *Dorimant . . . Loveit*: characters in Etherege's *The Man of Mode* (1676).

l. 153. *Cully, Cockwood, Fopling*: characters in Etherege's *The Comical Revenge* (1664), *She would if she could* (1668), and *The Man of Mode*.

5 l. 163. *Sedley*: Sir Charles Sedley (1639–1701), poet. He was said to have helped Shadwell with *Epsom Wells*.

l. 168. *Sir Formal's*: Sir Formal Trifle, a character in Shadwell's *Virtuoso*.

l. 170. *northern dedications*: Shadwell frequently dedicated his plays to the Duke or Duchess of Newcastle.

l. 178. *rail at arts*: Shadwell's *The Virtuoso* satirizes the science of the Royal Society.

l. 179. *Nicander's*: Nicander is a character in *Psyche*.

l. 181. *sold he bargains*. To 'sell bargains' is to reply coarsely to a question, as here in the idiom of Sir Samuel Hearty in *The Virtuoso*.

l. 188. *New humours*: parodying the Dedication to *The Virtuoso*, 'four of the humours are entirely new'.

ll. 189–92. *bias . . . will*: parodying Shadwell's Epilogue to *The Humourists* (1671):

> A humour is the bias of the mind
> By which with violence 'tis one way inclined:
> It makes our actions lean on one side still,
> And in all changes that way bends the will.

l. 194. *likeness*: to Jonson. *tympany*: 'a kind of obstructed flatulence that swells the body like a drum' (J).

l. 195. *tun*: a large wine cask.   l. 196. *kilderkin*: a quarter of a tun.

6 l. 204. *keen iambics*: sharp satiric verse.

l. 206. *acrostic*: poem whose initial letters spell out a word.

l. 207. *wings display and altars raise*: in shaped poems, such as Herbert's 'Easter Wings' and 'The Altar'.

l. 212. *Bruce . . . Longvil*: characters in *The Virtuoso*.

ll. 216–17. *prophet's part . . . double portion*: 2 Kgs 2: 9–13.

Absalom and Achitophel. The poem was first published in 1681.

The application of the biblical story (2 Sam. 13–18) to contemporary political events was common among both supporters and opponents of the king. Here, Dryden applies the story to the Exclusion Crisis of 1678–81. The Whigs, led by the Earl of Shaftesbury, advocated religious toleration for the dissenters and wished to exclude the succession of James, Duke of York, a catholic who, it was feared, would be autocratic. Anti-catholic feeling was further whipped up by the 'popish plot' of the same years, featuring a fictitious Jesuit conspiracy against the king.

At the time the poem was written (at the suggestion of the king, it was said), the exclusionist parliament had been dissolved, and Shaftesbury ('Achitophel') arrested.

l. 7. *Israel's monarch*: Charles II. 1 Sam. 13: 13–14.

l. 11. *Michal*: Catherine of Braganza, wife to Charles II. 2 Sam. 6: 23.

l. 14. *David*: Charles II.

l. 18. *Absalom*: James Scott, Duke of Monmouth (1649–85), bastard son of Charles II. 2. *Sam.* 14: 25.

7 l. 34. *Annabel*: Anne, Countess of Buccleuch (1651–1732), Monmouth's wife.

l. 39. *Amnon's murder*. This contemporary reference has not been conclusively identified.

l. 42. *Sion*: London.

l. 45. *The Jews*: the English.

l. 57. *Saul*: Oliver Cromwell (1599–1658). 2 Sam. 3–4.

l. 58 *Ishbosheth*: Richard Cromwell (1626–1712).

l. 59. *Hebron*: Scotland. Charles was crowned king by the Scots on 1 Jan. 1651, and by the English on 23 Apr. 1661. 2 Sam. 5: 1–5.

8 l. 82. *Good Old Cause*: the commonwealth of 1649–53.

l. 85. *Jerusalem*: London.

l. 86. *Jebusites*: Roman Catholics. Joshua 15: 63.

l. 88. *the chosen people*: protestants.

l. 94. *deprived*: by the penal laws.

l. 107. *eat and drink*: get their living.

l. 108. *that Plot*: the 'popish plot'.

l. 118. *Egyptian rites*: Roman Catholic rites. 'Egypt' is France.

l. 129. *fleece*: income from tithes.   l. 130. *God's anointed*: the king.

10 l. 150. *Achitophel*: Anthony Ashley Cooper, Earl of Shaftesbury (1621–83).

l. 175. *triple bond*: the alliance of England, Holland, and Sweden against France.

l. 200. *to possess*: of possessing.

11 l. 229. *Him*: Absalom.

l. 233. *Their cloudy pillar and their guardian fire*: Exod. 13: 21.

l. 234. *second Moses*: Exod. 14: 15–16.

l. 239. *The young men's vision, and the old men's dream*: Joel 2: 28.

12 l. 264. *Gath*: Brussels. 1 Sam. 27: 1–4.

l. 270. *Jordan's sand*: Dover beach. 2 Sam. 19: 9–15.

l. 273. *prince of angels*: Satan.

l. 544. *Zimri*: George Villiers, Duke of Buckingham (1628–87).

13 l. 632. *Corah*: Titus Oates (1649–1705), chief witness in the popish plot. Num. 16. l. 633. *monumental brass*: Num. 21: 6–9.

l. 643. *Stephen*: Acts 6: 9–15.

l. 645. *His tribe were God almighty's gentlemen*: Num. 16: 8–9.

l. 649. *Moses' face*: Exod. 34: 29 (the comparison is ironic).

14 l. 676. *Agag's murder*: possibly referring to the catholic Lord Stafford, imprisoned and condemned on Oates's accusation. 1 Sam. 15: 32–3.

From the Second Part of Absalom and Achitophel. The second part was published late in 1682. It was mostly written by Nahum Tate with some touches by Dryden. These lines (457–509) are indubitably by Dryden.

l. 3. *Og*: Thomas Shadwell; see notes to *MacFlecknoe* (above, p. 237).

l. 5. *link*: a boy with a torch ('link') of pitch and tar.

15 l. 36. *Doeg*: Elkanah Settle (1648–1724), author of *The Empress of Morocco* (1673).

ll. 50–1. *But of King David's foes . . . Absalom*: 2 Sam. 18: 32.

16 *To the Memory of Mr Oldham.* First published in *The Remains of Mr John Oldham*, 1684. John Oldham (1653–83) was a poet, satirist, and schoolmaster.

l. 9. *Nisus*. At the funeral of Anchises (*Aeneid* 5) two friends, Nisus and Euryalus run together in a race. Nisus, the older man, slips and falls, but manages to trip the next runner, allowing Euryalus to win. See 'The entire Episode of Nisus and Euryalus' which follows.

l. 14. *numbers*: harmony of verse, or simply versification.

l. 23. *Marcellus*: Augustus' nephew. His early death is celebrated in Virgil's *Aeneid* 6. 860–86, which Dryden echoes in this poem. Cf. his translation (6. 1196–9):

> Observe the crowds that compass him around:
> All gaze and all admire, and raise a shouting sound:
> But hovering mists around his brows are spread;
> And night, with sable shades, involves his head.

The entire Episode of Nisus and Euryalus translated from the Fifth and Ninth Books of Virgil's Aeneid. First published in *Sylvae* (1685). A translation of *Aeneid* 5. 286–361 and 9. 176–449.

Nisus and Euryalus 1

l. 1. *Trojan hero*: Aeneas.

17 l. 33. *well-breathed*: sound of wind.

18 l. 67. *cuts*: passes sharply through.   l. 81. *the prince*: Aeneas.

19 l. 100. *Neptune's bars*: the gates of a temple dedicated to Neptune.

Nisus and Euryalus 2

22 l. 108. *took the word*: spoke at once.

l. 136. *gave*: to Aeneas.

26 l. 302. *perplexing*: tangled.

27 l. 336. *brown*: dark.

l. 337. *poising from his ear*: balancing on a level with his ear.

29 *Translations from Lucretius*. First published in *Sylvae* (1685).

The latter part of the third book. Against the fear of death. De rerum natura 3. 830–1094.

l. 4. *Punic arms*: the three wars between Rome and Carthage in the third and second centuries BC.

30 l. 54. *offals*: carrion, waste.

31 l. 99. *brimmers*: goblets.   l. 104. *the god that never thinks*: Bacchus.

33 l. 185. *Tantalus*: he stole the food of the gods.

l. 189. *Tityus*: two vultures tore at his liver as a punishment for having assaulted Leto.

34 l. 200. *Sisyphus*: punished by having to roll a stone uphill perpetually.

l. 211. *smokes*: rushes.

l. 219. *fifty foolish virgins*: the Danaides, daughters of Danaus. At his command they killed their husbands on their wedding night. They were punished by having to draw water eternally in leaky vessels.

l. 222. *the dog*: Cerberus, guardian of the underworld.

l. 228. *the Tarpeian rock*: from which traitors and murderers were thrown in Rome.

l. 237. *Ancus*: Ancus Marcius, according to tradition the fourth king of Rome.

35 l. 242. *That haughty king*: Xerxes, who bridged the Hellespont.

l. 255. *Democritus*: fifth-century-BC philosopher.

37 *The Ninth Ode of the First Book of Horace*. First published in *Sylvae* (1685).

38 l. 32. *pointed*: appointed.

A Song for St Cecilia's Day, 1687. First published in 1687. Written for the concert on 22 Nov. 1687.

l. 2. *universal frame*: the physical universe.

l. 14. *compass*: the full range.

l. 15. *diapason*: the combination of all the notes sounding in a harmonious whole.

closing full: ending in a perfect cadence.

l. 17. *Jubal*: 'the father of all such as handle the harp and organ' (Genesis 4: 21).

39 l. 50. *sequacious of*: following. Ovid, *Metamorphoses* 11. 1–2: 'with such songs the bard of Thrace [Orpheus] drew the trees, held beasts enthralled, and constrained stones to follow him'.

40 l. 63. *untune the sky*: 'when this world and the heavenly bodies are destroyed, the music of the spheres will cease; thus *Music* (the blast of the divine *trumpet*) will untune (make incapable of harmony) the sky' (Noyes).

The Lady's Song. Published in 1704, in *Poetic Miscellanies*, part 5.

l. 2. *May-lady*: Queen of the May.

l. 7. *Pan . . . Syrinx*. For the myth see 'The First Book of Ovid's *Metamorphoses*' 951–87 (above, pp. 86–7); but 'Pan' and 'Syrinx' almost certainly allude to the banished James II and his wife Mary of Este.

41 *The sixth satire of Juvenal*. First published in *The Satires of Juvenal and Persius* (1693). Some of Dryden's notes are reproduced here.

play prizes: engage in a contest.

42 l. 71. *Ceres' feast*: 'when the Roman women were forbidden to bed with their husbands' (D).

43 l. 90. *Secure . . . of*: safe from finding.

l. 107. *quail-pipe*: the vocal organs. The Californian editors think there may be an obscene pun. 'Quail-pipe' translates *fibula*, a needle drawn through the foreskin to prevent sex taking place.

44 l. 118. *wondering Pharos*: 'She fled to Egypt which wondered at the enormity of her crime' (D).

45 l. 163. *The good old sluggard*: Claudius. Juvenal 'tells the famous story of Messalina, wife to the emperor Claudius' (D).

l. 179. *Britannicus*: son of Messalina.

46 l. 208. *Wealth has the privilege*. 'His meaning is that a wife who brings a large dowry may do what she pleases and has all the privileges of a widow' (D).

l. 231. *Berenice's ring*: 'a ring of great price, which Herod Agrippa gave to his sister Berenice. He was king of the Jews, but tributary to the Romans' (D).

47 l. 249. *Cornelia*: 'mother to the Gracchi, of the family of the Cornelii, from whence Scipio the African was descended, who triumphed over Hannibal' (D).

l. 255. *O Paean*: Juvenal 'alludes to the known fable of Niobe in Ovid [*Metamorphoses* 6, 165 ff.]. Amphion was her husband. Paean was Apollo who with his arrows killed her children because she boasted that she was more fruitful than Latona, Apollo's mother' (D).

l. 261. *thirty pigs*. Juvenal 'alludes to the white sow in Virgil [*Aeneid* 3. 390–3], who farrowed thirty pigs' (D).

l. 271. *the Grecian cant*. 'Women then learned Greek, as ours speak French' (D).

48 l. 282. Ζωὴ καὶ ψυχὴ: life and soul (terms of endearment).

49 l. 354. *plastron*: leather-covered breast-plate worn by a fencing-master.

50 l. 365. *magazine*: jewel-box. l. 369. *sarcenet*: fine silk.

l. 377. *play a prize*: engage in a contest.

l. 379. *curtain-lecture*: 'a reproof given by a wife to her husband in bed' (J).

l. 389. *tiller*: drawer.

51 l. 424. *eringoes*: the root of sea holly, thought to nourish sexual desire and performance.

l. 439. *the goddess named the good*: 'at whose feasts no men were to be present' (D).

52 l. 449. *flats*: moisture.

l. 450. *rubster*: either one who rubs or something one rubs oneself with.

l. 456. *Nestor*: 'who lived three hundred years' (D).

l. 467. *what singer*. Juvenal 'alludes to the story of P. Clodius who, disguised in the habit of a singing woman, went into the house of Caesar where the feast of the good goddess was celebrated, to find an opportunity with Caesar's wife, Pompeia' (D).

53 l. 504. *navel-string*. It was believed that the navel-string was bound up with prosperity. l. 510. *Carved*: castrated.

l. 522. *Pollio*: 'a famous singing boy' (D).

54 l. 532. *actors*: 'that such an actor, whom they love, might obtain the prize' (D).

l. 534. *haruspex*: 'he who inspects the entrails of the sacrifice and from thence foretells the successor' (D).

55 l. 586. *Tabors and trumpets*. 'The ancients thought that with such sounds they could bring the moon out of her eclipse' (D).

l. 593. *a mood and figure bride*: 'a woman who had learned logic' (D).

l. 601. *Priscian's ... head*: 'a woman grammarian who corrects her husband for speaking false Latin, which is called "breaking Priscian's head"' (D).

56 l. 622. *A train of these*: 'of she-asses' (D).

l. 641. *Sicilian tyrants*: 'are grown to a proverb in Latin for their cruelty' (D).

57 l. 672. *Bellona's priests*. 'Bellona's priests were a sort of fortune teller and their high-priest a eunuch' (D).

l. 684. *murrey-coloured vest*: mulberry-coloured vest. D notes: 'a garment was given to the priest which he threw into the river; and that, they thought, bore all the sins of the people which were drowned with it'.

58 l. 696. *Meroe's burning sand*. Meroe is an island in the Nile.

59 l. 738. *Otho*: 'succeeded Galba in the empire, which was foretold him by an astrologer' (D).

ll. 753–4. *Mars ... Venus*. 'Mars and Saturn are the two unfortunate planets; Jupiter and Venus the two fortunate' (D).

l. 761. *twelve houses, and their lords*: 'the twelve astrological divisions of the heavens, and the planets exercising influence in each' (Kinsley).

l. 767. *decumbiture*: horoscope for a bed-ridden person.

60 l. 790. *savin*: shrub used to procure an abortion.

l. 792. *Ethiop's son*. Juvenal's 'meaning is, help her to any kind of sleep which may cause her to miscarry; for fear she may be brought to bed of blackamoor, which thou, being her husband, art bound to father, and that bastard may by law inherit thy estate' (D).

l. 796. *His omen would discolour all the day*. 'The Romans thought it ominous to see a blackamoor in the morning, if he were the first man they met' (D).

61 l. 818. *Caesinia*: 'wife of Caius Caligula, the great tyrant. It is said she gave him a love potion, which flying up in to his head, distracted him and was the occasion of his committing so many acts of cruelty' (D).

l. 820. *mother's love*. If the hippomanes (a small black membrane on the head of a new-born foal) was removed before the mother could eat it, she refused to nurse her foal.

l. 827. *Agrippina's mushroom*. 'Agrippina was the mother of the tyrant Nero, who poisoned her husband Claudius that Nero might succeed, who was her son, and not Britannicus, who was the son of Claudius by a former wife' (D).

l. 848. *Drymon's wife*. 'The widow of Drymon poisoned her sons, that she might succeed to their estate. This was done in the poet's time or just before it' (D).

l. 853. *Medea's legend*. 'Medea, out of revenge to Jason who had forsaken her, killed the children which she had by him' (D).

62 l. 869. *the Belides*: 'who were fifty sisters, married to fifty young men, who were their cousins-german [first cousins], and killed them all on their wedding night, excepting Hypermnestra, who saved her husband Linus [Lynceus]' (D).

The First Book of Ovid's Metamorphoses. First published in *Examen Poeticum* (1693).

l. 5. *tenor*: continuance. l. 6. *Deduced*: brought down.

l. 10. *indigested*: disordered.

63 l. 26. *intestine*: domestic. l. 47. *bounding*: limiting.

64 l. 80. *frozen waggon*: the constellation of the Great Bear (Charles's Wain).

l. 82. *the unwholesome year*: the annual harvest.

66 l. 132. *guiltless of*: unacquainted with.

67 l. 174. *rummaging*: emptying.

68 l. 211. *Lycaon's guilt*. Lycaon was an Arcadian tyrant, impious to Jupiter.

69 l. 248. *nobler parts*: the heart and lungs. l. 256. *attempted*: assailed.

70 l. 297. *Molossian state*: the state of the Molossi, a people of Epirus.

l. 313. *famished*: wasted.

71 l. 346. *axle-tree*: axle-pin. l. 358. *flaggy*: limp.

72 l. 368. *Junonian Iris*: Iris the messenger of Juno.

l. 377. *The watery tyrant*: Neptune, god of the sea.

73 l. 426. *bound*: boundary. l. 449. *Tyrian*: purple.

74 l. 489. *our father*: Prometheus.

75 l. 506. *gradual*: 'an order of steps' (J).

76 l. 532. *diffides*: distrusts.

l. 565. *Pharian*: of Pharos. l. 568. *crusted*: covered with a crust.

77 l. 574. *temper*: mixture. l. 586. *Python*: a huge serpent.

l. 605. *promiscuous*: undifferentiating.

78 l. 646. *her father*: Peneus. l. 647. *son*: grandson.

79 l. 680. *a foe*: as a foe.

80 l. 693. *Delphos*: Delphi. l. 694. *Patareian*: of Patara.

l. 718. *slipped*: let loose.

l. 722. *turn*: 'a hare's change of direction, manœuvred by the dog' (Kinsley).

81 l. 736. *paternal brook*. Daphne's father was the river-god Peneus.

84 l. 871. *hardly*: 'not softly' (J).

85 l. 921. *his airy messenger*: Mercury (Hermes).

89 l. 1055. *daunted*: overcome with fear.

l. 1086. *levée*: rising from bed.

90 *The Fable of Iphis and Ianthe*. First published in *Examen Poeticum* (1693). A translation of *Metamorphoses* 9. 665–796.

l. 1. *of this*: of the preceding story in Ovid.

l. 3. *Gnossian*: Cretan.

l. 14. *tits*: girls (used playfully).

l. 37. *Osiris*: Egyptian god of fertility and husband to Isis.

l. 38. *The silent god*: Harpocrates, Egyptian god of silence.

92 l. 109. *daughter of the sun*: Pasiphae.

94 l. 199. *burnish*: increase in breadth.

95 *The Fable of Acis, Polyphemus, and Galatea*. First published in *Examen Poeticum* (1693). A translation of *Metamorphoses* 13. 750–897.

l. 31. *simagres*: grimaces.

98 l. 115. *Phaeacian*: ideal, like the gardens of Alcinous, king of the Phaeacians (*Odyssey* 7).

l. 127. *sweepy*: moving with a sweeping motion.

l. 137. *turtles*: turtle-doves.

101 *To my Dear Friend Mr Congreve on his Comedy called The Double Dealer*. First published as a commendatory poem in Congreve's *The Double Dealer* (1694). The poem was written in 1693. William Congreve (1670–1729) had been Dryden's friend for some three years.

l. 5. *giant race*: Gen. 6: 4.

l. 7. *Janus*: Roman god who introduced cultivation into Italy (Ovid, *Fasti*, 1. 63).

l. 14. *The second temple*: Ezra 5–6, and Hag. 2: 3.

l. 15. *Vitruvius*: Roman architect in the time of Augustus. As author of the only surviving ancient treatises on architecture, he exerted an enormous influence at the time of the renaissance.

l. 29. *courtship*: courtliness. Etherege was also a diplomat.

l. 30. *manly*: the name of the hero of Wycherley's *The Plain Dealer*.

l. 32. *foiled*: overdone, surpassed.

ll. 35–8. *Fabius . . . overcome*. 'Had Scipio been as loveable as you the envious Fabius would have rejoiced in his early fame and supported him, even though Fabious had in his own day been unsuccessful against Hannibal' (Kinsley).

102 ll. 39–40. *Romano ... taught.* Dryden is in error. Giulio Romano (1492–1546) was nine years younger than Raphael (1483–1520) and never his master.

ll. 45–6. *one Edward ... A greater Edward.* Edward II (1284–1327) was deposed and murdered. He was succeeded by his son Edward III (1312–77), 'greater', I suppose, because of his frequent wars against the French.

ll. 47–8. *Tom the second ... Tom the first.* When William of Orange came to the throne in 1688 Dryden lost his offices of Poet Laureate and Historiographer Royal to Thomas Shadwell (see headnote to 'MacFlecknoe' above, p. 237). Next as Historiographer (1692) came Thomas Rymer.

l. 49. *my patron's.* Dryden's patron was Charles Sackville, Earl of Dorset (1638–1706). As Lord Chamberlain, it was his duty to deprive Dryden of his offices.

l. 53. *High on the throne of wit: Paradise Lost*, 2. 1: 'High on a throne of royal state.'

l. 55. *Thy first attempt*: Congreve's *The Old Bachelor* (1693).

103 *An Ode on the Death of Mr Henry Purcell.* First published in 1696. Purcell died on 21 Nov. 1695.

l. 5. *the close of*: the closing in of. l. 6. *Philomel*: the nightingale.

l. 18. *sovereigns'*: Pluto and Prosperpina, 'here thought of as symbolizing disorder' (C). l. 25. *handed him along*: led him by the hand.

104 *Meleager and Atalanta.* First published in *Fables* (1700). A translation of Ovid's *Metamorphoses* 8. 270–545.

Meleager was the son of Oeneus (l. 5), king of Calydon, and Althaea (l. 243).

l. 4. *Cynthia's.* Cynthia was a name given to Diana, associated with Artemis, the virgin goddess of hunting. The cause of her displeasure is given at l. 13 below.

l. 28. *strove*: 'his tusks were as big as an Indian elephant's'.

l. 33. *intercepts*: stops from accomplishing its purpose.

105 l. 44. *crew*: Most are glossed by Dryden in the text. Only the more noteworthy are glossed here.

l. 46. *Leda's twins*: Castor and Pollux. They became the constellation Gemini.

l. 48. *Jason*: son of Aeson, a king of Thessaly. He 'manned' the *Argo* to recover the Golden Fleece.

l. 52. *Thestian sons.* Sons of Thestius, Plexippus, and Toxeus, brothers of Althaea, the mother of Meleager.

l. 53. *Caeneus*: of Thessaly. He was born a woman. See 'The Twelfth Book of Ovid's *Metamorphoses*' 260–87 (above, pp. 188–9).

l. 60. *twice-old Iolas*. 'Iolas was rejuvenated by Hebe at the instigation of his friend Hercules' (Kinsley).

l. 65. *Atalanta*: daughter of Iasus and Clymene. A virgin huntress.

106 l. 89. *toils*: large piece of cloth bordered with thick ropes, stretched round an enclosure to capture wild beasts or large nets for stags.

l. 108. *spend their mouth*: bark, give tongue, on discovering the quarry.

108 l. 178. *distains*: stains.

109 l. 213. *Nonacrine*: Arcadian.

110 l. 255. *fatal sisters*: the Moirai.

113 l. 398. *her whom heaven for Hercules decreed*. Deianira, sister of Meleager.

114 *Sigismonda and Guiscardo*. First published in *Fables* (1700). A translation of *Decameron* 4. 1. Dryden keeps close to Boccaccio (except for the addition at ll. 151–72), his main changes being: (1) Guiscardo's social rank is raised a few notches; (2) the lovers marry before their love is consummated.

115 l. 51. *blooming*: just coming to manhood.

l. 64. *rays*: glances. (Before the seventeenth century the eyes were thought to give out light.)

117 l. 143. *perplexed*: entangled.   l. 145. *to*: as a.

l. 151. *conscious*: privy to the secret. Lines 151–72 are Dryden's addition. Boccaccio has simply 'After giving each other a rapturous greeting, they made their way into her chamber, where they spent a good part of the day in transports of bliss.'

119 l. 215. *averse*: turned away.

120 l. 244. *meditates*: muses over.   l. 245. *thoughtless*: unsuspecting.

l. 270. *sensible of*: acutely perceiving.

121 l. 317. *people's lee*: the dregs of the people.

123 l. 372. *And little wanted, but*: there was little wanting but that . . .

128 l. 579. *Fixed*: resolved.

129 l. 625. *magazine*: storehouse.   l. 626. *Secure*: certain.

130 l. 670. *down*: immediately.

l. 694 *infection*: the 'catching' influence of sympathy.

131 l. 711. *genial bed*: marriage bed.

l. 718. *suborned*: usually 'bribed'. Here probably 'brought to her aid for a sinister reason'.

132 *Baucis and Philemon*. First published in *Fables* (1700). A translation of Ovid's *Metamorphoses* 8. 611–724.

l. 3. *Ixion's son*: Pirithous.

133 l. 36. *professing*: openly declaring themselves.

134 l. 57. *seether*: a utensil for boiling.

l. 77. *genial bed*: a marriage bed. l. 81. *alone*: only.

l. 90. *Pallas*. The olive was sacred to Pallas (Athene).

l. 92. *cornels*: the red fruit of the cornelian cherry tree.

l. 93. *lees of wine*: vinegary dregs of wine.

135 l. 111. *working in the must*: fermenting.

136 l. 141. *owned*: acknowledge himself.

l. 152. *floated level*: flooded surface.

l. 177. *sign their suit*: signal their agreement to what was asked.

137 l. 191. *Tyanaean*: a native of Tyana in Turkey.

Pygmalion and the Statue. First published in *Fables* (1700). A translation of Ovid's *Metamorphoses* 10. 243–97.

138 l. 23. *strained*: clasped tight.

l. 52. *Sidonian*. Sidon was near Tyre, famous for its purple-dyeing industry.

139 l. 93. *kiss sincere*: genuine kiss. There may be a pun: the old etymology of 'sincere' was from *sine cera*, 'without wax'.

140 *Cinyras and Myrrha*. First published in *Fables* (1700). A translation of Ovid's *Metamorphoses* 10. 298–524.

l. 16. *amomum*: a fragrant plant.

l. 21. *Her plant*: Myrrha, a shrub or plant yielding gum-resin, used in scent. See ll. 347–69.

l. 29. *ambitious of*: aspiring to.

142 l. 90. *the infernal bands*: the Furies, avengers of crime, especially crimes against the ties of kinship.

l. 100. *Observant of*: respectfully attentive to.

144 l. 181. *house*: kindred.

145 l. 201. *received*: heard.

146 l. 264. *Arctophylax*: Boötes. l. 268. *amazed*: horrified.

l. 270. *Icarius*: Icarus. l. 271. *Virgin sign*: Erigone.

l. 277. *Secure of*: feeling no care from.

147 l. 296. *His bowels*: his own flesh.

l. 303. *That names might not be wanting to the sin*: 'even the names were not wanting to complete the wickedness'.

l. 304. *Full of her sire*: impregnated by her father.

l. 318. *Panchaia*: an island east of Arabia.

148 l. 320. *mewed*. Properly 'mew' means 'to shed the feathers'; here, more generally, 'changed'.

l. 320. *her horns*: each of the pointed extremities of the moon as she appears in her first and last quarters.

149 l. 369. *convulsive*: shaken with convulsions.

The Cock and the Fox from Chaucer. First published in *Fables* (1700).

150 l. 10. *groat*: four old pence; about 1½ pence.

l. 13. *cattle*: livestock in general.

l. 24. *posset*: a drink made of curdled milk.

151 l. 62. *Ptolemies*: an incestuous dynasty of ancient Egypt.

l. 64. *dispensation*: alluding to 'Henry VIII's marriage with Catherine of Aragon, his brother's widow' (Kinsley).

l. 70. *feathered*: copulated with.

152 l. 90. *Solus cum sola*. 'The reference is to the monkish Latin proverb "Solus cum sola non cogitabuntur orare pater noster", which could be roughly translated "If a man is alone with a woman, neither of them would be expected to spend their time saying their prayers". *Solus cum sola* is the title of a Pavan for the lute by John Dowland' (Hopkins and Mason).   *all his note*: (1) the entire subject of his song; (2) what he was renowned for.

l. 91. *parts*: (1) accomplishments; (2) part-singing.

l. 106. *shrovetide-cock*: 'a cock tied and pelted with stones on Shrove Tuesday' (Kinsley).

153 l. 140. *Galen*: second-century physician, and influential writer on medicine.   l. 156. *Choler adust*: the humour of melancholy.

154 l. 182. *tertian ague*: 'an ague [fever] intermitting but one day, so that there are two fits in three days' (J).

l. 188. *the gods unequal numbers love*: Virgil, *Eclogues* 8. 75.

l. 190. *fumetery, centaury, and spurge*: medicinal plants of uncertain identification.   l. 202. *Homer plainly says*: Iliad 1. 63.

ll. 203–4. *Nor Cato . . . school*. 'The distinction is between the Roman Cato and the medieval school-book *Dionysii Catonis disticha de moribus ad filium*, vulgarly ascribed to Cato' (Kinsley).

l. 209. *An ancient author*: Cicero, *De divinatione* 1. 27.

156 l. 254. *sacred*: accursed. An echo of Virgil's *auri sacra fames* (*Aeneid* 3. 57).

l. 283. *deeds of night*: evil deeds.

158 l. 374. *Bede*: Dryden's error. Bede lived a century before Kenelm (l. 360).

l. 376. *Macrobius*: Ambrosius Macrobius, fifth-century Roman, who wrote a commentary on Cicero's fictional *Somnium Scipionis* (*Scipio's Dream*), in which Scipio's grandfather appeared in a dream and told him he would conquer Carthage.

159 l. 380. *Daniel*: Dan. 7.

l. 383. *Joseph*: Gen. 37.   l. 387. *butler*: Pharaoh's butler (Gen. 40).

l. 388. *he*: Pharaoh's baker (Gen. 40).

l. 389. *Croesus*: the fabulously rich king of Lydia in Asia Minor.

l. 391. *wife of Hector*: Andromache's dream is a medieval addition to the matter of Troy.   l. 417. *in principio*: 'in the beginning' (Gen. 1. 1).

160 l. 418. *Mulier . . . confusio*: woman is man's undoing.

l. 438. *trod*: copulated with.

l. 451. *Ephemeris*: a table showing the predicted positions of a heavenly body for every day during a given period.

161 l. 460. *man strutting on two legs and aping me*: alluding to Plato's humorous definition of man as 'a two-legged animal without wings' (Diogenes Laertius *Vitae philosophorum* 6. 40).

l. 479. *Book of Martyrs*: John Foxe's *Acts and Monuments* (1563).

162 l. 500. *Sinon*. See *Aeneid* 2. 57-194.

l. 501. *Gallic*: (1) French; (2) a cock's (Latin *gallus* = cock).

l. 502. *Gano*: he betrayed Charlemagne at Roncesvalles.

l. 523. *bolt . . . bran*: 'I can't make head or tail of it.'

l. 524. *Bradwardine*: Thomas Bradwardine (d. 1349), Archbishop of Canterbury.   *Austin*: St Augustine.

ll. 531-5. *The first . . . before*. 'The distinction is between (i) deliberate, rational choice of a course of action, and (ii) "spontaneous" or unreflective action in inevitable circumstances. The slaves do not initially choose whether to row or not; but constrained to work, they pull "willingly" under the natural prompting of a "prospect of the shore"' (Kinsley).

165 l. 633. *Maro's*: Virgil's.   l. 634. *Horace when a swan*: *Odes* 2. 20.

l. 636. *Brennus*: leader of the Gauls who overran Italy in 390 BC. *Belinus*: a god of the Gauls.   l. 648. *saint charity*: holy charity.

l. 652. *solar people*: people born under the influence of the sun.

166 l. 693. *Gaufride*: Geoffrey de Vinsauf, who mourned the Friday death of Richard I.

167 l. 707. *Asdrubal*: Carthaginian leader whom Scipio (note to l. 376 above) overthrew in 146 BC.

l. 728. *Talbot with the band.* Chaucer speaks of Talbot and Gerland. Dryden was misled by his corrupt text.

l. 742. *Jack Straw*: a leader of the Peasants' Revolt of 1381.

170 *Ceyx and Alcyone*. First published in *Fables* (1700). A translation of Ovid's *Metamorphoses* 11. 410–748.

l. 26. *face*: surface, appearance.   l. 41. *comport*: behaviour.

171 l. 51. *present what I suffer only fear*: 'being with you, fear only what I am really suffering' (Kinsley).

172 l. 93. *atrip*: hoisted up.

l. 100. *denounce*: announce.   l. 102. *Strike*: lower.

l. 109. *laves*: bails out.

173 l. 130. *Stygian*: hellish.

l. 131. *flatted*: made calm.   l. 134. *sublime*: elevated.

174 l. 181. *whom their funerals wait*: those dead already.

175 l. 203. *Pindus . . . Athos*: famous ancient mountains.

l. 241. *fumed*: 'perfumed with odours in the fire' (J).

176 l. 254. *tainted*: because until a dead man had been given proper burial his home and family were regarded as unclean.

l. 256. *Iris*: Greek goddess of the rainbow, and messenger of the gods.

l. 268. *Cimmerians*: an ancient people living on the edge of the world.

l. 275. *provoke*: rouse.

177 l. 299. *bearded ears*: prickly spikes of corn.

179 l. 392. *blubbered*: swollen.

181 l. 470. *mole*: dyke.

182 l. 491. *obnoxious*: exposed to.

l. 494. *compressed*: pregnant.   l. 499. *nephews*: grandchildren.

The Twelfth Book of Ovid's Metamorphoses. First published in *Fables* (1700).   l. 7. *Spartan queen*: Helen.

183 l. 27. *gratulates to*: congratulates on.

l. 37. *disobeyed*: held back (from aiding the Greeks).

184 l. 101. *Neptunian Cygnus*: Neptune's son Cygnus.

185 l. 110. *in act to*: just about to.   l. 117. *Goddess-born*: Achilles, son of Thetis.   l. 149. *Lyrnessian*: Lyrnessus'.

186 l. 181. *bored arms*: pierced armour.

187 l. 203. *his name*: swan; Latin *cygnus*.

188 l. 239. *Othrys*: a mountain in Thessaly.

l. 252. *Neleides*: Nestor, son of Neleus.

l. 272. *power of ocean*: Neptune.

189 l. 294. *cloud-begotten race*: the centaurs.

l. 307. *little wanted . . . employ*: and it had nearly happened that all had wished her joy in vain.

190 l. 337. *double-formed*: centaurs, half-man, half-horse.

193 l. 440. *Stygian*: of Styx.

l. 463. *cubit-bone*: elbow-joint.

194 l. 480. *Athenian knight*: Theseus.   l. 491. *Their king*: Amyntor.

195 l. 524. *form*: beauty.

196 l. 582. *house*: covering attached to saddle.

197 l. 629. *card*: comb wool.

202 l. 815. *The god*: Vulcan.   l. 828. *Laertes' son*: Ulysses.

The Speeches of Ajax and Ulysses. First published in *Fables* (1700). A translation of *Metamorphoses* 13. 1–398. Ajax and Ulysses contend for the shield of Achilles.

l. 2. *master of the sevenfold shield*: Ajax.

203 l. 38. *This thief*: Ulysses.

204 l. 53. *one more cunning*: Palamedes. He exposed, and was killed by, Ulysses. See ll. 77, 478 ff.

l. 63. *Philoctetes*: son of Poesas; possessor of a deadly bow. He was left wounded on Lemnos, and later persuaded by Ulysses to join the Greek expedition against Troy. See ll. 484 ff.

208 l. 215. *he*: Ajax.

l. 245. *uncle's name*: Peleus, father of Achilles.

209 l. 293. *general's*: Agamemnon's.   l. 294. *daughter's*: Iphigenia's.

210 l. 311. *mother's*: Clytemnestra's.

211 l. 341. *lines*: trenches.

212 l. 384. *spy*: Dolon.

213 l. 457. *Undipped in seas*: by Juno's request Neptune was not to allow these constellations to bathe (set) in his waters.

l. 457. *Orion's angry star*: Ovid has 'Orion's gleaming sword'.

214 l. 468. *mother*: Thetis.   l. 469. *wife*: Penelope.

215 l. 510. *prophet*: Helenus.   l. 516. *maid*: Minerva. Her image is the Palladium.   l. 536. *Tydides*: Diomede.

216 l. 546. *more moderate Ajax*: Ajax son of Oileus; 'Ajax the lesser'.

l. 547. *Cretan king*: Idomeneus.

217 l. 609. *flower*: the hyacinth.

l. 611. *whom unaware Apollo slew*: Hyacinthus (*Metamorphoses* 10. 162).

l. 612. *letters*: Ovid plays on AIAI, a cry of woe, and AIAΣ, Ajax.

Of the Pythagorean Philosophy. First published in *Fables* (1700). A translation of Ovid, *Metamorphoses* 15. 1–484.

219 l. 61. *Alemonides*: Alemon's son Myseclos (l. 26).

l. 62. *Alcumena's son*: Hercules. l. 77. *man divine*: Pythagoras.

221 l. 134. *cyclopean feasts*: *Odyssey* 9 tells how the cyclops Polyphemus eats the followers of Odysseus two by two.

222 l. 196. *meal betwixt his temples cast*: barley was sprinkled as part of the ritual of sacrifice.

223 l. 232. *Euphorbus*: a Dardanian. He wounded Patroclus, and was killed by Menelaus (l. 234).

224 l. 260. *Tiphys*: the helmsman of the Argo; see ll. 505 ff.

225 l. 326. *fermented*: 'excited', stirred up.

226 l. 351. *Milo-like*: Milon was a renowned athlete from Croton. He was caught in the trunk of a tree he was trying to split open and was eaten by wolves.

l. 357. *To force her twice*. Helen was abducted by Theseus and, after her marriage, by Paris.

227 l. 401. *our metal*: iron.

228 l. 418. *Lycus*: river of Colchis. l. 420. *Erasinus*: river in Argolis.

l. 442. *Zancle*: Messana in Sicily.

229 l. 467. *Ammon*: the Egyptian equivalent of Jupiter.

l. 469. *Athaman*. Ovid has 'the Athamanians'.

l. 490. *Proetides*: daughter of Proetus.

232 l. 618. *conquering god*: Bacchus.

233 l. 649. *goddess-born*: Aeneas, son of Venus.

234 l. 680. *Thyestean meal*. Thyestes' brother served up his sons to him.

235 *Aesacus Transformed into a Cormorant*. First published in *Ovid's Metamorphoses in Fifteen Books* (1717). A translation of Ovid, *Metamorphoses*, 11. 749–95.

l. 3. *shows*: points out. l. 7. *Tros*: father of Ganymede.

l. 8. *Laomedon*: father of Priam.

236 l. 44. *Tethys*: sea goddess, wife of Oceanus. l. 55. *his name*: Mergus, a diver.

Further Reading

(The place of publication is London unless otherwise specified.)

EDITIONS

The Works of John Dryden, ed. E. N. Hooker *et al.* (Berkeley and Los Angeles, 1956–). In progress.
The Poems of John Dryden, ed. James Kinsley (4 vols., Oxford, 1958).
'Of Dramatic Poesy' and other Critical Essays, ed. George Watson (2 vols., 1962).
John Dryden: Four Comedies, and *John Dryden: Four Tragedies*, ed. L. A. Beaurline and Fredson Bowers (Chicago and London, 1967).
The Letters of John Dryden, ed. Charles E. Ward (Chapel Hill, NC, 1942).

LIVES

Samuel Johnson, 'Preface to Dryden', in *Prefaces, Biographical and Critical, to the Works of the English Poets*, vol. 3 (1779). Standard edition in G. B. Hill (ed.), *The Lives of the Poets* (3 vols., Oxford, 1905); widely reprinted.
James A. Winn, *John Dryden and his world* (New Haven, Conn., 1987).
Paul Hammond *John Dryden: a literary life* (1991).

CRITICAL

T. S. Eliot, *John Dryden: The Poet, the Dramatist, the Critic* (New York, 1932).
David Hopkins, *John Dryden* (Cambridge, 1986).
Earl Miner (ed.), *John Dryden* (1972).
William Myers, *Dryden* (1973).
David Wykes, *A Preface to Dryden* (1977).

Glossary

abate, to lessen

abroad, out of the house, this way and that

accord, agreement

Achates, the faithful companion of Aeneas

achievement, escutcheon granted in memory of some distinguished feat

Acis, son of Faunus and a river-nymph; lover of Galatea

admire, to wonder, to wonder at

adown, down

adulterate, impure

Aeacus, father of Telamon, son of Jove, who made him judge of the underworld

Aeneas, Trojan prince, son of Anchises and Venus

Aeolus, god of winds

afeard, frightened

affect, to desire, to seek

affright, fear; to frighten

Agamemnon, son of Atreus, king of Mycenae, husband of Clytemnestra

Ajax, Greek warrior, son of Telamon

Alcides, Hercules

Alexander (356–323 BC), called 'the great', king of Macedonia, conqueror

alga, seaweed

alienate, to convey title to another

allege, to cite

allow, to approve

alluded, mentioned

Almain, Germany

alow, low

amain, vehemently; immediately

amaze(ment), wonder, consternation

Amazon, warrior-woman

ambient, surrounding

amomum, odoriferous plant

Anchises, father of Aeneas

annoy, vexation

Antenor, Trojan counsellor of Priam

antic, strange, grotesque

Apollo, god of poetry, prophecy, archery

appeach, to accuse

appoint, to equip

Araby, Arabia

Ares, Greek god of war

Argives, Greeks

Argo, Jason's ship

argument, subject-matter

Arion, Greek musician saved from drowning by dolphins

armado, army

armipotent, powerful in arms

arose, arisen

arow, in a row

Artemis, Diana

Ascanius, son of Aeneas

assay, to try

assert, to claim

assist, to be present

assistant, one who is present

Atalanta, virgin huntress

Athene, Greek goddess of war

Atlas, a titan who bore the world on his shoulders

atone, to reconcile; to harmonize

Atrides, Agamemnon, son of Atreus

attend, to wait for; to watch

attent, attentive

Augustus, grandnephew of Julius Caesar; Roman emperor

Aurora, goddess of dawn; the morning star

auspice, patronage

Auster, the south wind

authentic, authoritative, genuine

award, decision, judgement

awful, feeling awe, awe-inspiring

Bacchus, god of wine and revelry

bad, past tense of 'bid'

baffled, disgraced, dishonoured

band, bond

bane, poison

Batavian, Dutchman

bate, to lessen

beak, prow
beamy, large, wide
becoming, properly suiting
beholding, indebted
beldam, old woman
Belgian, Dutch
belie, to counterfeit, to feign
bent, hill, bare field; inclination, bias
beshrew, to wish a curse on
bias, predominant disposition
bid, to count
bid beads to pray
big, pregnant
bilk, to cheat
blatant, bellowing
bleaky, bleak
bloomy, blooming
boding, auguring
boisterous, strong
bolt, shot
boon, what was asked
Boreas, the north wind
botch, boil
boult, to sift
bowels, offspring
box, wind instrument
boyism, puerility
brave, bully
breathe, to lance
breathed, rested
brew, to mix
bristled, covered with bristles
broke, broken
brown, dark
bubby, breast
buxom, pliant

Calchas, Greek seer
callow, unfledged
candid, white
cant, jargon
cantlet, fragment
caparison, cloth covering over saddle
captive, to make captive
car, chariot
careful, attended with care
cast, to require
Castor, one of the Argonauts who brought back the golden fleece
castor, a beaver

cates, provisions
caul, fold of fat
Cecilia, patron saint of music
cense, to scatter incense
censure, judgement
centaur, descendant of Centaurus, son of Ixion; half man, half horse
Ceres, goddess of harvests, agriculture
chaffer, to haggle
Cham, Ham, son of Noah
champian, of the country
chapman, merchant
charge, accusation
charger, horse; flat dish
Charon, ferryman of souls of dead across Styx
chaw, to chew
cheer, appearance; rich food, food and drink
cherubims, cherubs
cherubin, cherub
Chimera, three-headed monster
choir, company
chose, chosen
chuck, to call together with a clucking noise
circular, perfect, complete
cit, citizen (contemptuous)
clench, pun
clenched, clamped
clew, thread, cord, line
clip, to fly
clog, obstacle
close, secret
Clytemnestra, wife of Agamemnon, whom she killed
cockle, weed in corn
colewort, cabbage
coming, forward
common, general, universal
compass, to encircle
complexion, disposition (mental or physical)
composure, study, composition, reconciliation
conceit, conception, idea
concernment, care
conch, shell
condition, nature, character
confidant, person confided in

confining, bordering
congee, bow
conglobutate, compressed into a globe
connatural, of the same nature
conscious, knowing, privy to a secret
consequent, consequence
considering, reflecting
contain, to keep oneself within
contemn, to disdain, to despise
contended, contended for
content, on content, without examination
conversation, behaviour
converse, talk
convert, to change
convict, convicted, guilty
convince, to prove guilty
cot, dwelling
couch, to lay down
couchee, evening reception
counsel, sagacity
course, of course, to be expected
courser, horse
courtship, courtliness
convent, thicket, shelter
cozen, to deceive, cheat
cozenage, deception
crack, noise, crash
crazy, sickly, flawed
cross, across; to contradict
crotch, fork, support
crowd, rabble
cudden, clown, dolt
cumber, distress, encumbrance
Cupid, child god of love
curious, elaborately wrought
cyclops, a one-eyed giant
cymar, a long loose robe
Cynthia, Diana

dame, wife, woman, girl
dared, frightened, bewildered
darkling, in the dark
dart, spear
dash, to dilute
dauby, sticky
debonair, complaisant
decease, to die
deceive, to frustrate
deck, to adorn
decline, to deviate

deducement, deduction
defy, to repudiate
dell, dale
delude, to evade
deplore, to lament
describe, to survey
designment, design
despite, spite
destined, doomed
detort, to twist
Deucalion, son of Prometheus
devoted, doomed
Diana, daughter of Jupiter and Latona, goddess of childbirth and the moon; a virgin huntress
digestive, digesting, methodizing; aid to digestion
dint, force
Diomede, Diomedes, son of Tydeus; Greek warrior from Argos, friend of Ulysses
dip, to immerse
discover, to make known
disembogue, to flow, to pour out
disheir, to deprive of an heir
disherited, disinherited
dishonest, shameful, hideous
dismission, dismissal
dispose, disposal
distinctly, separately
distraction, madness
doddered, having lost branches through decay
dome, temple
doom, judgment; to decree
doted, doting
doubt, to suspect; to hesitate
doubtful, dubious, uncertain
dryad, wood-nymph
dug, pap, udder
dungeon, tower

earthy, of the earth
economy, arrangement
effect, result
Elysium, the abode of the blessed
embrown, to make brown
empiric, quack
emptiness, vacuum
endlong, straight on

engine, machinery, rack, mechanical device, instrument of war
enterprised, undertaken
enthusiast, fanatic
entranced, unconscious
envy, ill-will
Epicurus, Greek philosopher (341–271 BC) who was believed to advocate the pursuit of pleasure
equal, just, impartial, unruffled
equipage, equestrian trappings
erring, wandering
essay, first effort
estate, condition
etherial, heavenly
event, outcome
evidence, witness
evince, to prove
exact, perfect
exception, objection
exclusive, excluding
exequies, funeral rites
exercise, to try severely; to practise
exert, to bring out, to reveal
expect, to await
expire, to rush forth; to breathe out
explicate, to explain

fabric, building, structure
fact, action, deed, feat, crime
factor, agent; observer
falchion, broadsword
fame, rumour, reputation
fanatic, enthusiast, nonconformist
fane, temple
farmost, furthest off
fatal, fated, fateful
fell, fierce
fix, to determine
flame, passion
flix, fur
flood, river, sea
foin, to lunge, to thrust
forbear, to abstain from, to withhold
forbid, forbidden
forceful, strong
forelay, to waylay
forfeit, forfeited
forfent, to forbid
forgot, forgotten

forslow, to retard
forthright, straightforward
fougue, fury
fowl, bird
fraischeur, freshness
freak, whim
free, courteous, liberal, generous
frequent, crowded
fret, to erode
fright, to frighten
frock, tunic
front, face
frontless, shameless
froze, frozen
fry, to burn; to foam
Furies, snake-haired goddesses in Greek mythology
fustian, bombast

gage, pledge
Galatea, sea-nymph loved by Acis
gale, breeze
galled, rubbed, hurt
gaudry, finery
gaudy, splendid, fine
gem, bud
generous, noble, of good stock; strong, vigorous, high-spirited
genial, natural; what gives cheerfulness; contributing to propagation
genius, tutelary god
gentle, noble
give on, to go violently
glad, to gladden
glebe, land, a field
grabble, to grope after
gramercy, thanks
grant, permission
grateful, agreeable
gratulate, to congratulate
grave, to engrave
graver, engraver
grisly, horrible, nasty
gross, in gross, in a body
gull, to cheat
gust, the height of sensual pleasure
gyves, shackles

halcyon, legendary sea-bird bringing good weather

Hannibal, (247–182 BC) leader of the Carthaginians against Rome

happiness, successful aptitude

happy, propitious

hardly, with difficulty

hardy, courageous

haste, to make haste

hatch, to build

hateful, full of hate

heap, on a heap, into one mass

hear, to obey

heartless, destitute of courage

Hector, Trojan hero, son of Priam and Hecuba

Hecuba, wife of Priam, king of Troy

heir, to inherit

Helen, wife of Menelaus, king of Sparta; she was seduced by Paris

Helenus, Trojan prophet, son of Priam

Helicon, mountain in middle Greece sacred to the muses

Hercules, Heracles, Greek hero, son of Jove

Hermes, Mercury, messenger to the gods

hie, to hasten

hight, is called, was called

hind, farm labourer, peasant

hire, reward

hoary, white

hobby, hawk

hold, to abstain

homely, humble

honest, decent, respectable; glorious

hope, to expect; to wait for

horrid, bristling

Holland, cloth from Holland

humid, moist

humour, fancy, temperament

husband, one who tills the soil

Hydra, a many-headed monster

Hymen, god of marriage, son of Bacchus

Ilium, Troy

imp, to repair wings

impassible, insensible to pain

impassive, not subject to pain

impudent, immodestly presumptuous

inartificial, clumsy

increase, offspring; accumulation, growth; size

incumbent, pressing upon

Inde, India

indignant, angry

inform, to make known to

informing, animating

infuse, to pour

infused, poured in

inly, inwardly

inmate, foreign

innocent, harmless

innovate, to introduce for the first time

insensible, imperceptible

inspire, to breathe into or upon

instop, to fill up

insult, to exult proudly (over), to assail, to triumph over

insulting, exulting

intent, purpose; anxiously diligent

intercept, to stop, to obstruct, to cut off

interlude, play

invidious, envious, malignant

involve, to wrap

Io, daughter of Inachus

Iphigenia, daughter of Agamemnon

Isis, Egyptian goddess whose cult spread to Rome in the early centuries AD

Ixion, king of the Lapiths, and the first parricide; he fathered the centaurs

jambeux, armour for the legs

Janus, god of doors and gates

jar, harsh sound, clash, conflict

jealousy, suspicion

Jove, Jupiter, king of the gods, husband of Juno

joy, to make joyful; to rejoice

judgment, judge, critic

Julus, Ascanius, son of Aeneas

Juno, wife of Jove; goddess of marriage

Jupiter, Jove, Zeus, king of the gods

jupon, close-fitting padded tunic

ken, sight, gaze, view; to see, to know

kern, Irish peasant, Irish foot-soldier

kind, nature; *by*—, naturally

kindness, infatuation

kindred, kinship

kine, cows

king-at-arms, chief herald

knare, knot in a tree, gnarled
  protuberance
known, well known

Lacedaemon, Sparta
lade, to load
lag, laggard
lard, bacon
lares, household gods
large, generous, free
laund, clearing
lave, to wash, to bathe
laveer, to tack about
lazar, filthy deformed person, leper
leave, to leave off
lee, sediment of wine
leech, physician
left of, left by
legator, testator
lenitive, sedative
let, to hinder
levée morning reception
liberal, free, generous
lightsome, gay
like, to please
limbec, alchemical still
limber, pliant
limbo, space
line, the equator
linstock, match-holder to light cannon
liquorish, randy
litter, to cover with straw
lively, like life
loll, to stretch out
loon, scoundrel
lubber, clumsy, idle fellow
lubric, slippery, immoral
Lucina, goddess of childbirth
lug, to pull, to drag
lust, desire
lusty, stout, vigorous
luxury, lust
Lyaeus, Bacchus

Macedon, Macedonian
machine, mechanical device
magazine, storehouse
make, to do
manes, dead ancestors who are
  worshipped

manifest of, guilty of
mannerly, well-mannered
many, crowd; retinue
marling, small tarred line for winding
  round ropes
Mars, god of war
martlet, swallow
massy, heavy
mate, equal; to equal
maw, gut, stomach
mechanic, vulgar
medicinal, having the power of healing
mend, to improve upon
mien, look, manner
millenary, of the millennium
Minerva, Athene, goddess of wisdom
mingle, mixture
mint, place of assay
mischief, a bringer of mischief; hurt,
  harm
miserable, fraught with misery
miss of, to fail to secure
missioner, ambassador, missionary
missive, missile
mistaken, misconceived
morion, helmet
motion, movement
mould, form, shape; material
moulted, affected by moulting
mumble, to chew toothlessly

naked, unprotected
nard, an aromatic plant
nasty, foul, filthy, unclean
naughty, bad, wicked
nereid, Greek sea-nymph
nervous, sinewy
Nestor, king of Pylos, of great age and
  wisdom
nice, (over-)fastidious, precise
nick, to hit; to censure
noblesse, nobility
noiseful, noisy
nose, to annoy; to detect
notched, marked
note, stigma
now, moment
numbers, metrical feet; versification
nursery, training place for young
  actors

oaf, simpleton
Oberon, king of the fairies
obligement, obligation
obnoxious, liable to punishment; subject to punishment
obscene, loathsome, horrid
obsequious, obedient, compliant
obstinate, determined
obtend, to allege; to hold out; to present in opposition
occasion, opportunity
o'erinformed, filled to overflowing
offend, to attack
officious, obliging, serviceable
once, some time
or . . . or, either . . . or
orient, bright-coloured; of superior value
ostent, portent
overpoise, superiority of weight
overwatched, weary from lack of sleep
out, to oust
outrageous, violent, excessive, extravagant
owe, to own
owing, indebted

pad, to go out robbing
pain, labour; to exert violently
Pales, Roman goddess of flocks
Pallas, Athene, goddess of war
palm, palm leaf worn as symbol of victory or triumph; victory
Pan, fertility god, god of the country
pard, panther, leopard
pardalis, panther
Paris, son of Priam; he abducted Helen, thus beginning the Trojan war
parlous, formidable, perilous
paronomasia, pun
parts, abilities
Patroclus, Greek warrior, Achilles' lover
pay o'er, to spread over
peccant, injurious
peevish, querulous
Pegasus, a winged horse
Pelides, Achilles, son of Peleus
pencil, paintbrush
pennon, small forked streamer
pent, confined
period, conclusion
Philomel, nightingale

philosophy, natural science
Phoebe, the moon-goddess Diana
Phoebus, Apollo, the sun
physic, to heal
picture, art of painting
pile, troop
pimp, to pander
pious, dutiful
place, office
plagiary, plagiarist
pleasure, to please
plume, pen; to pluck
plump, flock
Pluto, god of the underworld and death
poise, to weigh; to steady
Polyphemus, a cyclops, son of Neptune
pomp, splendour, show, pageant
pompous, splendid
ponderous, heavy
port, demeanour
Portunus, god of harbours
post, to travel, to hurry
pounce, claw, talon
practice, plot, intrigue
practise, to frequent
prelude, to usher in
presage, omen; to predict
pretend, to claim
prevail, to avail
prevent, to go before; to anticipate
Priam, king of Troy
pricking, riding
prime, spring, dawn, early morning
procedure, proceeding
process, trial
proclamation, proscription
prodigious, ominous
prodigy, portent; something monstrous
prolific, generative
Prometheus, a titan, son of Iapetus and father of Deucalion; he made mankind out of clay
prompt, to urge
proof, trial
proponent, propounding
Proserpine, goddess of the underworld
prospective, telescope
protend, to stretch out
protractive, protracting
prove, to try

provident, frugal
Pruce, Prussia
Punic wars, wars between Rome and Carthage, 264–146 BC
punk, whore
purchase, acquisition
purfled, bordered
pursue, to follow
pursuivant, attendant

quail-pipe, throat
quantity, length
quarry, game
queazy, squeamish
quick, flesh

rabbin, rabbi
rack, driving clouds; to move around
rage, fit of madness
rail, to abuse
raillery, abuse; mocking
ranch, to tear
rapt, snatched
rathe, early
raven, to hunger
rebate, to blunt
receipt, prescription
reckless, heedless
reconcile, to appease
recourse, expedient
recreant, cowardly; confessing oneself overcome
reeking, oozing blood
refer, to restore
reflective, reflected
regalio, choice entertainment
regorge, to swallow back
rehearsal, repetition, recitation
rehearse, to relate, to number
relent, to soften
remember, to remind
Remus, twin brother of Romulus
rend, to destroy
renown, to make renowned
repair, resort
repeat, to reseek
repose, to place as a trust
reprise, reprisal
republic, republican
require, to seek again; to demand

resolve, to melt, to dissolve
resort, assembly of people
rest, remainder
resume, to revoke
retire, to draw back; to take away
rheums, watery humours
rivelled, dried, shrivelled
Romulus, legendary founder of Rome
room, place
ropy, sticky
ruin, fall
ruminate, to muse on

salve, to excuse
Sappho, woman poet of Lesbos (sixth century BC)
savourly, with savour
sawtry, psaltery
scan, to examine closely
scandal, to scandalize
scape, escape; to escape
school, scholastic
scour, to race over
scud, to run away
secure of, secure from
Seneca, (*c.*4 BC–AD 65), Roman philosopher and writer
sennight, week
sentence, maxim
sequacious, following
seraphims, seraphs
sere-wood, dry wood
set, to put down a stake
several, various, different
shade, ghost
share, ploughshare
sheer, to cut, to cut through
shent, destroyed
shore, sewer
show, appearance; to appear
shrieval, sheriff's
sign, sign of the zodiac
simples, medicinal herbs
sincere, unmixed, pure: unhurt
sincerely, purely, without alloy
Sisyphus, son of Aeolus, famous for cunning; putative father of Ulysses
slavering, with running mouth
snip, scrap
sophisticate, artificial

sort, number, collection
sot, fool
sounding, resounding
souse, to swoop down
sovereign, all-powerful
spleen, melancholy; ill-humour
spring, to set going
sprite, spirit
spurn, to kick, to kick up
spurt, to squirt
squander, to disperse
stay, to wait
steep, steep height
steepy, steep
stew, brothel
stickle, to dispute
stickler, umpire
still, always
stint, proportion
stoles, robes
stoop, to swoop
strain, race, stock; to constrain
strait, narrow
strict, tight
stub, stump of a tree
stubborn, hard, rigid
studied, carefully contrived
studious of, concerned for
stum, new wine used for fermenting old
stupid, stupified
style, to describe
Styx, river of the underworld
suage, to assuage
submit, to lower
suborn, to procure secretly
succeed, to make to follow; to prosper
success, outcome
successive, by succession
suit, petition, favour, prayer
suiting, suitable
surcoat, outer coat
surety, pledge
sustain, to endure
swain, attendant, youth, labourer
swound, swoon
sylvan, of the woods
sylvans, wood gods

table, tablet
tale, number, calculation, tally

tally, counterpart
tarnish, to become stained
tawny, yellow
tax, to accuse
Telamon, son of Aeacus and father of Ajax
tell, to count
Tethys, wife of Oceanus
Thebes, Greek city, north-west of Athens
Themis, goddess of justice
theologue, theologian
Thetis, sea-nymph, wife of Peleus and mother of Achilles
thick, quickly following
threat, to threaten
throughly, thoroughly
timbrel, tambourine
timely, in time
tine, to kindle
tire, row of guns
tissue, rich cloth
toil, trap, snare
took, taken
towardly, promising
traduction, transmission
train, procession, retinue
tralineate, to get out of the line
translate, to transplant, to transfer
traverse, to oppose (in law)
treasonous, treasonable
treat, entertainment
trim, adornment
trine, two planets positioned 120° apart: a favourable omen
Triton, Greek merman, son of Neptune
trump, trumpet
try, to test
Tully, Cicero
tumbril, farm cart
tun, large cask
twist, cord
tympany, flatulence; swelling

Ulysses, Greek warrior, king of Ithaca; famous for cunning
uncouth, uncanny
unctuous, oily
uncumbered, unencumbered
undecent, unbecoming
ungodded, having no gods

unhappy, unfortunate
unhoped, unexpected
unknowing, ignorant
unlade, to empty
unrooted, insatiable
unshorn, unclipped
unspell, to disenchant
unteach, to destroy the teaching of
unthrift, prodigal
use, to practise, to be accustomed to

vale, valley
value, good opinion
vapours, hypochondria, hysteria
vare, staff
various, variable, many-coloured
Varro, Roman general defeated by Hannibal at Cannae
vegetive, having the potential of growth
Vesper, the evening star
vest, to clothe
villanize, to make villainous
vindicate, to defend against interference
virelay, poem or song with interlaced lines
virtue, power, force, valour
virtuoso, one skilled in some branch of knowledge
virtuous, curative
volume, coil

vulgar, common people

wain, waggon, carriage
wait, to attend, to accompany
wallow, a rolling walk
want, to be wanted; to be without
wanting, poor
wanton, frolicsome, sportive
watch, constable(s) patrolling streets at night
weal, well-being
weeds, clothes
well-breathed, with good lungs
whilom, formerly
whirlbat, gauntlet
wilder, to bewilder
wilding, crab-apple
wit, intelligence, felicity of thought, propriety of thought
without, outside
withstand, to gainsay, to oppose
witness, evidence
woe, woeful
wreak, to avenge
writhen, twisted

yeaning, just born

zealous, fanatical
Zephyr, the west wind
zone, girdle

Index of Titles and First Lines

(Titles are set in italic.)

OXFORD POETRY LIBRARY
WILLIAM WORDSWORTH
Edited by Stephen Gill and Duncan Wu

Wordsworth was one of the most illustrious of the Romantic poets. In this selection generous extracts are given from his important work *The Prelude*, together with many of his shorter poems. The reader will find classics such as *Tintern Abbey*, *Westminster Bridge* and 'I wandered lonely as a cloud' well represented. Notes and introduction are provided by Wordsworth's biographers, Stephen Gill and Duncan Wu.

OXFORD POETRY LIBRARY

ALEXANDER POPE

Edited by Pat Rogers

Pope has been acknowledged as the most important poet of the first half of the eighteenth century. This selection includes his brilliant poems *An Essay on Criticism*, *Windsor Forest*, and his masterpiece of social satire, *The Rape of the Lock*. Together with a representative sample of Pope's other verse, Pat Rogers gives an eloquent defence of Pope's poetic practice.

OXFORD POETRY LIBRARY

SAMUEL TAYLOR COLERIDGE

Edited by Heather Jackson

Coleridge was one of the most significant figures in the development of Romantic poetry. This new selection represents the full range of his poetic gifts, from his early polemic poetry such as the *Sonnets on Eminent Characters*, to the maturity of the blank verse poems, *Fears in Solitude* and *Frost at Midnight*. Also included are the wonderful works, *Kubla Khan* and *The Rime of the Ancient Mariner*.

OXFORD POETRY LIBRARY
LORD BYRON
Edited by Jerome J. McGann

Byron was one of the most acclaimed writers of his time, and he continues to be a highly popular Romantic poet with readers today. His mastery of a sweeping range of topics and forms is clearly reflected in this selection, which includes extracts from all his major poems such as *Childe Harold*, *Beppo*, and *Don Juan*, together with many shorter lyrics.